MASTERING THE ART OF SELLING REAL ESTATE

MASTERING

the Art of Selling Real Estate

FULLY REVISED AND UPDATED

TOM HOPKINS

Portfolio

PORTFOLIO

Published by the Penguin Group, Penguin Group (USA) Inc., 375 Hudson Street, New York,
    New York 10014, U.S.A.
Penguin Books Ltd, 80 Strand, London WC2R 0RL, England
Penguin Books Australia Ltd, 250 Camberwell Road, Camberwell, Victoria 3124, Australia
Penguin Books Canada Ltd, 10 Alcorn Avenue, Toronto, Ontario, Canada M4V 3B2
Penguin Books India (P) Ltd, 11 Community Centre, Panchsheel Park, New Delhi - 110 017, India
Penguin Group (N.Z.) Ltd, Cnr Airborne and Rosedale Roads, Albany, Auckland, 1310,
    New Zealand
Penguin Books (South Africa) (Pty) Ltd, 24 Sturdee Avenue, Rosebank, Johannesburg 2196,
    South Africa

Penguin Books Ltd, Registered Offices: 80 Strand, London WC2R 0RL, England

This edition published in 2004 by Portfolio, a member of Penguin Group (USA) Inc.

10   9   8

Original edition published under the title *How to Master the Art of Listing & Selling Real Estate*.

PUBLISHER'S NOTE
This publication is designed to provide accurate and authoritative information in regard to the subject matter covered. It is sold with the understanding that the publisher is not engaged in rendering legal, accounting or other professional services. If you require legal advice or other expert assistance, you should seek the services of a competent professional.

LIBRARY OF CONGRESS CATALOGING-IN-PUBLICATION DATA

Hopkins, Tom.
    Mastering the art of selling real estate / Tom Hopkins.
        p.   cm.
    Fully rev. and updated edition of: How to master the art of listing and selling real estate. 1991.
    Includes index.
    ISBN 1-59184-040-6
        1. Real estate business.   2. Real estate listings.   3. Real estate agents.   I. Hopkins, Tom.
    How to master the art of listing and selling real estate.   II. Title.

    HD1375.H78 2004
    333.33'068'8—dc22   2004040076

This book is printed on acid-free paper. ∞

Printed in the United States of America
Designed by Fritz Metsch • Set in Adobe Garamond

To all the brave and creative souls who choose the wonderful,
exciting field of real estate as their career path

Acknowledgments

I must acknowledge the late, great J. Douglas Edwards. His teachings about the exciting field of sales not only inspired me but are also the foundation on which my entire life's work has been built.

I thank all of my early clients who invested in real estate through me—even when I didn't know what I was doing. Your patience made the difference. Your continued business was a blessing.

Special thanks go to my students of these thirty plus years who have the burning desire to succeed without limits. Your feedback and input on keeping my training current are invaluable.

I thank my team at Tom Hopkins International, especially Judy Slack, who manages the huge library of content we have created over the years.

I'm grateful for the wonderful people at Portfolio, especially editors Stephanie Land and Megan Casey for their guidance as we fine-tuned each page.

Contents

Introduction

Welcome to the wonderful world of real estate! I began my career in real estate in the 1960s. It was wonderful then and has evolved into something even more wonderful today. What a joy it is for people to own real property—to have a place they can truly call home. And you get to delight in helping people achieve their dreams of home ownership, while earning a good income for yourself and your loved ones. It's a truly satisfying career choice.

Back in the 60s, real estate was primarily an older man's business. There were few young men choosing real estate as a career and even fewer women.

Fortunately for all of us, times have changed. I know of some young people these days who got their real estate licenses while still in high school and had a jump start on their careers on graduation day! Due to its flexibility of working hours, the field has provided excellent opportunities for thousands. I've seen many exciting changes over the years and congratulate you on your choice of a career in real estate.

When I wrote the first version of this material, it was actually two separate books. One just covered the listing aspect of real estate. The other, selling. They were first printed in the 1980s—back before computers, wireless phones, pagers, and the Internet. You are so fortunate today. Much of the research you need to do is available with the click of a few keys—and in minutes. I used to invest hours in researching data for Comparable Market Analyses, and reading through the Multiple Listing Service book (yes, it was a book, back then).

While the times have changed, some important aspects of buying and selling real estate have not. These include: the reasons people need your services; motivations for wanting a particular type of home; how husbands and wives relate to each other during real estate transactions; and how you must relate to them. That's the power of this book. In it are step-by-step strategies for getting started in this business, for finding people who need your services, for helping them like and trust you and your expertise in the field, how to prepare for a listing presentation, what to expect from potential buyers, what to say when they give you the most common questions or objections, how to negotiate offers and counteroffers, and how to close people on either listing their property with you or buying the home you've helped them find that best suits their needs.

In this revised edition, I have kept the best of the original books, deleted old strategies that may not be as effective today as they once were, and have added strategies that work phenomenally well in today's marketplace. I cover the use of technology to save you time and increase your appearance of competence with clients. This book is designed to help you achieve a certain level of comfort within the real estate industry—being comfortable with the knowledge of what to expect and how to succeed in this truly wonderful career. Treat it as a textbook. Read it with a highlighter, a pen, and a notebook. Let it become your quick reference guide and your study guide as you grow. There is enough material here to help you through many years in this business. And, to help you find the success you dream of more quickly than you would without it.

My wish for you is to find as much joy and satisfaction from your real estate career as I did mine.

MASTERING THE ART OF SELLING REAL ESTATE

CHAPTER 1

Portrait of a Professional Real Estate Salesperson

If you are reading this book, you may already have had a day that stands out as your worst day in real estate. If you're new to the business and haven't had such a day, don't worry, you will. Just don't let it deter you. Perseverance has made all the difference in my life.

My worst day is one I will always remember. I was new to real estate, nineteen years old, and I didn't own a suit. So, I wore my black and silver high school band uniform to work. My car was a beat-up, old convertible with holes in the roof and springs popping through the back seat. Needless to say, I didn't present the most professional image.

Like most new licensees, I didn't know what to do with myself. The training program in my office consisted of the sales manager giving me the thumbs up signal and telling me to "hang in there." I was warm and friendly with all my prospects, but didn't know how to close a sale. In fact, I was so nice that sometimes when people didn't buy from me, they would send apologetic notes to my broker, saying how nice I was.

Until I discovered that there was such a thing as sales training, my earnings averaged $42 per month. That was for my first six months! It doesn't matter how you budgeted, even in the early 1960s, $42 a month didn't make it.

My enthusiasm was beginning to fade. In fact, there was a low period during which I decided real estate wasn't for me. Three sales had fallen out in one week. One day I walked into my broker's office and said, "I'm thinking about quitting." He had no answer for me—the thumbs up signal wasn't good enough anymore.

I was so depressed that I went back to my desk and started looking at the classifieds. Then the telephone rang. To my surprise, through the receiver came, without a doubt, the most beautiful voice I have ever heard. It was an absolute melody. She said something that I had never heard before. "Sir, my husband and I would like to buy a home." I thought someone was playing a joke on me. Then, she said, "Sir, we'd like to spend around $200,000." This really shook me up because the area I worked in was Simi Valley, California, and then the average home sold for between $18,000 and $20,000.

I felt like saying, "Ma'am, would you like half of the valley, a quarter of the valley, or what?" I didn't though. Somehow I kept my composure and set an appointment for 2:00 P.M. that day.

To say I was nervous after this phone call would be a terrible understatement. I didn't even know of a home that was worth that much in Simi Valley. After driving around for a few hours, I finally found the right home on the top of a hill. It was absolutely perfect! It had a phenomenal view. It was a $187,000 mansion. My career finally looked like it was turning around.

On the way back to the office, they announced on the radio that it was the hottest day of the year—105 degrees, 75 percent humidity. I didn't care, though. My enthusiasm was zooming off the charts! Back in the office, I pulled out a piece of paper, like any starving real estate person, and figured out what 6 percent of $187,000 was. People around me could hear me say, "All right! I'm going to make some big money here!"

Right at 2:00 P.M., in walked this gorgeous creature. She had on a $300 outfit and diamonds everywhere. Her hair was beautifully styled, her makeup exquisite. It must have taken at least two hours to put it on. I jumped up to meet her.

Being such a nervous wreck, I don't even remember how I got her into my car. As we drove down the street, I couldn't think of a thing to say to her. I was embarrassed by my car and nervous about the possibility of selling such a high-priced property.

All of a sudden, my car started to jerk. In my excitement about finding the right home, I had forgotten to check my gas tank. It was empty! Rolling the car to a stop at the side of the road, I turned to my potential new client and said, "Ma'am, I've never had anything like this happen before. Please forgive me. There's a gas station only half a mile away. I'll be right back."

There I was in my newly dry-cleaned, wool band uniform jogging down the street with my gas can. I wish you could have been there when I got back to that car. Not only was I a sweaty wreck, the woman had sat in that closed car at 105 degrees the whole time I was gone. Everything that had been on her face was now on her chest. Her hair even looked like it was melting. "Ma'am, I'm so sorry," I said. "I've never had this happen. You can have all the air." I turned all the vents on her and drove on to the house.

By the time we got to the house, I had decided nothing could be worse than selling real estate as a career. Trying to regain my composure, I thought I'd show her the beautiful view from the patio. She would have to be impressed with it and might forget what had happened with the car.

Walking over to the sliding door, I said, "Ma'am, I think you'll enjoy this view." I held the curtain back for her to see it. Well, she thought the sliding glass door was open and walked right into it. She hit her head hard and was obviously stunned. She looked at me for a split second with an expression I cannot describe and ran to lock herself in the bathroom.

Luckily, the sellers were gone. But now I had to get her out of the bathroom. I began knocking on the door, pleading with her to come out. Upon hearing a noise behind me, I turned to see that the sellers had returned ahead of schedule. Needless to say, they wanted to know what was going on. With the help of the sellers, the lady came out of the bathroom, and I got her back to my car. Not a word was spoken on the trip back to the office. When we got there, like a zombie, she got out of my car, walked to hers, and drove away.

I went into the office and took some aspirin. This was definitely the end of my real estate career. Nothing could be worse than what I'd just gone through. Out came the classifieds again. Then, there was a phone call for me. When I answered, the man on the other end said, "Yes, Mr.

Hopkins, you just showed my wife a home. I just can't believe what she's told me. I want to see it, too." I felt like fainting dead on the spot!

They were both coming to the office right then. This time I had a goal for when they arrived. My goal was to get them from the front door to my desk without incident.

Now, there are certain types of people that we instantly like—people we can build a rapport with very quickly. This lady's husband was one of those types for me. After a few minutes, he and I were talking easily and getting along really well. All the while, his wife watched us both very carefully.

All of a sudden, this horsefly flew by. We had each shooed it away a couple of times during our conversation. This time, though, as a joke, I reached out for the fly, acted like I had it, and popped it in my mouth. Much to my surprise, I really did have it! It was moving around in there.

Now, I could do one of two things. I could swallow it and say something like, "Mmm, we love them here!" Or, I could spit it out. I chose the latter. When I looked up, that couple had this amazed look on their faces. The wife was nudging the husband with her elbow and saying, "I told you so."

Needless to say, I didn't make that sale. In fact, a letter came from them a day later that said, "Based on our short exposure to the people in Simi Valley, we're staying where we live!"

Around that time, I found out there was such a thing as sales training. I invested my last $150 of savings on a seminar to learn how to sell. If that didn't work, I was going to quit for sure. I was amazed by the things I learned at that seminar. Now that I could see where I'd been going wrong, I started getting my enthusiasm back. I took notes and memorized them until my brain ached. Once I was able to apply the material, I was thrilled with the results. My career really started turning around.

Hopefully, you will never have as terrible a day as I did. Unfortunately, some of your days may be just as bad or, even worse. What's important is to anticipate those days and learn in advance the best ways to handle them. You've made the first important step just by picking up this book. By reading and internalizing this material, you can become more prepared to meet the daily challenges of a career in real estate and succeed.

As a real estate salesperson, you are paid in direct proportion to your ability to communicate with people and serve their needs. If you can't do that, you'll go nowhere in this business—fast. I'm assuming you've already learned that lesson the hard way and that's part of the reason why you are now reading this book. You want to learn how to become a real estate *professional*.

Every profession has certain tools, which, once mastered, will allow you the opportunity to become one of the great ones in that field. For example, a professional golfer is paid in direct proportion to his or her ability to take a piece of steel at the end of a stick and bring it down to touch a small, white ball at the right time and place to send it hundreds of yards, eventually dropping into a small hole. Someone like Tiger Woods is a very successful professional because he has mastered the use of his tools.

A professional fighter is paid for how well he uses his fists; a surgeon—a scalpel; a carpenter must master the use of saws, hammers, and power tools. The people in each of these lines of work develop their skills through years of study, practice, and experience before they consider themselves professionals. If they're smart, they learn not only by their own experiences but through the experiences of others.

The same thing applies to you in real estate. You can't become a real estate professional without learning what one does, can you? My goal in this book is to make you realize that you're no different from any other professional. As a real estate agent, you must primarily learn how to use your eyes, ears, and mouth because one of your most important tools is your ability to create exciting, colorful images, thus leading people to the decision to own real estate.

You see, selling real estate is no different from any other profession. As I mentioned above, people in most professional fields are paid in direct proportion to the amount of service they give. You, as a real estate salesperson, are as professional as the income you earn. So, in other words, if you're not making enough money, you're not giving enough service.

To learn how to give more service, you must learn from a professional—someone who has done what you want to do: real estate. The problem with too many people is that they are taking advice or "training" from people who are not professionals. How can they teach you something they've never accomplished themselves? Why would you want to learn from someone who's not a top producer? I'm not saying you can't learn from someone else, but be aware that you are limited to their experience. If they're already way ahead of you because you're new, go ahead and let them help you. However, once you begin to master what they teach, you'll likely find yourself needing to learn from someone who is better at this business—that is if you plan to achieve the most you can from it.

You might be concerned about how well you'll do in this business because you're not a natural born salesperson. You just don't have that gift of gab. Trust me, there's no such thing as a natural born salesperson. All you're doing if you accept that myth is keeping yourself from achieving your true potential. We all start out with pretty much the same abilities. It's what we do with them along the way that counts. In other words, great salespeople are not born, they're trained. If you love the idea of helping people sell their homes and find new ones that are just right for them, you'll do well. The first key to success in any sales position is that you must be enthusiastic about your product. Everything else can be learned.

You have the ability right now to learn what it takes to become one of the top salespeople the real estate business has ever known. You just have to be willing to change and grow beyond who you are now. Begin by finding successful people and surrounding yourself with them. Be with the people whom you'd most like to become. If you want to be average, then stick with average people. If it's your desire to achieve greatness in real estate sales, then learn what the great ones do, and do it!

What Is a Professional Salesperson?

A professional salesperson is a person who earns more money than the average salesperson. If you are not earning two to three times more income than the average real estate salesperson, you are not as professional as you could be. If you are unwilling to make the changes necessary to achieve this level of professionalism, you should consider getting a job where someone pays you a salary.

In a salaried position, you have a lot of security. However, you also have someone else determining exactly how much money you will make. In most cases, that person is going to be working too hard at becoming rich to worry about whether or not you do.

The exciting thing about real estate is that you can get rich helping other people to get rich. You see, the people who own the real estate have more than you do. You get your brokerage, but they get to keep the real estate, the value of which is going up faster than inflation. So, they're hedging inflation, building equity, sheltering income, and building estates—all because of you—the professional real estate salesperson.

I hope you want to become rich. You may not realize it, but there are people who don't want to be rich. Maybe there are some in your office—people who are literally afraid of success. You hear them say things like this:

"I don't want to be rich. Rich men are sick men."

Believe me, I know a lot of healthy, wealthy people.

"Money isn't important."

It isn't. Unless you don't have any.

Money is the by-product of the service you render to other people. If you give no service, you get no money. When you give lots of excellent service, you get lots of money.

It is important you realize that when I say the word *rich,* I mean the fully matured, happy, and successful human being, who is striving to get rich in all areas of his or her life. A truly successful life has much more to it than money.

Let's break the term *rich* down into four key areas:

1. EMOTIONAL RICHES.

This means coping with life's daily challenges and crises. It includes keeping a balance in life between business and family priorities. Don't booby-trap yourself into thinking that you could or should be happy all of the time. Things happen in everyone's lives that make them unhappy. It's how you handle those things that will matter in the long run. Experience everything life has to offer, but determine that you will pick yourself up after every downer, learn from it, and get back to being happy the rest of the time.

I know this may sound simplified. There's much more to it that I just can't cover in this book. For more help in this area, you might consider my book, *The Official Guide to Success* and audio series titled *Balance Your Life*.

2. FINANCIAL RICHES.

My definition of financial wealth is the ability to live comfortably, that means debt-free, off the monthly income generated by your net worth at a given date and time using the talents God has given you to be productive.

Earning a high income is truly possible in this business. What you do with that money after you earn it determines how financially rich you become. Be money smart. It pays!

3. PHYSICAL RICHES.

This means taking care of your body through exercise and proper eating habits and striving to live a long, healthy life overall. If you have a challenge with smoking, alcohol, or drugs of any sort—legal or illegal—set a goal to become free of the habit. Then seek out the best help you can find to start working toward that goal.

4. SPIRITUAL RICHES.

I strongly believe in the importance of having a satisfactory personal relationship with God, and that it has helped me achieve professional success. One thing I know is true. I was fortunate at a young age to achieve what most people consider material success and I can honestly tell you that *things* don't make you happy once you have them. It is spiritual satisfaction, balanced with material gain, that brings total fulfillment.

It seems that too often today we see people who want more for less. Sure, they want more. Doesn't everybody? But, they also want to know how they can get it the easy way.

Fifty years ago in America people thought differently. They wanted more, but they also understood that to get it, they would have to give more, to work harder, to work smarter. By understanding what people did fifty years ago, you and I have the opportunity to get rich today.

Common Characteristics of the Pros

There are many characteristics common to real estate professionals. To become more professional, adopt these traits. If you already have them, good for you. Consider what it would take to improve them.

One particular quality that separates the average from the great can be expressed by one simple word—*desire*. Most of the great ones have an overwhelming desire to prove something to someone. They know they can be the best in their field and are out to prove it to the world, or maybe just to themselves and their families. This desire burns so strongly within them that it keeps them moving in the right direction. It keeps them cheerful with their clients and fellow sales-people. It's the fuel that keeps their engines running in top condition.

Now, I can't tell how much desire you have to make it in this field. Only you know that. The question is how much stress, anxiety, and pain can you handle before you quit? Do you have a low threshold for rejection? Think about what you're willing to give or do to achieve what you really want. Can you accept ten or twenty nos in order to get the one yes that earns you a big fee? If you're not sure, consider looking at it differently. Take the ten nos and divide them into one fee you'll receive from a listing sold or a sale you make yourself.

For example, let's say you end up with $5,000 in your personal bank account after a sale. And, let's say you were rejected in some way or another by ten people before making that sale. That makes each no you received worth $500 to you. Each no brought you $500 closer to the final yes and your fee.

Selling is a game. You must make a game of the negative aspects of it in order to be a winner in the long run. Learn ways to brush off the negatives, the rejection, and the canceled sales in order to stay focused on the gold ring—the closed sale that does eventually come about if you stick with it. That's how to increase your desire to succeed in this business.

Professionals pay close attention to details. They ask questions that help them get a better understanding of what their clients are looking for in a home. They have their paperwork in order. They return phone calls promptly. They keep their promises and have answers ready when questions are asked.

Professionals are highly goal-oriented. They strive for a certain number of homes listed and sold each month, a certain income, a trophy, or an award. They know exactly what they're working for and when they'll achieve it.

Do you have your goals in writing? If not, you are a wisher and a dreamer. You haven't really committed yourself to achieving anything. You're like those average people in your office who say, "Sure, I want to make more money, but after the day I had yesterday, I'm not leaving the office today."

You see, the successful ones, the true professionals, begin where the failures stop. They do what the failures are afraid or too lazy to do.

The great ones understand that they must strive daily to improve their skills. I hope you're not one of those people who says, "If I don't make it at this, I can always . . ." That's a plan for failure. If you anticipate it, you will probably get it. Instead, be one of the great ones who says, "If I don't do well enough this time, next time, I'll try _____ to do it better." Have a plan for success instead of one for failure.

Top professionals in real estate give excellent service. They know they are paid in direct proportion to the amount of service they give their clients. They understand they are in the people business. They don't sell homes. They get people happily involved in owning property by satisfying their real estate needs.

Steps to Professionalism

There are ten basic, overall steps to professionalism I'd like to share with you. Follow them and you will be able to achieve the level of success you desire.

STEP 1. Professionals keep a positive attitude when the world crumbles around them. A little bit of the world crumbles around each of us at times, and we must learn to anticipate it. If you allow life's challenges to get you down, you won't be ready for the next positive thing that happens to you, and you just might miss a fantastic opportunity.

STEP 2. Professionals have a certain look about them. What's your vision of what a professional real estate salesperson looks like? Envision every detail from the hairstyle down to the shoes. Now, look at yourself in a mirror. Do any of the details in your ideal picture fit you? If not, maybe it's time to make some changes. Start with minor changes and watch yourself grow into that professional image you have in mind.

STEP 3. Customers and clients relate business success with competence. A professional surrounds himself or herself with images of success. Do your car, briefcase, desk, and office communicate a successful business career?

STEP 4. Organization is an important image to clients. This means being on time, having answers ready, handling details, and following up diligently. All these things tell people that you are a person worthy of their confidence. How organized are you?

STEP 5. Talk like a professional. Avoid shop talk at all costs. Ask questions about your clients. You must show an interest in them and their needs to get them to open up to you. Choose your words carefully so as not to offend. Plan your presentation from your prospect's point of view.

STEP 6. Stay in tune. The real estate profession is constantly changing. Devote a regular part of your week to learning of new developments in the field and sharpening your skills.

STEP 7. Respect your fellow salespeople. Others in this profession have the same challenges you have. They deserve the same credit and recognition when they succeed and the same help and encouragement when they fail. Everyone wins when the team gets stronger.

STEP 8. Remember your family and friends. They want and need a high-quality relationship. Be sure to plan time for family and social needs. It will help you gain their understanding when business takes you away evenings and weekends.

STEP 9. See the people. There are literally thousands of people in your area who need and deserve professional assistance with their real estate needs. If you don't take it to them, they might be shortchanged by someone less professional. The more people you meet, the more you can serve.

STEP 10. **Keep your integrity intact.** Almost every day an opportunity to take unfair advantage of someone arises. A professional knows that a dissatisfied customer today will cost him or her several possible transactions in the future. A professional knows how important selling with the facts is. Stretching the truth, omitting information, and avoiding present problems by stalling or blaming someone else is for amateurs. Sell with the facts, and you only have to sell them once.

If you'll use these ten steps as a guideline, when someone asks what you do for a living, you can say: I am a real estate professional!

Chapter 2

What to Do When You're New

Okay, you've passed the licensing exam and been hired by a local real estate brokerage. You have invested a good bit of your time, effort, and savings account in getting this far. Now, you're ready to make some money. Or are you?

Do you know that many agents lose all chance to take the listing before they even open their mouths? You might feel that this is rather hard to do. But it's easy. Happens all the time.

How is this feat managed? By arriving for appointments sloppily dressed, poorly groomed, and empty handed. Some losers aren't content with taking three strikes; they also get themselves thrown out of the game by being late.

The successful agent not only gets there on time, he or she is professionally dressed and well-groomed. Adding to these subtle but powerful indications of competence, the successful agent has the tools for getting the job done right there in his or her hand. By favorably impressing the client at first glance, the successful agent lays the foundation for a productive session before a word is spoken.

In many areas, professional dress for men is a suit and tie in a pleasing blend of fabrics that are quiet rather than loud in color and pattern. The professional's shoes don't yell for attention either. If you want your clients to trust you, if you want them to listen to what you're saying, don't fascinate or frighten them with your footgear.

The same holds true for your entire outfit. Loud ties, bright shirts, clashing colors, and bold patterns are associated with the huckster kind of salesperson in many people's minds. Most salespeople who dress this way feel the need to bolster their appearance of aggressiveness. Others do it out of ignorance. A few have a desperate need to show individuality. Winners don't let any of these considerations enter into their professional clothing decisions. They indulge their individuality and preferences during nonworking hours only. For business, they choose clothing that will help them make money.

When there are ensembles for business wear that project authority, stability, and competence, why put on clothing that projects eccentricity, instability, and incompetence? You are, after all, asking them to trust you to market what is probably their largest investment. If you're unsure of your wardrobe, visit the nearest large financial center and notice how the men and women who work there dress. Window shop the best clothiers in the area. Then make the best choices you can afford.

On the question of women's professional dress, I have just two suggestions: 1. when in doubt as to what to wear for an appointment, choose the conservative alternative; 2. avoid anything that will compete for attention with your face and what you're saying. That includes jewelry and too short a hemline on your skirt.

Stepping into Business

Now that you're ready to begin, here are the most important steps to take:

1. Have a professional photo taken. This will appear on everything you put your name to except, of course, legal documents that are part of the listing or sale of properties.

2. Get a cell phone. You have to have a number where people can reach you when you're out and about. Be sure to subscribe to voice mail services on this telephone and any other number you plan to give out. Make it a habit to listen to all of your messages—from clients and to yourself—twice each day at the very least.

3. Record an effective, powerful outgoing voice mail message. Here's a suggestion: "This is Mary Jones. Thank you for calling. I'm serving the needs of another client at the moment. However, your call is important to me. Please leave a message, and I will return your call as soon as possible." This demonstrates your desire to serve and your professionalism. Try a few different versions of the message until you come up with one that both suits your personality and gets the job done.

4. Get access to a computer and some good contact management software, such as ACT!, Goldmine, or Top Producer. Your broker or a top agent in the office might also have good recommendations.

If you don't already have a computer or easy access to one, you will want to consider investing in one. You will be using it quite a bit. If making this initial investment isn't in your budget, talk with your broker about what might be available in the office for your use.

5. Select a time management device such as a daily planner, PDA (Personal Data Assistant), or time-planning software for your laptop or other computer. These are necessary to help you keep your daily schedule and commitments up to date and accessible.

6. Get an e-mail address. Check it at minimum twice daily. Less than 6 percent of real estate agents with e-mail addresses do this. You'll set yourself apart as a dedicated professional by responding to all inquiries within twelve hours or less.

In a study conducted by the California Association of Realtors, more and more buyers are seeking information about properties online, and a large percentage of them are choosing real estate agents after a response to a Web inquiry.

7. Get access to the Internet. Become familiar with the many resources it has for real estate agents including training, industry news, information from public records, lead generation, and so on. Most importantly, become very familiar with your company's Web site. Make sure your personal contact information, including your e-mail and cell phone number is on it. If they don't have a Web site or an area in the site to list information on their agents, create a Web page that shows your photo and tells why you're the best agent to help a potential client.

Another key resource for real estate agents is Mapquest.com to provide you with driving directions to any location. As a backup, you might also want to keep a copy of your local street guide in your car. Don't risk your reputation on not being able to find a property.

8. Have magnetic signs made for your car. Put them on whenever you're out driving around town. Don't be afraid to be creative with your signs, unless your office dictates a standard style. One real estate agent invested in an unusual color of purple for the paint on her car. It drew attention wherever she went and when folks in her area thought of real estate they remembered her purple car *and* her name.

9. Purchase or gain access to a digital camera. You'll use this both in self-promotion—getting pictures of yourself at events you sponsor—and in promoting the homes you will list.

10. Have your business cards printed. When you receive them, take ten minutes to handwrite the words, *Thank You* on as many cards as you can. The handwritten thank you gives clients a quick impression that you're courteous. It will also allow you to present a professional image as you hand your card to someone: "You might notice that I wrote thank you on my card. I'm thanking you in advance for the opportunity, hopefully, to someday serve your real estate needs." This is a great way to break the ice with new contacts.

11. Mail out simple flyers or postcards announcing your new career and telling people how to contact you.

Now that you're set up in business, you need to find ways to reach out and get business. The first thing you want to do is to start campaigning for yourself. Just as political candidates gain support and find their way into the news, so must you.

Enter all the contact information for everyone you know into the software management program you've chosen. Don't leave anyone out. This is your first list of potential clients, as well as your list of key campaigners. Once the list is completed, you'll mail either a postcard or letter to each of them, telling them that you're now a part of the XYZ Realty Team, and that you're ready, willing, and able to serve their real estate needs.

Chances are that not too many of these people will call you right away to help them with selling a property. They may call to congratulate you, and that's just fine. The reason for sending them the announcement is to have your smiling face pop into their heads the next time they are involved in a conversation with anyone they meet about selling real estate. They are to become your eyes and ears—your scouts, if you will—for referring people to you.

Call a short list of key people—ones with a fairly large network of friends, relatives, and acquaintances—and offer your services to them or others they know. Offer to give them a free market analysis of their property as a way of thanking them in advance for keeping you in mind. This demonstrates to them that you have the ability and resources to handle the real estate business.

Now that you've taken the initial steps to let the world know you're in business, it's time to learn as much as possible about working the business.

What You Can Learn at the Office

Participate in any training the company has scheduled. If there's nothing scheduled, watch and learn from those around you in the office who are more experienced.

Volunteer for floor duty. This means you are responsible to take incoming calls from new potential clients who do not already have an agent representing their needs. Since the large share of real estate agents get their business by referral, this probably won't be a significant portion of your business, but it is a good place to start. To learn how to convert these callers into clients, read Chapter 20.

Get Out There

Offer to help out with another agent's open house. In most areas, there are open houses nearly every weekend. Experienced agents love to have help at these open houses. If a qualified buyer comes to the open house but finds the property is not what they're looking for, the real estate agent is free to further qualify their needs and possibly show them other properties while you take over the open house. Open houses are a great way to meet people interested in either buying or selling property. Even if their need isn't "hot" today, if you build rapport, establish trust with them, and follow up properly, you should be the one they call when their need does become urgent. Again, more about open house opportunities is covered in Chapter 21.

Select a specialty. This could be a particular neighborhood, school district, size of home, or town if you work in a small town area. Talk with other agents about their specialties. Learn the pluses and minuses of each. When driving through subdivisions pay attention not only to the homes but also to the amenities of the area such as parks, shopping, schools, churches, etc., that will be important to people moving in.

Take tours or canvases of properties that have recently become available for sale. Talk with other agents while on canvas. Take detailed notes on each property. It could very well be the new kitchen sink and faucets that help one of your buyers decide between two properties. Walk through each home, checking for details as if you were going to live there yourself.

Buddy up. If your broker allows it, go out on different types of appointments with several experienced agents in the office. You may visit a for-sale-by-owner with one; an appraisal or home inspection with another; the final closing on a property with a third.

Get familiar with your paperwork. Practice creating comparable market analyses, filling out listing forms, purchase agreements, etc. Familiarity will prevent you from making mistakes on the paperwork that could cost you or your client money or even lose a sale.

Get Public Notice

Send an announcement to the local paper for a section that might be titled, New Faces in Business. If your local area publications do not have such a section, you may want to consider taking out a small ad to announce your arrival in the real estate business and your readiness to serve the needs of your community. Some companies will split the investment for such an ad with new agents. See if your broker is open to this.

Be a part of your community. Attend chamber of commerce functions; get involved with some type of community action group or a local school function; consider sponsoring a sports team such as a local youth soccer team or little league. Get your name and face out there where the people are. When they see you in action, you'll begin building a positive reputation as a can-do person.

You're going to be very busy during the first few weeks of your real estate career. The key to success is in understanding that activity leads to productivity.

CHAPTER 3

Selling with Emotions

People don't buy logically. They buy emotionally, and then justify their purchases logically. Some real estate salespeople logically try to convince their prospects to purchase a property. That's why they don't make many sales. In actuality, people will get involved in a property emotionally first. Then it's up to you to provide solid, logical reasons they can use to justify their purchase.

Everything you have ever bought has been an emotional purchase. Take the clothes you're wearing. You must wear clothes, right? That's a logical point. However, the individual items of clothing you wear have been chosen with your emotions.

What about food? Why do you buy a certain brand of something when there are six others just like it on the shelf? You do it because of national advertising, because your mother bought that brand, or for some other emotional reason. You don't logically decide which brand to choose unless you're a super-frugal shopper and only buy the least expensive brands of everything. Even then, it's the emotion that arises when you practice thrift that makes the buying decision.

In real estate, each person or family you come in contact with needs shelter of some sort, right? That's a logical point. The type of shelter they own is an emotional decision. They may want something just like the home they grew up in. They may want a home of a certain size in a certain location for status reasons. That's still an emotional decision.

For others, the decision is based on economy—what they can afford. You might think that's logical, but emotions and money are linked together by a very strong chain. So you must effectively handle the emotions of your buyers to become a top real estate professional.

Creating Positive Images

To sell to our prospects emotionally, we must create positive images in their minds all the time. We want them to like us and trust us so they will relax and not keep anything back so we can help them find the home that suits them physically, emotionally, and financially. So we have to eliminate those things that create fear or tension and replace them with words, phrases, and images that will make clients want to invest their hard-earned money in a particular piece of real estate and with our help.

To begin with, you'll have to overcome the sad fact that most people just don't trust sales professionals. Why? Because everyone has heard about people who called themselves salespeople treating their customers poorly, even dishonestly. That means you're going to have to work extra hard to win their trust. The better you serve them, the more likely it is that you'll be able to make a career of serving them, their families, and their friends for many years to come. Therefore, you must overcome their initial wariness or fear by creating positive emotions if they're going to let you help them.

There are certain words in the vocabulary of the average real estate salesperson that literally scare prospects away. I call them rejection words. They create a desire in the heart of the client to reject whatever you say. You must soften the images associated with these words. Replace them with the words and phrases I will give you, and you'll be amazed at the results.

The first rejection word is *commission*. The moment they hear the word commission, what do your prospects think of? "Oh, yes, that's the money you make if we buy a home from you. So, obviously, everything you're telling us is so you earn one of those, you silver-tongued devil." This is not always done on a conscious level. Their thoughts are likely subconscious but still are affecting their emotions and desire to purchase.

A professional salesperson calls it the *brokerage* or the *fee for service*. You see, people understand that they must pay a fee to obtain service. They accept that but somehow when it's called a commission, it's like you're taking their money from them.

The next phrase is *down payment*. Don't ask people for a down payment. They don't want to give you one because they know they'll be obligated to a long string of payments before they will ever actually own the home. That's why we call it the *initial investment*. People know that making an investment is a good thing to do. The dictionary defines investment as "putting money into something for the purpose of making a profit." Therefore, when people hear investment, they think of profit, which generates a positive emotional response.

Professional salespeople never use the term *monthly payment*. What do you visualize when you hear that term? A big stack of bills you have to pay, right? Call it the *monthly investment*. People like being investors, but no one wants to be a payer.

The next rejection word might surprise you. It's the word *contract*. Most people know that when they get involved in a contract, they must go to court to get out of it. So, a contract is something to stay away from. A pro calls the contract or listing form the *agreement* or the *paperwork*. It's amazing how they'll let you go ahead and "draft up their feelings on the paperwork" to help them analyze the details before making a decision. But they'd be petrified if they thought you were filling out a contract. When it comes time for them to put their name on the paperwork, you do have an obligation to let them know it's a legal, binding agreement.

Another word that will destroy you is *sign*. What have your mother and father taught you from the time you were old enough to write your name? Don't sign anything unless you read the fine print! If the average human being takes a real estate agreement and reads the fine print, they'll want to see their lawyer. That's why we say *okay, endorse, approve,* or *authorize*. It's amazing that people won't sign anything, but they will approve it.

Just a note for you here that if you ask a client to okay the agreement, make sure they put their name on it. One fellow I know had a buyer okay an agreement, and when he presented it to the seller, they thought "Okay" was a mighty strange name.

Don't use the word *buy*. Emotionally, the prospects are not there with you to buy a home. They'll fight you if they hear that word. They want to *own* a home.

Please remove the words *sell* and *sold* from your mind. The moment your prospects hear either of those words, they'll immediately think, "We're not here to be sold." That's why we use the phrases *got them involved* or *helped them acquire*. Then, the image is of you being helpful rather than pushy or forceful.

If you love real estate as I do, you won't want anything to detract from the professionalism of our industry. That's why we don't make anyone a *deal* as in, "Boy, do I have a deal for you." When I think of the word *deal*, I think of the one I've always been looking for and never found. A professional real estate salesperson offers people magnificent *opportunities*. Now, once they take advantage of this opportunity, it's not a *deal closing*. Call it a *pending transaction*.

People know as soon as they hear the words *cost* or *price*, someone is about to try to take their money. So let's call it the *total investment* instead. Remember, an investment is something positive.

This next word is one of my pet peeves. Never let it leave your lips! The word is *pitch*. When I hear someone say, "I made a pitch today," I picture them throwing something at their prospect. What we, as professional real estate salespeople, do when we explain a property to our prospects is to give them a *presentation* on the property. Or we *demonstrate* the property. We don't throw it at them.

There will be times when your potential client, whether listing a property or seeking one to own, will state an *objection* to something you've said or shown them. The mental image is of a roadblock going up—something that stalls the forward movement of the transaction. If you have to discuss their objections, refer to them as *areas of concern* or *concerns*. It's a subtle difference, yet it implies something to address rather than overcome.

Often you'll have things arise that you used to call *problems*. Not any more. You're going to think of them as *challenges* from now on. Problems get in your way. Challenges are put in your way for you to overcome—becoming a better real estate agent in the doing.

Since attitude has a lot to do with success in any business, but especially in any form of sales, let's stop calling the people we haven't met yet *prospects*. Instead, we're going to refer to them exclusively as *future clients*. Thinking of them as clients before they actually become clients will have a positive impact on how you treat them when you first meet.

Speaking of meetings, let's stop making *appointments*. We're going to ask for an opportunity to *pop by and visit* with them. Do you see the difference? Appointments are for doctors and dentists. Popping by makes it sound like your visit won't take a lot of time—that it will be less formal. And, who doesn't like to visit? It implies getting to know you better, which will, in turn, allow you to better serve their needs.

If one of your potential clients doesn't qualify for the type of home they are wanting—let's say they have champagne tastes with a beer budget—never, ever suggest that they look for a cheaper home. The word *cheaper* connotes something that might be run down or in a lesser neighborhood than they desire. Instead, use the phrase *more economical*. Economy with someone else's money is never a bad thing.

When the prospect decides to go ahead, don't call what they give you their *deposit* or an *offer*. It's a *commitment* or *proposal*. Those terms sound more concrete than offer and will increase the confidence the seller has in your abilities.

If there is a charge to refinance the property prior to the maturity date, don't call it the *prepayment penalty*. Who wants to be penalized? No one. Call it the *prepayment privilege*.

And, if the seller chooses to carry back a secondary position in financing, which will be due in a few years, don't call it a *balloon payment*. What does the buyer see hanging over their home? Let's call it the *deferred initial investment*.

You might want to consider enlisting the help of another associate or a family member and giving them your usual presentation. Have them make notes on any of the rejection words that you use. Or, you may want to record your presentation either in an audio format or on video. You can then review your vocabulary and any other weaknesses so you can learn how to correct them.

You should know by now that repetition is the mother of learning. Therefore, the only way you're going to be able to improve yourself is to consciously replace the negative words and phrases in your vocabulary with the suggestions I've just given you. Repeat, repeat, repeat until the new, positive words flow naturally from your mouth.

In some offices where our training is mandatory, brokers or managers have been known to charge fees for each usage of a rejection word. As you might imagine, those replacement words become a natural part of your vocabulary rather quickly once you place a dollar figure on what the rejection words are costing you. The sad part is that few people realize how much more they cost them in lost sales or repeat business because the clients just didn't feel comfortable with your language—even though they probably didn't realize that's what caused the negative emotion at the time.

Professionals in all fields must continually hone their skills to stay on top. That's all I'm asking you to do.

Building Your Reflexes

Now that you know the words to use, you need to learn exactly when to use them. Professional salespeople have a polished, ready answer prepared for every objection—or concern—they hear. The average salesperson, on the other hand, relies on just saying whatever comes out of his or her mouth. They don't learn what to do or say when they hear an objection, even if it's one they've heard twenty times before and know they'll hear again, such as, "We're just looking," "It costs too much," or "We have a friend in the business."

You might not believe in using a canned presentation. I felt that way too, when I was broke. Yet if you take the time to learn my words, words that have been proven to work, you can use them until you are comfortable enough to come up with your own words that will then also work. But for now, use my words.

You can use index cards or make tapes to listen to in the car, or you can try my real estate audio program, which includes a review segment similar to what I'm telling you to create here. Whatever method you use, you've got to PDR—practice, drill, and rehearse. Whether you do it by yourself or with a family member, friend, or business associate doesn't matter. The idea is not to practice on good, qualified buyers. The lesson becomes too expensive if you try to learn that way.

Part One

Becoming a Listing Champion

CHAPTER 4

Why You Should Become a Listing Champion

The primary reason is money. Champion listing agents have the potential to earn as much as other professionals, such as doctors and lawyers—without the huge investment of time and money in formal education. But they don't do it without effort, or without first learning their business.

Please understand that I'm talking about *champions* at listing real estate, not *average* listing agents. The truth is shocking: The average salesperson doesn't make enough to stay in the business. Worse yet, thousands of new licensees quit real estate before they've made their first dollar.

It's so unnecessary.

Everyone who has enough intelligence and discipline to acquire a license can be successful in real estate. All it takes is the proper training and a reasonable amount of effort. The training I can give you; the effort you must provide.

If you regard real estate as just another job, you'll certainly fail to achieve much, and you're not likely to be in business next year at this time. When you hang your new real estate license on a broker's wall, you go into business for yourself. You plunge into a battle to survive that's far keener than most people experience while working for wages or a salary. Real estate is not a position in which you build up seniority, accrue company benefits, and go on strike for more money. When you want more money in real estate, you just go out and make it.

"But they don't train me," many new people in real estate say. "How am I supposed to know what to do if my company won't train me?"

I had that misconception too. I thought my company would train me. Every company I'd ever worked for ran me through an on-the-job training program first. When I went to work as a bridge deck specialist, they trained me. It went like this: "See those steel bars over there? Carry them up that ramp." That's on-the-job training. And you know what? Nobody pays much for jobs you can learn in four seconds. But they will pay you while they train you.

Since you're essentially in business for yourself when you get your license, the training falls on your shoulders. As I mentioned in Chapter 2, you'll need to take the initiative to seek out classes, books, audio programs, mentors, and top producers and learn from them. If you're fortunate, you'll start out with a company that has at the very least a mentoring program where you work beside an experienced agent for a while to learn the ropes. If you're really fortunate, you'll start with a company that offers in-house training classes covering all aspects of real estate listing, sales, and industry changes as they come along.

Another reason why you should become a listing champion is power. Champion listers and strong listers control the business. Sellers come to them because of their reputation for getting houses sold; buyers come to them because of their reputation for having desirable properties—many to choose from. Wise brokers treasure agents who get their share of salable listings over those who don't.

Why? Because one of the unique features of the resale housing brokerage business is that we have to create our own stock in trade. That's where about half the income lies, in the inventory-creating activity known as listing. And it's the more secure half. Without listings, a brokerage office has nothing to sell of its own. Buyers tend to work with the offices that have signs on interesting properties. The office without a good inventory of listings soon feels its sales drying up. Unless you're a strong lister, you'll always be hanging by your fingernails in real estate.

Another reason why you should become a listing champion is that listings can make you money even when you're out of town. As a buyer's agent, you must be with those buyers while looking at homes and making the necessary decisions. As a listing agent, you can list the home and let every other real estate agent in the world work on selling it—without having to be present. There's nothing sweeter than having your vacation paid for by a listing that sold when you were skiing down a mountain or wiggling your toes in the sand thousands of miles from home. Nice things like this frequently happen to listing champions.

How do you achieve that level? To explain that, we first need to talk about listing banks.

If you've just started to think about a career in real estate, this concept may be new to you. Perhaps you're not positive exactly what a listing is. Skip the next two paragraphs if you are familiar with these terms.

The agreement between a broker and an owner wanting to sell property is called a *listing*. It must be in writing and conform to many laws and regulations. The most commonly used kind of listing agreement states that the seller will pay a fee if the property is sold within a limited time for the specified price and under the specified terms. The listing also shows (1) how the fee is to be calculated and (2) how it is to be divided between the listing office representing the seller and the selling office representing the buyer. (Brokers have separate written agreements with their agents spelling out how the fee will be divided between the office and the agent.)

A *listing bank*—often called a *farm*—is a group of up to five hundred houses assigned to or selected by one agent as his or her special territory.

A *listing champion* is a real estate agent who earns more in listing fees from his or her listing bank than any other agent in the office does.

A *listing superchampion* earns more than all other agents combined do in their listing banks.

And in this book, *champion* refers to an agent who is trained in the Tom Hopkins method.

Can this really happen? Do listing superchampions actually exist?

Certainly. I was one myself for several years in my listing bank in Simi Valley, California. After that, I managed a real estate office and developed a team of strong listers, champions, and superchampions of listing.

Did you notice that I didn't say your listing bank will be your *exclusive* territory? Companies that own the products they sell may give exclusive territories, but real estate brokers are in an entirely different position. Only rarely do they own what they sell. Since they lack a manufacturer's absolute control of inventory, they must adopt rules that are realistic for their own operations.

In addition to the competition you'll face from other real estate firms, you'll probably find that, under certain circumstances, agents from your own office can take listings in your bank. Expect this to occur frequently. Then, it won't be such a terrible shock when you discover that there's a new listing in your territory, and it was taken by an agent whose desk is just down the aisle from yours. But the rules that allow him to do that also allow you to take listings all over town under the same circumstances. So learn the rules. Get comfortable with them by understanding their logic. Think positively. Concentrate on what you can gain rather than what you can lose.

Another powerful reason why you should become a listing champion is to gain what I call mobile security. This is one of the great benefits of professional status. It means that you can take your specialized knowledge and skills wherever you like and earn a professional's income with them.

And here's yet another reason for attaining championship listing power. Real estate brokerage has to be performed by local people. No development overseas can drive your company out of business, and no one anywhere can invent a gadget that will make you obsolete. The practice of real estate gets more complicated every year, and this trend has to continue. Why am I so sure? Because our population is increasing, but our land area is not. This means that the pressure of people on the available space will intensify, leading to more and more complex real estate arrangements. The need for ever more skilled and knowledgeable real estate professionals will continue to grow throughout your career. Everything positive that you learn about real estate not only contributes to your present prosperity; it also contributes to your future security as well.

The price of becoming a listing champion is high. Most people think that it takes too much effort and demands too great a sacrifice of free time. Maybe you're one of those who won't pay the price. That's all right. If money is your only concern, you'll always be poor in spirit no matter how much wealth you accumulate. So make the choice that's right for you. We all have to decide at what point making more money becomes less valuable to us than having more time for ourselves and our families.

But remember that you don't have to pay the high price of becoming a listing champion in order to earn a substantial income from listing fees. The thousands of strong listers I've trained are proof of this.

You may be thinking, "I'll bet none of those successful people had to overcome my handicaps and disadvantages, or fight my problems."

You're right.

None of them had exactly your personal situation or set of challenges—many of them had far worse troubles of their own. I know strong listers who get around on crutches. Others are blind. Gary Wahlquist was a listing champion throughout his losing fight against leukemia.

Edie Roman didn't do well in school because of her heartrending childhood. So when her first marriage ended and left her with small children to support, Edie had no job skills to support them with. After a rough period of low-paid menial work and welfare, this determined lady became a strong lister.

Many of today's listing champions had to learn English first, and some came to real estate with no previous work experience except manual labor in farmer's fields. Other listing winners had to battle various kinds of prejudice along their road to achievement. Life gave every one of these people plenty of excuses for failure, but they chose success anyway. You too can find excuses in your life, or you can turn your back on excuses and opt for success.

It's your choice. What will it be?

Please realize one vital point: It truly is entirely your choice whether you fail or succeed. Once you accept this fact, nothing can deny you every bit of success that you're willing to earn.

In the chapters that follow, you'll find all the techniques you need to acquire listing power.

CHAPTER 5

How to Acquire Listing Power

If you've worked the list of campaigners you started with in Chapter 2, you will be receiving names and contact information about people who want to sell a home. Or, just as good, having the people your campaigners meet give you a direct call with their real estate questions.

Refer to these leads as quality introductions. The new people you meet through your friends and acquaintances will already have a positive impression of you because of what those friends told them about you. Now, all you have to do is live up to your reputation.

These leads, most commonly called referrals, are the best source of new business. A referral is a fee that calls up or walks in and says, "Take me, I'm yours." But if you don't have the proper knowledge and skill, they will walk right out again and leave you empty handed.

How do you avoid this? By acting on my first method of acquiring listing power: Gain knowledge. You should know everything about:

THE INVENTORY.

A thorough understanding of the real estate that's available now in your service area is essential. This knowledge is your basic expertise. The more formidable your fund of inventory knowledge is, the more formidable your listing power will be.

FINANCING.

Sellers will be impressed if you can guide prospective buyers through a practiced discussion about their financing options.

YOUR SERVICE AREA.

Sellers want to know that you are aware of and appreciate the benefits that your area offers prospective buyers.

THE FORMALITIES.

You must have full understanding of the legal requirements, forms, and business procedures involved in the transfer of real estate ownership.

The second way to acquire listing power is to learn to work with people, to get them to like and trust you, to lead them to decisions that are truly beneficial to them and earn your fee. We'll cover this thoroughly in later pages.

The third requirement for acquiring listing power is to get yourself out in the community and put your skills and knowledge to work. But what about referrals? Can't you wait for people to come through the door on a referral?

Sure you can. Thousands of new licensees do; it's one of the most popular ways to fail in this business. Don't confuse the referrals and walk-in traffic that your company generates with the true referral that comes specifically to you because you've earned it.

This is an easy pitfall. If you depend on your company's leads, call-ins, and walk-ins for your basic income, you're not lift to that firm, you're drag. When they start losing altitude, they'll have to get rid of the drag.

Look on company-provided business as a bit of gravy that makes your meat and potatoes taste better, but never think of it as the main course. With this attitude and a determination to develop several dollars in fees on your own for every dollar you make from company-generated activity, you'll truly be in business for yourself. Only by believing in and acting on the premise that you're a business of your own can you develop the professional skills that will give you high income and mobile security.

The fourth and most important way of acquiring listing power is to deserve referrals. You do that by using superior knowledge and superior skill to render superior service. The referrals will come when you've earned the right to ask for them and not before. Many new salespeople do such a good job on their first transactions that they start getting referrals very early in their real estate careers. Make that your goal. Without a steady flow of referrals, high earnings are difficult to achieve.

There are many sources for gaining high-performance listing power. It's practically impossible to enact all of them at once. You'll want to select one or two to begin with and add others as needed. I'll list them briefly here so you can start thinking about which appeals most to you. Later chapters will explain each of these systems in detail.

Getting Behind Closed Doors

The money in real estate is behind the doors that line your town's streets. To get whatever share of that money you want, you have to get yourself known behind those closed doors.

When I started in real estate, we got to know the people in the neighborhoods where we wanted to work by walking door to door, knocking or ringing the doorbell, and introducing ourselves to Mrs. Housewife. Obviously, times have changed and there are very few homemakers at home during the day. If they are, they're likely to be working a home-based business or coordinating volunteer work in the community or at their children's schools.

In most areas where people are at home during the day, many will be sleeping because they work night shifts. Others may be tending small children. Few will feel comfortable opening their door to strangers. But sometimes it does work if you're able to get their attention.

Turning Doorbells into Dollars

Most people hate ringing strangers' doorbells. But when you're prepared, when you know how, when you've had a lot of success doing it, you won't hate ringing doorbells any more. Maybe you won't love it—but you'll get out there and do it regularly without feeling any distress.

To make doorbell ringing easy, have a reason for doing it. Something that's truly beneficial to the person on the other side of the door. This would include information on real estate values, or things that could or are being done by others to increase values in the area.

Then rehearse plenty of things to say. You must be warm, friendly, and sincere in order to get them to like you and trust you. Be prepared to talk about the neighborhood, the local shopping, employment opportunities in the area, and so on.

Finally, have the right attitude. We're going to talk a lot about attitude in Chapter 29 because attitude is where most real estate people—and salespeople of all kinds for that matter—destroy themselves. For the time being, accept the fact that this book will give you many ways to enhance your attitude so that you can do whatever it takes to succeed in this business.

Canvasing That Counts

We're concentrating on listing real estate in this part of the book, and in part two, we'll concentrate on selling real estate. But the two functions often mix in actual practice. When you're canvasing, you're not only looking for people who want to sell their homes, you're also looking for people who want to buy real estate. Champion listers also sell a large volume of real estate, which is the fifth source of listing power: the ability to sell what you list.

In the following chapters we're going to explore the techniques of money-making in detail. I'm going to show you how to act and what to say so that you'll get the opportunity to visit with and to work face to face with qualified people. Then and only then do you have the opportunity to earn a fee.

In other chapters, I'll detail exactly how you turn that visit or meeting into a listing. Acquiring listing power is a process of learning a variety of skills and facts and then putting them all together in a series of smooth performances. That is, you learn a method that works, and then you keep using it over and over. You'll find it all in these pages.

Getting People to Like and Trust You

Champion listers have an aura of integrity. People feel comfortable with them. People believe they can rely on the champion or strong lister's word. They respect the lister's knowledge of real estate. All through the book, we're going to be studying this basic skill of getting people to like and trust you. You'll find many hints, insights, and specific techniques for making this happen. For years, I've been telling my audiences that being able to get people to like and trust you is an essential part of real estate success. This quality is the sixth source of listing power.

Converting For-Sale-by-Owners into Money-Making Inventory

Sellers of real estate who try to go it alone without professional assistance are one of the top sources for listings. At least once in their lives, a large percentage of owners try to market their own properties. Few succeed. But the myth that it's easy persists. Why? Because that's what many sellers want to believe. Their purpose, of course, is to save the fee. What they don't face up to is that the buyer also intends to save the fee. Why else should he or she bother negotiating directly with the owner instead of having a knowledgeable agent do the scouting and bargaining for him? And then there are the complex details to handle and all the pitfalls to avoid.

Few by-owners understand the fears that grip many people facing the challenge of selecting a home. The reality is that most buyers aren't decisive enough to go through with the purchase of a home without the emotional support of a capable salesperson. By-owners don't give much thought to another reality: that the buyers they're most likely to get an offer from are people whose credit won't carry the purchase. These so-called buyers usually have been told by several real estate offices that they can't qualify for the necessary financing. Do they go home and start saving their money and improving their credit rating? No. First they try their luck on the by-owners.

Most real estate transactions hit snags at some point between a qualified buyer's first visit and the day he or she assumes ownership.

Unless a skilled real estate professional is constantly monitoring the transaction, any of these snags can hold the transaction up and then destroy it. By-owners don't realize how often problems arise during the time transactions are open. Nor do they realize how difficult it will be for them to resolve matters directly with the buyer.

Why? Because the problems generally boil down to one thing: Who pays for curing this new difficulty?

By-owners also underestimate the difficulties of financing the sale of their home. They don't know about title insurance, proration of taxes, and a host of other questions that a strong agent is well informed on and can cope with. For-sale-by-owners often enter into transactions that fall out of escrow (fall out of the closing or settlement) and are never completed. Such fallouts usually are a disaster for the by-owner. Fallouts often tie the sellers' property up during the best selling season. They often cause the sellers to default on the purchase of their next home or force the sellers into costly double moves or into making payments on two houses at the same time. What a vital service you render to by-owners when you list them for your highly skilled professional service!

The reasons why by-owners won't save money add up to a compelling argument. All you have to do is explain the facts and take the listing. Sounds easy, doesn't it? It is when you've paid the price for knowing how.

The truth is, listing by-owners demands special skills that come only from special training. We'll give you that training in Chapters 11 and 12. If you'll make these skills yours, you'll find that working with by-owners is one of your most dependable and rewarding activities. Though it's the seventh source of listing power given in this chapter, many high-earning agents consider by-owners to be their primary source of income.

Gathering Listings on Open Houses

When done well, holding open houses is a marvelously effective strategy. Unfortunately, it's not done well very often. This provides you with great opportunities, because holding successful open houses is a simple, step-by-step process. Doing it well enough to make big money requires work the week before. Unless you do that work in time, your weekend open houses have little chance of being worthwhile.

Many new or unsuccessful people in real estate don't understand that open houses often are better for listing than for selling. Some of these people have only one thing in mind: to sell the house they're holding open. This attitude puts them in the same position as the by-owner: that of trying to fit just one house to everybody who walks in.

At the opposite extreme, other agents try desperately to hook onto everyone who comes through, giving little thought to protecting their sellers' interests. These experts in unprofessional conduct are as quick to knock the price of the house they're showing as they are to close it up and take off to look at other property with any possible buyer. The results range from wasted time to calamity.

In Chapter 21, I'll tell you how to avoid calamities and cash in on the exciting opportunities that professional open house techniques offer you. This is your eighth source of listing power, and it's one of the best.

Creating a Profitable Listing Bank

Call it a farm if you like. That's a good name. It implies that you work your group of up to five hundred houses with the diligence of a successful farmer working his acres. Like him, you prepare the soil, plant the seeds, and nurture the growth of the crop you're raising. You work with people. The farmer works with plants. Your seeds are the words you speak and the notes you write. Both of you have to cope with things like insects and rodents before you can take in your harvest. His crop may be corn or cotton; yours is a steady flow of salable listings.

But I think it's more inspiring to look on your special territory as a listing bank because every time you go in there and work, you make a deposit. (Don't forget, bank withdrawals must be preceded by bank deposits.) After you've made frequent enough deposits in your listing bank, the value you've built up there will support you in the style you'd like to become accustomed to.

Think of your listing bank as your ninth and last source of listing power. Why last? Because a rich flow of employment agreements (listings) won't surge into your control from your bank until some of the first eight sources are delivering results from your efforts. Your listing bank won't be ninth in terms of income produced for you when that happens. Then it'll be one of your top sources of income. I'll show you exactly how to develop your listing bank into a money gusher in Chapter 16.

For most high earners, the largest source of listing fees is referrals. This entire book tells you how to get referrals by increasing your professional skill and knowledge.

CHAPTER 6

Liquidating Your Listings

What do you want more of in your bank? Both at the bank where you do your checking and in the bank where you do your listing, you want to have more things that can quickly be turned into cash. Things like salable listings.

How do you do that? Well, in order to earn money to invest *for* yourself, you must invest *in* yourself. True education marries knowledge to skill. Their child is power. Power is money. Every time you go into your listing bank, you have the opportunity to convert your education into money in the bank.

If you don't educate yourself on the most common situations you'll encounter and how to handle them professionally, you risk the potential hazard that you will load yourself up with five or ten listings priced too high to sell. When that happens, the uneducated work hard. They take a great amount of abuse from their unrealistic sellers who can't understand why they aren't getting their unreasonable prices, but they can't make any money. Listings are like sirloin steaks. Barbecue them properly and they're delicious; leave them on the coals too long and there's not much enjoyment.

How to Lose by Winning

Listing runs smoothly when your properties are priced right in the beginning. Your clients are happy because their equity money comes fast; you are happy because your fee money comes fast. Fewer challenges develop over the shorter time span. Listing the right way means pricing the right way.

You lose by winning by being top poodle in a dogfight over who'll take a listing at the highest price. Who will your clients blame when their dreams of extra thousands of dollars fade? How patient will they be when there's no action? Who will they bad-mouth around town? Your prize is a listing that'll sour your enthusiasm and damage your reputation without paying you a cent. The only way you can come out ahead in a bidding contest is to persuade the sellers to give their overpriced listing to another agent for thirty days only. Then, when the market proves you right by ignoring that property, you have a chance to take the expired listing at a salable price.

Servicing Your Listings with Style and Control

In an active market, and when your listings are priced right for that market, you won't spend much time servicing listings. You'll spend more time monitoring transactions through to completion. But we aren't always in an active market. And, in any market, there are properties that appeal to only a small percentage of the available buyers. So you'll need to know how to service listings over a period of time until the right buyers are found.

The champion sets the sellers up for a smooth-running relationship at the time the listing is taken. He tells them what to expect, what the market is doing, and how prospective buyers and the agents working with those buyers will operate. Then the champion stays in regular contact with those sellers until the listing sells. During the first week, he contacts them every three days to tell them what he's done behind the scenes. This might include:

Getting the listing in the MLS (Multiple Listing Service).

Telling other agents in his office, and other offices, about the newly available property.

Telling the sellers whether or not an open house is scheduled and when.

He never lets a week go by without phoning, never lets three weeks slip by without stopping for a personal visit. This is the minimum program. Some sellers may require more attention. What should the champion communicate to them?

How the market for housing is behaving.

Changes in the interest rates.

Competing properties newly on the market.

Comments from people who have seen the house.

Similar properties that have sold. Sellers hate to discover for themselves that a house like theirs just sold two blocks away. They want to hear it from the real estate expert they've employed.

Plans for additional selling efforts.

And reminders, as required, of how the process works.

An important part, perhaps the most important part, of this communication process is listening. The sellers are living in a changing world. Their emotions can be volatile. Many sellers feel that they have plenty of time to move when they list. However, the act of listing punctures the balloon of security that their home had given them. Keep them talking to you about their feelings. When they start looking for a new home to make them feel secure again, their nonchalance about timing can vanish. Maybe they can't find the home they really want. Maybe they have doubts arise about making a move at all. The relaxed, confident sellers become the tense, worried buyers of another house. Buyers, that is, if they can get their money out of their old home. The tabby becomes a tiger. Every day that goes by feels like a week. Listening to their needs and their fears will allow you to reassure them that they're normal in having those feelings. You will be the calming voice in the upheaval they've created in their lives by putting their biggest security up for sale.

How and When to Get Price Reductions

When we refer to the need to get price reductions, we're talking only about in reasonably steady market conditions. If prices are changing rapidly, today's market price listing may be tomorrow's no-action headache.

How do you get sellers to lower their asking price? By setting it up when you agree to take the high-priced listing. You tell them that if it doesn't sell within a certain time frame, you'll ask them to lower it. That's what the champions and superchampions I've trained do. Set it up going in. Do that every time you take a listing unless you get it at market value when the general outlook and seasonal pattern indicate steady or rising prices.

If you don't set them up to realistically lower their asking price, you're asking for trouble. By confirming your sellers' unrealistic expectations, you have set yourself up for this disaster: Your sellers have already mentally, and maybe even actually, spent the money they're not going to get because you let them shove an unobtainable price onto the listing agreement.

Keep in mind that you approved the listing agreement, too. You're the real estate *expert*. Your name on that agreement gives their price the stamp of validity in their minds. Your credibility as a real estate expert rides on that price. When it gets thrown out, you get thrown out, too. If you have set up all of your listings in this way, your best move might be to start over in a new listing bank in another part of town.

Contrast this with the champion's method of operation. She researches the value and presents her findings. If she agrees to test the market at a higher price, she does so only after making sure that her sellers understand that she is not endorsing that amount. She gets the seller to initial a comment to that effect on the CMA (comparable market analysis) while taking the listing. The wise agent also gets a commitment from the sellers to consider a price reduction if no genuine buying interest has developed after an agreed period of time.

When should you seek the price reduction?

Just as soon as it's apparent that the seller's price is too high. Establish that answer for each listing with your sellers. When you walk in for the listing presentation, you should already have a clear idea of how long property in their price category remains on the market when it's listed at market value. Your Multiple Listing Service or your office's files will give you this information. Having this information on hand puts you in the power seat and lets the sellers know they're dealing with an expert.

Documenting facts is one of the successful real estate agent's primary methods of impressing his expertise on clients. New agents need aids of this kind more than established agents do. Yet new agents generally have less of it.

Here's a document you can create in a short time to help impress your clients with your real estate expertise. It is also a powerful aid in setting the client up for a more realistic price now, or for a significant reduction later.

Keep a running list of the days on market (DOM) for all properties that sell in your office's service area. Break this information down by price categories. Keep it simple. You can handwrite this data on a legal pad, but it will look more professional in an Excel document. Gather the information only on the hottest-selling price categories, and don't bother with unnecessary details.

Let's say there are ten properties on your DOM study. To get the average number of days on market, take the total days all ten were offered for sale (say 587) and divide by ten. The answer is 58.7 days, which we round to 59 days.

This information will make motivated sellers think. Are they willing to wait fifty-nine days—almost two months—to see their property sell?

Please remember that the timing of their sale is of great importance to most sincere sellers, and timing is the overriding consideration with some. In fact, if your sellers say they're in no hurry, be wary. All your selling efforts may go for nothing because they're not emotionally committed to selling at any other price.

Of course, whatever you tell your clients must be the absolute truth. Be aware that your MLS book will often only show the days on market of the most recent listing; if the house was previously listed with one or several other offices, that information may not show on the list of sold properties. Sellers need to know what it will cost them in terms of time if they choose to test the market with an unrealistic price. One of the most important services that you can perform as their real estate expert is to advise them how much time they can lose trying to get $21 for a $20 bill.

In Chapter 19, I'll give you a sample script to use when trying to get your sellers to agree to a realistic price using a DOM study. You'll be halfway home to liquidating that listing and adding to your liquid assets in the bank.

DOM STUDY
(Days on Market)

4 BEDROOMS	UNDER $200,000		SOLD DURING MARCH	
Address	**Date Sold**	**Selling Price**	**Original Asking Price**	**DOM**
2814 Lambert	3/2	$159,500	$159,500	26
302 Konya	3/4	$151,000	$151,000	3
2212 Willow	3/5	$172,000	$200,000	314
2874 Ganado	3/8	$174,500	$174,500	19
906 Knollview	3/12	$168,500	$168,500	7
202 Whiting	3/15	$155,900	$158,500	31
811 Rubio	3/18	$154,300	$156,500	33
892 Elm	3/12	$165,000	$165,000	28
1991 West	3/27	$170,900	$172,500	37
1679 Ashley	3/29	$164,450	$169,500	89
				587

AVERAGE DAYS ON MARKET

Overall	59
When 2 longest are disregarded	23
When 2 longest and 2 shortest are disregarded	29

CHAPTER 7

The Typical Seller's Pricing Method

When you get to a listing appointment, you'll only be as good as your preparation. Great preparation lets you give a great presentation; mediocre preparation limits you to a mediocre listing presentation; no preparation dooms you to flounder through what can't really be called a presentation at all. If this book convinces you of only one thing, I hope it's that to make money listing real estate, you must prepare effectively before working with sellers.

Unless you do, the sellers know more about the property than you do. They're in control of your meeting. They set the price. And you aren't playing a real estate expert's part. You're playing the part of a clerk.

To illustrate what you're up against in the usual listing opportunity, let's run through one as it develops. The specific facts differ in every case, but the basic realities are the same, and the emotional responses that people have to those realities fall into the same pattern.

As you read the situation that follows, picture the people in your mind. Share their feelings. The more you do, the better you'll understand the feelings of your future clients when they put their homes on the market. Understanding how your clients think and feel is an important step toward mastering the art of listing real estate.

My clients are Mr. and Mrs. Watt. An electrical engineer who's been with the same firm for twenty years, Jack Watt is a tall, skinny fellow with an intense manner. His goal in life is to become a vice president at his company. Over the years, management has given Jack a lot of encouragement, and six times he's moved to different states at their request. But now Jack and his wife Gloria have lived in their present home for five years. They like it and the community. They've put down roots. Taking another transfer is a touchy subject for them. In fact, Jack promised Gloria that they won't move again—unless it's for a really good promotion.

Then one day that kind of promotion comes through. As is so often the case, Jack's new opportunity is a thousand miles away. So Jack doesn't pick up the phone and call Gloria: "Guess what, honey? You get to move to another strange town." Instead, Jack decides to wait until they're face-to-face.

When he starts home that night, Jack has some doubts. He wonders if the promotion is worth all the emotional upheaval, all the effort of getting resettled and finding new friends, and he worries about the effect of the move on his family. But he knows he's going. Then he starts thinking about his largest investment, his home. Now he'll have to market it. He's spent a lot of weekends working on the house, getting things just the way he and Gloria like them. Remembering all they've shared in their home, Jack feels resentful. He knows he has to sell, but he doesn't want to do it.

When he reaches his neighborhood, Jack starts seeing things he never paid much attention to before. Turning a corner, he notices a for-sale-by-owner sign. Jack has the vague feeling that it's been there for quite a while. "I wonder what that house is worth," he says to himself, and makes a mental note of the phone number on the sign.

The house Jack noticed belongs to Mr. and Mrs. Tweety, and it's been on the market since they moved in eight years ago. Mr. Tweety is a perpetual by-owner. Everything he has is for sale at all times. If he gets his price, he'll be happy to move. Not all by-owners are like that, but in every community there seems to be one Mr. Tweety.

On another street, Jack takes a close look at the XYZ Realty sign on Herman and Wilma Mildue's front lawn. He and Gloria know the Mildues. When he sees the red SOLD rider on XYZ Realty's sign, Jack feels a stab of excitement. Since Gloria and Wilma bowl on the same team, Jack figures he can get the straight story from the Mildues.

A couple of blocks farther on, there's another sign. This is the Simpson home, listed with Pathetic Realty. It's been on the market for seven months now, but, since Jack doesn't know the Simpsons, he doesn't remember how long it's been for sale.

When Jack turns into his own driveway, he's feeling a little better about selling his home. Without going out of his way, he's found three houses to base his price on. He starts off with this premise: his home is nicer than the other three.

Our minds are like computers. Put garbage in your mind about a specific subject, and you'll get garbage out of your mind on that same subject. That's what's called a GIGO (garbage in, garbage out). If Jack puts the wrong facts about the value of nearby houses in his head, he'll get the wrong answer about the value of his house out of his head. After squaring things with Gloria and the kids about the move, Jack gets busy gathering his GIGOs.

First, he calls Mr. Tweety. That gentleman now has eight years of experience in handling sign calls, so Mr. Tweety is very persuasive when he says that his home is worth $285,000 if it's worth one thin dime. Jack catches his first sack of garbage.

When he gets off the phone, he's bubbling with delight. "Gloria, if that guy on the corner can get $285,000 for his place, we're going to start at $300,000. I didn't think houses were worth that much around here, but I've been hearing rumors. Honey, XYZ Realty just sold the Mildue's place. Why don't you give Wilma a call and see how much they got."

Gloria says, "Do I have to? Wilma's kind of a loudmouth. She'll yap it to everybody we know that we're moving."

"Don't let on," Jack tells his wife. "Just say that maybe we might be moving sometime in the next few months. Look, we're talking big dollars now. Knowing what property sells for around here can make us several thousand more. It'll be like finding a bundle of money in the street. We need that information."

"Okay, okay," Gloria says, "I'll call her."

She does. "We noticed that you've sold your home. How'd you come out?"

"On top like we always do," Wilma says. "We got what we wanted."

When Wilma and Gloria were bowling a few weeks before, somebody asked Wilma how much they had their house listed for. Wilma did what many people do when she answered: She added about 15 percent to get a better sounding figure.

In the bowling center, Gloria had been surprised at how high Wilma said their price was. Now, on the phone, Gloria is thinking a little dubiously about that price, but Wilma's manner keeps her from pressing to confirm the exact figure the Mildues sold for. She puts the phone down and tells Jack, "I think the Mildues might've sold for about $290,000."

"Wow," says Jack, catching his second sack of garbage.

"Aren't you glad you called Wilma? You probably just made us at least $10,000. I'm almost positive we'll be able to get $300,000." Now Gloria starts getting excited about all the money they're going to make, and she forgets her doubts about Wilma's truthfulness.

Here's what actually happened. When the Mildues decided to sell, Herman called in an agent he respected, and he insisted that their house was worth $265,000. The agent agreed to list their house at $265,000 on condition that the price would be reconsidered if 30 days passed without action. There wasn't any. After a month, the Mildues reduced their price to the market figure recommended by their agent, $249,500. Two weeks later, they accepted an offer of $248,000. That price gave them a profit of $13,000—more than Herman had hoped to make on the house when they moved in three years before. In that sense, Wilma told the truth when she said, "We got what we wanted." But, knowing that she'd spread the $290,000 figure all over town, Wilma isn't about to admit to anyone that they actually were glad to get $248,000.

Jack says, "That one sold for $290,000, and Tweety is selling himself for $285,000. All right! Now let's call Pathetic Realty and find out what the real estate experts can tell us about values in this neighborhood."

Jack gets through to Pathetic the next day. After half an hour (because it takes them that long to find the listing) someone calls back and says the Simpson house is beautiful, it's priced at $297,500, and would Jack like to see it sometime?

He says no and gets off the phone quickly. Not realizing that he's just caught his third sack of garbage in two days, Jack is overjoyed. A real estate "expert" has confirmed his hopes.

The truth about Pathetic's listing wouldn't support Jack's optimism. The Simpsons' property has been on the market seven months now because their motivation to sell isn't strong enough to make them realistic about price. They aren't leaving town. The only way they'll move is if they can sell well above market and buy well below market.

The Simpsons didn't list their home until they talked to Fred Blodgett, who works at the butcher shop in the grocery store where they shop. The Simpsons like the way Fred cuts meat. So, when he told them he'd just received his real estate license, they asked him to come over and list their house.

That's been the extent of Blodgett's real estate career. He's still working in the butcher shop for a living. Whenever he thinks about it, Fred wishes the Simpsons' house would sell. If that happens, Fred thinks he might start working at real estate a couple weekends a month. He doesn't want to rush into anything that might not pay. As it is, Fred figures that real estate already owes him for at least two weeks' work because, if he doesn't round up some of his relatives twice a month and take them through the house as though they were buyers, the Simpsons complain about no action. Sometimes Fred wonders why SOLD signs always pop up on other people's listings, but never on his. He thinks it's just dumb luck, and someday his will change. In the meantime, Fred's main worry is that he's running out of relatives.

I've just detailed the general method that most sellers use in pricing their homes. They talk to other sellers in ways that are guaranteed to give them unrealistic values. They listen to every rumor that raises real estate prices, and there's always at least one real estate adviser where everybody works. You know the type. He bought a vacant lot once that sold for a profit after nine years. Then he went to real estate school three nights in a row for a whole week. He knows everything about all real estate everywhere.

Here's how the seller's pricing method works: The average seller contributes three GIGOs when he calls in the average real estate agent. If that agent hasn't done his homework, he can't hose off the three garbage in, garbage outs. So he adds his part of the formula: one scientific wild guess. Then what do they have?

$$3 \text{ GIGOS} + 1 \text{ SWG} = 1 \text{ OPT}$$

An Overpriced Turkey.

The natural-as-breathing formula, GIGO + SWG = OPT, never

gives you a fast-selling, priced-at-the-market listing. It never results in the bargain-priced buy of the year. It traps you in the turkey cage every time you let a seller run it off on you.

Please realize that this is not the fault of the sellers. They can't help feeling that their home is worth 10 to 30 percent more than the market will carry. They're not real estate professionals. But, they all feel their home is better than the neighbors'; that they've done more to the home that added value to it. They don't earn their living with real estate knowledge. But you do—or, at least it's your aim to. The point is that you must know more about the property's realistic value than the owners do and expect them to have unrealistic expectations. How well you do in this business will depend on the accuracy of your information and the delicacy with which you relay it to hopeful sellers.

CHAPTER 8

Being Prepared and in Control During
Your Listing Presentation

What follows isn't a set of handy little hints that you can ignore if you feel like it and still make some money in this business. If you're interested in making big money, the tips that follow are the essence of real estate success.

1. FOOLS RUSH IN.

Every time you rush over to take a listing before you've prepared adequately, you guarantee that you'll lose money instead of making money. The seller will set the price, and he or she will always set it too high. It won't sell, so there'll be no income. But there will be expenses, which you'll pay. There'll be time spent servicing the listing, which you'll put in for free. Doesn't it make more sense to put in a few hours preparing and then take the listing at a price that will sell? Make a commitment to yourself that you will know more about the property than the owners do because that knowledge will make important money for you.

2. SET A TOP PRICE FIRST.

Before you go in for the listing appointment, know the top figure at which you'll take the listing. If they insist on going above that amount, you'll walk away without the listing. Setting a top price demands confidence in your own powers. If you don't develop that confidence, you'll have a tough time making it in real estate. Keep in mind there are markets that are so hot that a listing for a higher price than you'd like for thirty days might not be a bad idea. You just have to know your area and the current market activity.

3. STRUCTURE YOUR PRESENTATION FIRST.

Then learn it word for word. I know this might seem like an awesome challenge right now if you're new to real estate. It isn't. Later in the book, you'll learn various scripts that have been proven to work. Memorize them and you'll be halfway to your dream of real estate success.

4. PROMISE YOURSELF THAT EVERYTHING YOU DO MUST PRIMARILY BE GOOD FOR YOUR SELLER.

You must go into every listing performance with this attitude firmly in mind. Insisting that what you do must always be for the good of the seller will frequently cause you to pass up what seems like a good chance at a fast buck. All too often, those chances aren't really there. Even more often, they can be reputation-destroying issues.

One of the most powerful ways to make people like and trust you is to be committed to doing what is best for them. To be convincing in your fiduciary relationship as the seller's agent, you must believe in your own integrity. If you know you aren't trustworthy, how can you convince others that you are? It all starts with your own internal commitment to giving honorable service.

They used to say to me at the office, "Tom, you can really close." But I'd never agree. It seemed they were implying that I could talk people into bad decisions with closing tricks. I'd answer, "If it's good for the sellers, they need it. So I didn't close them, I simply helped them understand what their true interests were. Leading people to the decisions that are primarily good for them is what my profession is all about. So when you said that I can really close, you're actually telling me that I give professional service by showing my sellers what's best for them and I agree with that statement."

Now let's talk about the tools you should carry in for a listing presentation, not only because you'll need them, but also to help convey that you possess a high degree of professional expertise.

The Tools for Getting the Job Done

The doctor has her little black bag, the repairman his toolbox, the accountant his calculator and forms. The successful lister carries:

1. THE COMPARABLE MARKET ANALYSIS.

Take my word for it, you're only 25 to 50 percent effective if you don't use one. Later, I'll show you precisely how to make this powerful persuader work.

2. THE ASSUMPTIVE LISTING FOLDER.

The CMA and a partially filled out listing form are the two most important ingredients in this effective listing tool. Assume you're going to get the listing, and have a folder ready to hold all of the information the seller will need to keep.

3. PRESENTATION MANUAL.

Like the doctor's black bag, the listing presentation manual enhances credibility. Champion listers always carry them into their presentations, and they almost always use them. There may be cases where you're meeting with a referred contact and they won't need a lot of convincing that you're the right person to help them sell their home. However, you should still always have your presentation materials at hand just in case you do need them.

4. A CLIPBOARD OR LEGAL PAD.

This shows the sellers that you're planning to take lots of notes, that you're organized, that you're efficient. Every note you take is a subtle compliment to them.

5. A MEASURING TAPE.

Get the cloth kind that won't scratch furniture. Or one of the latest laser measuring devices. A laser measure will show that you're up to date plus it's fun for sellers to play with if they haven't seen one yet. If you're one of several agents competing for the listing, you'll probably be the only one who takes a tape in and measures the rooms. What does this demonstrate? That you're competent, that you're painstaking, that you get your facts straight.

6. A CALCULATOR.

Today, people believe numbers displayed by calculators more readily than computations scribbled on paper. A small, thin calculator takes up hardly any space and adds a firm touch of professionalism for very little cost or trouble. When you reach the money part of your presentation, put it on the table and take control.

7. A DIGITAL CAMERA.

When you list this home, you're going to want photographs of the exterior and any special amenities it might have to use on your advertising flyers and Web site.

Chapter 17 will give you detailed techniques for using all these tools for greatest effect. Sellers want to work with an agent who takes his or her business seriously, who is knowledgeable and effective, and who cares about them and their property. The tools you bring to the listing appointment demonstrate that you have these qualities. Conversely, the lack of them shows that you don't.

Using Your Listing Tools with Flair

In this book you're going to learn more listing techniques than you'll have time to use effectively. So, when you're ready to start, I suggest you select the listing techniques you want to begin with—perhaps those that seem easiest to incorporate into your current style. Then, practice, drill, and rehearse every aspect of them. Practice every question you plan to ask; drill yourself on how you'll handle every response you're likely to get; rehearse every statement, gesture, and movement you expect to make.

Moving yourself to a level of professional earning power takes a professional level of practice, drill, and rehearsal. That, in real estate, requires very little except time and effort. You can do it all in the privacy of your home.

Balanced Research

You can do so much research that you never get out of the office and put it to use. You can do so little research that you aren't effective when you are working with people. Strike the balance between these extremes for an effective, well-paid performance.

The exciting thing about the research approach to strong listing is that it gets easier as you go along. When you're the champion lister in your listing bank, you'll already know many of the facts that a beginner would have to dig out because they're about your own sold listings.

When you're the superchampion, you'll fill out some of your CMAs (comparable market analyses) from memory. Why do superchampions write out CMAs when they have all the facts memorized? For the same reasons you should: Written numbers have more impact; they are more readily believed. When clients look at the figures you're talking about instead of just hearing you say them, they're more easily convinced.

Better yet, print out the information on each sold listing from your MLS or company records. These often include photos of the homes and details that are valuable in making comparisons to the home you'll be listing now.

When you're well prepared and well rehearsed, you'll use your listing tools with power. You'll ask the right questions, respond effectively to sellers' objections, quiet their fears, gain their trust, and cause them to like you. You'll put on a polished performance that will have a high success rate. You will, in a word, be a professional.

How can I be so sure?

First, the average person who enters the real estate business never puts much effort into acquiring expertise. He or she may work hard but at doing the wrong things. They may put in long hours but not work effectively at becoming an expert lister and seller. Since the average new person is out of the business in less than a year, they aren't much competition to someone like yourself who's resolved to succeed.

Then what is your competition?

Usually, it's a collection of people who are satisfied if they get by. When any of them go out on a listing presentation, what they put on is not a practiced, polished, professional performance. Your average, hanging-in-there real estate agent gets to the appointment late, wings his way through what he's pleased to call his listing presentation, and gets by because most of the time he's only competing against other come-late wingers.

If you'll practice, drill, and rehearse these ideas, it's not a question of whether or not you'll succeed in real estate, it's only a question of how great your success will be. And that decision, too, you make for yourself. It's all in your hands and mind. The more I travel and speak and train salespeople, the more convinced I become that the most important element of success is your level of discipline and determination to succeed. It's not good health, looks, education, or connections that decide who succeeds and who fails—it's determination.

CHAPTER 9

Reflexive Listing Techniques

A reflex is something you do without thinking. A trained reflex is something you do fast and well without thinking. In sports, in business, in almost all areas of active life, if you have to think before doing it, you're too late most of the time.

All professionals have trained reflexes, and it is the speed and accuracy of those reflexes that determine how successful each professional will be. When a boxer's reflexes slow down, he's through. The same thing is true of all professional athletes, but there's an exciting difference between the eye-hand coordination required in sports and the eye-and-mouth coordination required in real estate listing and selling: Our reflexes get faster as time passes.

When the seller says certain things, the strong lister instantly says the right thing in reply—and moves closer to success with that seller. When your reflexes are trained, you'll be a strong lister. It's that simple.

Using reflexive listing techniques means communicating effectively with your sellers. Communicating effectively means leading your sellers to the conclusion that listing with you is the wisest decision they can make. When you lead them by using reflexive listing techniques, they arrive where you want them to go. When you try to force them without using skillful techniques, the sellers are likely to run off in some other direction.

The Asking Secret

A listing is nothing more than a major decision that's reached through a series of minor agreements. The big yes is the listing. How do you get it? By first getting a lot of little yeses.

The professional athlete doesn't expect to win the game on the first play. He has a plan. His game plan calls for achieving victory through winning a series of plays. The big yes is the game win, reached through a lot of small yeses won over the entire period of the game.

In real estate, the beginner often fails to realize that there is a game period involved in taking each listing. Not realizing that, he gets overly anxious. He presses too hard too soon. And he starts off telling the seller things rather than asking.

Some of the most common phrases beginners say to sellers are:

"We are the finest real estate company in town."

"I'm the most professional salesperson you'll find."

"I know more about the real estate around here than anybody."

"By-owners can't sell homes now—and if they do, they always get less."

"You better list with me 'cause we're the best."

"We've got the biggest signs in town."

That is not how you win people over or gain their trust with the biggest single investment they've ever made. To become a strong lister, you need to get some of the same points across, but you do it differently. You do it by asking questions.

The automatic yes technique: "You'd like to do business with a professional, wouldn't you?" What are they going to say to that? "Oh, no, I'd like to work with the dumbest jerk in town." Of course they won't say that; they'll agree that they want to work with a professional. And as they give you that minor yes, aren't they also accepting the fact—telling themselves in reality—that you are the kind of professional they want to work with?

Here's a variation on that statement: "A reputation for professionalism is important, isn't it?" When you say that, they aren't going to come back with, "If you've built up a fine professional reputation, we're not talking to you anymore."

Use these two with sellers who've just been transferred:

"Wouldn't it be convenient to move as a family?" Most of them will agree with that, just as they will with, "Today, double moves are expensive, aren't they?" As always, sensitivity counts. Sometimes one of the spouses wouldn't mind looking the new town over by him- or herself for a month. If you suspect that one of them has an adventurous spirit, it might be better not to get into the question of them moving together.

"As a specialist in this area, I could better serve you folks, couldn't I?" If you've already displayed an impressive knowledge of the real estate in their neighborhood, what's their natural conclusion? That it's a good decision to give you the listing and benefit from your knowledgeable service.

If you've decided to turn pro in real estate, I hope that you'll make a commitment to listen twice as much as you talk. Do that and you'll double your effectiveness. You'll double your effectiveness again if you ask the right questions.

Keep on asking. And listen to the answers. They'll lead you to further questions. To further minor yeses. Let's get back to specific questions you should ask. This is what I would say if I were sitting across the kitchen table from a couple who needs to sell their home, like Don and Helen Lohman:

"Mr. and Mrs. Lohman, before we get started this evening, I'd like to—if I may—ask you some questions to see if our firm is the kind of firm that you'd like to represent you. Because, you see, if we don't have what you're looking for, then you should call another firm. May I ask, would you like a firm that is known in this community to have a reputation for professionalism?"

When they nod or say yes, I go on to the next question: "Would you also like a firm that invests a considerable amount of time and money advertising and exposing real estate to attract qualified purchasers?"

The Lohmans don't argue with that idea either. "Would you also like the firm that serves you to have hundreds of different financing sources at its fingertips to assure that qualified buyers can obtain the funds they need to purchase your house at the least amount of expense to you?"

Again I wait for the Lohmans to indicate agreement before proceeding to the next question. "Would you like your real estate representatives to screen possible buyers so that only those who are qualified, that is, who can afford and have the money to buy your house, are shown your property?"

The Lohmans nod assent, so I ask the next question in my sequence: "And would you also like a salesperson who is full time?" When I say that, I hand each of them one of my cards. "As you can see, my card has three phone numbers: my home, my office, and my mobile phone. Would you like to be able to contact your representative twenty-four hours a day? Six days a week?"

Am I making them feel important? Certainly. Mr. and Mrs. Lohman have been giving me a lot of small yeses, haven't they?

And my last question is, "Do you want as much money out of your home as you can possibly get?"

Believe me, they're going to say yes to that one. So we're certain to end on a yes. That's when I go in for my wrap-up: "Mr. and Mrs. Lohman, this is exciting. Based on what you've told me, I truly believe that we'll be able to do business because the things you've asked for are the things my firm offers. And now I'd like to go over my comparable market analysis with you."

I didn't tell the Lohmans anything. They told me that what they wanted was what I had to offer because I asked the right questions. By asking the right questions, I pulled out the right answers, answers that turned them around to "Yes, let's go."

There's an essential quality that all right questions for listing or selling real estate must have: The seller must know the right answer to them.

Don't laugh. If you ask them a question they can't answer, they feel stupid. If you make them feel stupid, will they want to work with you? No. A truism, yet many real estate salespeople ignore its reality. They feel that if they can just make their prospects feel they don't know enough about real estate to sell their front stoop, they'll also make them feel dependent. It doesn't work very often. The majority of people you'll work with want you to make them feel smart.

In the listing interview with the Lohmans, I asked them seven questions that all had only one answer, the automatic yes. But overuse makes any technique abrasive. So, before you rub them raw, switch smoothly to another technique. Here's one of the most dynamic listing techniques ever devised:

The Alternate of Choice System for Success

An alternate of choice is any question that has two answers, either of which confirms they're going ahead or agreeing to something that moves you forward in your attempt to list or sell a property.

Each minor yes leads to another small yes, and finally to the big yes. That's why the strong lister doesn't ask, "Can I come by and see you folks tonight?" Why? Because it's too easy for sellers to say no. Here's what the pro, the champion, asks:

"I'll be in the neighborhood this evening. Would it be more convenient if I stopped by at 6:00, or would you prefer 8:00?"

Give them two choices, either of which confirms that you have their permission to pop by. This works beautifully on an incoming call from an ad. "I have an appointment open this morning, or would this afternoon be more convenient?"

If the potential client says, "Oh no, we won't have any free time until the weekend," the champion is ready with another alternate of choice.

"I have some time open on Saturday and some on Sunday. Which day would you prefer?"

"Well, we'll have to wait until Sunday."

Noon divides each day into two parts, so the pro asks the next alternate of choice question: "Would you like to make it in the morning, or would the afternoon be better for you?"

"The afternoon, I think."

"Shall we say one o'clock, or would you rather show me your home around 3:00 P.M.?"

"We can be here at one," says the seller.

After just four smooth alternate of choice questions, the pro has the listing presentation appointment. In the same situation, the average salesperson will ask questions that suggest a negative answer until he gets a final no. Here's how he drives his car into the wall:

"Can I come out to see the house today?"

"No, you can't."

"Er, uh, do you know when I can stop by?"

"Well, that's hard to say. I'm kinda busy this week."

"How about on the weekend. I can come down there sometime then, can't I?"

"No, I'm afraid not. I think we're going away this weekend. Tell you what, I'll give you a call when we have some free time." And, of course, you never hear from them again.

Piggybacking

This is an excellent conversational tool. I suggest you use it all the time, not just with your clients. It stimulates the person you are with, as much as yourself, by developing your listening skills. Piggybacking is nothing more than asking your next question about their last answer. Too often, we're so busy thinking about what we're going to say next that we don't really listen to what the other person is saying. This can be embarrassing. It can destroy any credibility you've built with them to this point. When you use the piggybacking technique, you're truly listening to what they say. They'll know it and appreciate your attention. An example of this technique follows.

> SALESPERSON: "Where do you live now?"
> PROSPECT: "Palmdale."
> SALESPERSON: "What do you like most about living in Palmdale?"
> PROSPECT: "We like to sail."
> SALESPERSON: "Have you been sailing long?"

By using this simple technique, the people you meet will feel that you truly have an interest in them because you are obviously listening to everything they say. Just remember to direct your questions to get the answers you need about what they're looking for in a home—what type of lifestyle they want.

Logical Listing

A logical listing never happens. You know that people list their homes emotionally, and then they justify what they've done with logic. We're all the same on this. As you work through the process of getting the listing, seize every opportunity to bring legitimate emotions into play. Do it with alternate of choice questions:

"Helen, you know your home better than anyone. If you were marketing your home, would you bring buyers in through the front door or the side door?"

Either answer helps you, doesn't it?

"I love our entry hall, Tom. I'd bring them in from the front."

"Then that's where we should put the lock box, don't you agree? Let me make a note of that." Look how far a small yes here takes you toward winning the listing. Now watch this one:

Don Lohman is a landscaping fanatic. When I walk outside with him, I see every container plant. I praise every flower bed. I admire his fig tree. Then I say, "Mr. Lohman, you know your home and area better than anybody. One of the keys to a good, fast sale is to catch the eye of possible buyers—or of their friends—who drive past your home. Do you think it would be wise to place the sign this way (I indicate with my hands) or this way?"

Mr. Lohman says, "Well, Tom, the way the traffic moves by here, I think I'd place it both ways."

"Then you'd like two signs. Okay, that's a good idea. We'll do it. Let me make a note of that." If I can get them to agree to a sign in their yard, I'm halfway to taking the listing.

Your Biggest Challenge with the Listing Form

The biggest challenge most salespeople have with the listing form is that they never fill it out. Why don't they? Because they're afraid the seller will tell them not to. So they hide the form, planning to whip it out after they've somehow talked the sellers into saying, "Okay, write it up." But most sellers will never say that unless they are handled skillfully. They'll procrastinate; they'll wait to talk to the next real estate agent; they'll sleep on it—anything to keep from making the decision.

Nearly all strong listers use the listing form as an integral part of their listing sequence. Simply by learning how to use the listing form during listing interviews, you'll acquire more real estate expertise than most people entering the profession ever do.

Let's start with the basic assumption that it's almost impossible to take a listing without writing on the form. And it's equally difficult to write on a form that's locked inside your briefcase. So the first essential for using the form effectively is to expose it to the air.

Keep the form ready in your assumptive listing folder. What's an assumptive listing folder? You are going to assume you're getting this listing, so you're going in prepared as if you have it. Before you get there, fill in all the information that you're sure of: the address; the sellers' full legal names, etc. Then you're ready to use the minor closes when the time is right.

Let's take a moment to review a vital point: Minor closes are an essential part of successful listing. Learn the two that follow, word for word, and work them into your standard listing scenario. Let's suppose that you're at a listing interview with Chuck and Midge Jones. Here are the two closes:

"Mrs. Jones, would you want us to call for an appointment before showing the home, or shall we just stop by?"

"Mr. Jones, which do you feel would better suit your plans—a 30- or a 60-day possession date and close of escrow?"

They don't sound too difficult to deliver, do they? That's part of their strength: they're nonthreatening, and they're dynamite when they're used right. Here's how you use them to take a long step toward nailing down the listing. When your sellers answer—and it doesn't matter which alternative they choose—say this: "Let me make a note of that."

And then write their answer on the listing form. You may think "But they'll jump all over me if I try that. Couldn't I just scratch a note on a legal pad so they'll know I'm not using the listing form and copy it later when the heat's off?"

That's not what the strong listers think. They're *hoping* the sellers will try to stop them when they slide the listing form out and start writing on it.

How Strong Listers Keep Moving When the Sellers Try to Stop Them

A strong lister is ready when the seller sees him writing on the listing form and says, "What are you doing? We're not ready to give anyone the listing yet."

Listing champions move forward instead of being stopped cold when this happens. You can, too. Memorize the following words. Practice, drill, and rehearse until you can deliver them smoothly and with conviction.

"I organize my thoughts and keep everything in the proper perspective. I do that on the paperwork so I don't forget anything, particularly anything that might cost you money."

Are they excited that you won't forget anything that might cost them money? You bet they are. You are projecting competence when you respond confidently like that. This is why the pro thinks the listing form is a nice place to write notes.

Notice that we don't talk about the listing form to the seller. We call it the *paperwork*. Because paperwork is a nonthreatening detail; a listing form is a contract, and contracts are frightening. (Be aware that the seller does need to know that the form *is* a binding contract before they put their signature on it. Just during the initial conversations would you refer to it as paperwork.)

Let's go through that again. "Mrs. Jones, would you want us to call for an appointment before showing the home, or shall we just stop by?"

"You can just stop by," Mrs. Jones says.

"Let me make a note of that," you say, and write your note on the listing form.

"What are you doing?" Mr. Jones says.

"I organize my thoughts to keep everything in proper perspective," you say. "I do that on the paperwork so I don't forget anything, particularly anything that might cost you money."

"All right," Mr. Jones says, "Go ahead. But we haven't decided to list with you yet."

"I know," you say, "but I want to be sure of my facts in case you do decide to employ my professional skills and let me serve you."

Isn't that easy? And are you miles closer to taking the listing after that exchange? You can count on it.

How to Tie the Minor Yeses Down

As I already mentioned, listing is the process of building up minor yeses in the minds of your sellers. When the total weight of your minor yeses exceeds the total weight of your sellers' indecision and built-in negative feelings, their resistance crumbles. Then you can close for the listing and walk away with it every time. On your way to that critical point, you must win many minor yeses, but unless you tie those yeses down, much of their weight is lost. Your sellers have a lot on their minds, don't they? You'd like to break through their emotional stress and score solid points with them, wouldn't you?

Isn't it true that, if you can get your sellers to voice their agreement with the points you're making, they'll be far more likely to remember and believe those facts? Won't knowing how to do that make your success easier and more certain? Shouldn't you incorporate this technique into your listing sequence right away?

By this time, haven't you noticed the tie-down technique that I'm using on you right now? They're so simple you can work them into almost any situation.

The Four Styles of the Tie-Down

As you can see from the three previous paragraphs, there are several tie-down styles. A tie-down is a question at the end of a sentence that demands a yes answer. The most common forms of tie-downs are contractions such as "isn't it," "doesn't it," "wouldn't it," "couldn't it," "can't you see," "don't you agree," and "haven't they." The standard style places the tie-down last and *demands* a yes reply; the inverted style places it first, thus *suggesting* a yes; the internal style uses the tie-down in the middle of the sentence, for more subtlety and warmth. The fourth form of the tie-down is the tag-on. Use this whenever your sellers say something you want to reinforce in their minds, usually something that's positive to the idea of their listing with you. Simply tag your tie-down onto what they just said.

SELLER: "I see your company's sign all over town."
LISTER: "There certainly are a lot of them around, *aren't there?*"

But you don't have to stop there. Why not tag on a second sentence about the topic and double the reinforcing effect?

SELLER: "I see your company's sign all over town."

LISTER: "Many of my clients have told me that. By the way, *doesn't* all this heavy sign activity tell you a great deal about our company's effectiveness and reputation?" Wham and double wham.

Memorize the following tie-down zingers. You need to have them ready for instant use in your tool bag.

"A reputation for professionalism is important, *isn't it?*"

"You have noticed our signs and activity in your area, *haven't you?*"

"You're interested in your home having complete exposure, *aren't you?*"

"It would be convenient to move as a family, *wouldn't it?*"

"Double moves are expensive, *aren't they?*"

"As a specialist in this area, I could better serve you, *couldn't I?*"

These six tie-down zingers can be used word for word during most interviews. When you can honestly say nice things about the sellers' property, tailor comments such as the following to fit the situation. If possible, use these tie-downs to the other spouse when the husband or wife being praised can hear you.

"She's done a lovely job of decorating, *hasn't she?*"

"He's created a beautiful landscape here, *hasn't he?*"

All the elements of strong listing, when you practice, drill, and rehearse them, become part of a developed performance that you'll then find ridiculously easy to run through. You'll also find that it's fun—for two powerful and basic reasons: Achieving anything worthwhile by using great skill is one of life's greatest pleasures, and so is the knowledge that you'll be well paid for doing it.

Some final thoughts about tie-downs. Mix the four styles up as you say them. Most of us tend to overuse the standard form, don't we? It easily becomes a habit that annoys our listeners, doesn't it? But we have the other forms, don't we?

Shouldn't we use the inverted style just as often? Isn't the inverted form worth practicing? And, while we're rehearsing our tie-downs, wouldn't it be better if we blended in a few of the internal style to give our speech variety?

When you've practiced the tie-down technique adequately, don't you agree that you'll use the internal form as often as the other two? As soon as you reach that stage of development, won't mixing all three add a great deal to the interest and eloquence of your words? And, in order to make these points, haven't I had to overuse the tie-down technique? Certainly. When your technique is obvious and abrasive, it hurts you more than it helps you. So use the tie-downs liberally, mix them well, but don't overuse them.

The Importance of the Planned Pause

Once you've mastered these questioning techniques, you'll be in control during the demonstration of the property. However, there's one more extremely important factor for you to be aware of before using any technique. As I've mentioned several times already, you can't let your prospects know you're using techniques. If you respond too quickly to their comments or questions, you'll startle them. They'll wonder how you came up with that answer so fast and sooner or later, they'll figure you out. That's why any professional speaker or salesperson uses the planned pause.

By pausing before responding to them, they'll get the feeling that you're thinking about what to say next. They will be less likely to recognize your comments and questions as techniques. The planned pause also works to get their attention. I'm sure you've heard the phrase *pregnant pause*. It means that whatever is going to happen or be said next is full of meaning. The use of the planned pause really gets their anticipation built up. Try it a few times and you'll see what I mean.

Please don't overuse these techniques. You don't want to answer every question with a question. You don't need to tie down every statement. That would be foolish. You only need to use these techniques once or twice to get them mentally committed to going ahead with the purchase.

CHAPTER 10

Learning to Love Objections

The day you turn pro is the day you start loving objections and thinking of them as concerns, the way we discussed in Chapter 3. That's
right, love 'em. I can hear you now: "Come on, Tom. Don't expect me
to believe that you *love* objections." I do expect you to believe me on
this. It's important that you do. I'll say it again. I love hearing my potential clients' concerns. *I Love It!*

Why? Because I can't get a yes until someone gives me a no. In other
words, if I can't get any nos, I can't make any money. If they're completely agreeable, if they go along with everything I say, what are they
probably doing? Picking my brain. And when I try to close after an
hour of that, I can't hook onto anything solid. They keep on smiling
and agreeing as they walk me to the door.

I don't like it when people pick my brains that way. I want to be of
service—and then get paid for it. Being used and then trashed like an
empty milk carton is not my idea of fun. When you've made all the
skills in this book yours, you'll be a champion who can say, "I'm not
going to be used anymore. I'm not staying away from my family nights
without getting the listings." That's my philosophy: If you keep me
away from my family, you're going to pay for it. Shouldn't that be your
philosophy, too? To be a pro, you have to be able to put the whole jig-
saw puzzle of the real estate selling process together in that hour and a

half. One of the essential pieces is understanding and addressing concerns.

How to Address Concerns

First of all, most sellers forget their concerns if you don't interrupt what you're doing and talk about them when they come up. Sellers usually throw out concerns to slow the process down. Knowing that, when the sellers start pitching a few at you, you'll realize that you're coming in too fast, and all you have to do is shift gears and slow down a bit. Do that, and you'll get home quicker.

Now let's talk about one of the finest techniques for handling minor concerns: feedback. Using this magnificent minor close is a simple process. All it involves is taking the objection and warmly feeding it back to the client in the form of a question, thus demanding clarification or elaboration.

When people begin to elaborate, several things happen. One, they often realize how flimsy their objections sound. Two, they tell you what their real fears are. Until you know what's really bothering them, you won't be able to address it. Three, when you're dealing with a couple, you'll find they often have differing opinions about the concern and will talk each other out of it or at least diminish its importance. In other words, their concern will no longer be strong enough to keep you from getting the listing.

Getting Permission to Place a Sign on the Property

When someone tells you, "We don't want a sign on our home," and you agree by saying, "Well, we don't need to put a sign on your property if you don't want one," whom have you hurt? The sellers. Do you want to begin your relationship by hurting the people you'll be working for?

If there's no sign, the best potential buyers may drive right by and never think of purchasing that listing because they don't know it's available. The same applies to the lock box. If there's no lock box with a key or combination, the selling agents will pull that listing out of their books and take their clients to houses that are quickly and conveniently seen. Why won't they take the time to wrestle with getting hold of a key? Because their experience tells them that if the sellers won't give out a key, they aren't very eager to sell or the listing agent doesn't know his business. Either way, it spells trouble. They can find enough trouble on their own without your help. The pro knows that she or he has an obligation to the sellers and to the agents representing buyers to get them a key and to put out a sign that identifies the property as being for sale.

So when sellers balk at putting up a sign, be ready with the right reflexive. Here's how you might handle it:

Champion: "Quite a few of our clients tell us that our sign is distinguished looking and that it compliments the community's architecture. Do you agree?"

Seller: "We don't want a sign."

Champion: "You don't want a sign? Can you share with me why you feel that way?"

As you feed the concern back, it's vital that your tone and manner be warm and friendly. If there's a trace of argument in your voice, you'll get argument back. You're not trying to win an argument here (you never argue with a client); you're employing professional skills to persuade clients to do what's best for them. You don't really care why they're reluctant to have a sign, of course. Their reasons are certainly trifling compared with their need to do everything reasonable to help get their property sold. Ninety percent of the time, they don't want a sign because of something to do with the neighbors.

Let's pick up our example again.

Champion: "You don't want a sign? Can you share with me why you feel that way?"

Seller: "Well, Midge and I would just as soon the neighbors didn't know right away that we're moving."

Champion: "We don't *require* a sign. However, a large percentage of our buyer activity comes from properties with our signs on them. You know—I have an idea—if we're fortunate enough to arrive at the market value based on the comparable market analysis, we may not even need a sign. We may have the home sold in the next three weeks. Now, why don't we hold the sign off for three weeks, and let's see what happens, shall we? Let me make a note of that—no sign for three weeks." (Writes on the listing form.)

Seller: "What are you doing there?"

Champion: "I'm organizing my thoughts and keeping everything in proper perspective. I do that on the paperwork so I don't forget anything, particularly anything that might cost you money."

Getting a Key to the Property

Now another common obstacle you'll run into are sellers who don't want to give you a key. Why not? It's an emotional issue; they get nervous thinking about strange people coming through their home—and, believe me, they consider it their home until the day they move out. The cocoon of security and privacy that a home provides is precious to everyone. Logically, giving up a key is necessary if the house is to sell; emotionally, doing so violates a seller's innate sense of territory. Part of your job as a professional is to persuade them to break through those emotional barriers and get on with selling the house.

> MR. JONES: "We don't want to give out a key."
>
> CHAMPION: "Oh, you don't want to give out a key? Can you elaborate on that?"
>
> MRS. JONES: "We have lots of valuables."
>
> CHAMPION: "Fine. It's not mandatory that we have a key. Are you both home most of the time?"
>
> MR. JONES: "Well, no. We both work during the day. I don't get home until the evening, but Midge is often home before I am."
>
> CHAMPION: "What time do you usually get home, Midge?"
>
> MRS. JONES: "Usually around 4:00 P.M."
>
> CHAMPION: "It would be a shame to have a buyer unable to see the home earlier than 4:00 P.M. on a weekday, don't you agree? I have an idea. Have you ever seen one of these?" (Take a lock box out of your brief case or flip to a photo of one in your presentation manual.) "This is what we in the industry call a lock box. We have these to assure as much privacy and security as possible. Let me show you how it works. In fact, Chuck, to prove to Midge how

concerned we are with your security, would you take out your house key for me? Chuck, drop it in there. Go on. This will hang on the front door. Any agent who wants to show your home, must sign out the key or combination to this lock box. That way your key isn't accessible to anyone that's not supposed to have it. That's rather secure, isn't it?"

Now, where's his key? In the lock box. Where's it staying? In the lock box.

I think I'm reading you right now. You're thinking, "I couldn't do that." Let me tell you something: you can do it easily—very easily, if you do it warmly, softly, and persuasively. You can say them like that, too. All it takes is practice.

What is the normal reaction when you use the feedback technique?

They sell themselves out of it. Many times I've had the wife say, "Now Tom, we don't want to give out a key."

I'd say, "Okay. It's not mandatory that we have a key. Are you both home most of the time?"

And then the husband, knowing they're both gone a lot, says, "Oh, come on, honey. We can go ahead and give them the key. They wouldn't be in this business if they weren't trustworthy." Who sold whom? Spouses will close each other if you'll let them.

Here's my favorite technique for addressing concerns of all kinds:

The Porcupine

Let me ask you a question. If I walked in to where you're sitting right now and threw a live, prickly porcupine in your lap, what would you do?

Let me tell you something. You wouldn't cuddle him and say, "Isn't he a cute little fella." Oh, no. You'd throw that porcupine right back at me. When a seller asks you a prickly question, he's tossed you a porcupine. Toss the porcupine right back. How? By answering the seller's question with one of your own. Then write his answer to your question on the listing form.

When you put this technique in gear, it'll go so well that you'll chomp at the bit for an objection to be raised.

For example, have you ever worked with a couple when the husband is the abrupt kind who's in a big hurry to get things over with as fast as possible? I love this type because they'll close themselves if you'll let them.

Here's one of these hurry-up husbands, Barry Bevier, talking:

"All of this that you're telling me is well and good, but what I really want to know is, can you have our home sold in 60 days?"

What did he just throw at us?

A porcupine.

How would you answer him? Would you say something like, "Oh, the market is so good now, I'm positive that we can." Or, "We'll do our best; we'll give it our best shot." Say that kind of thing and you've got nothing.

The champion, the pro, the strong lister, loves that question.

He or she just smiles and says, "Barry, are you interested in giving possession in 60 days?"

Barry: "Well, I think we need to be out by then."

Champion: "Fine. Let me make a note of that." You know where the champion is going to write that note.

"What are you doing there?"

"I organize my thoughts and keep things in proper perspective. I do that on the paperwork so I don't forget anything, particularly anything that might cost you money. Barry, there are no guarantees your home will sell within 60 days. However, based on our research and findings in the Comparable Market Analysis and Days on Market study, if we list your home at the right amount, it appears likely to sell within that time frame. The more information, such as your desire to move in 60 days, that I put on the listing form, the more likely other agents will take notice and bring their buyers who have similar needs."

If you'll just run Barry Bevier through a few of those minor closes, he'll see that you know what you're doing. When that happens, you'll earn his trust in your competence and he'll lose interest in checking out other agents and tell you to write it up.

Here's another common opportunity:

Barry: "Will you put a sign on the property?"

Weak lister: "Will we! We've got signs you won't believe. They rise up out of the ground and hang over the house—you can see them for miles."

"We don't want a sign."

"Duh, well, we don't, uh, actually require a sign." Weak lister lets the seller shear his oars off again. Here's how the pro plays the same scene:

"Will you put a sign on the property?"

"Would you like a sign?"

If Barry says yes, the pro uses the let-me-make-a-note-of-that zap it on the listing form technique again. If Barry says no, the pro uses the sign close given previously.

You see the method: You always end with a close. Contrast that with the usual course of simply answering their question by giving them the information they've asked for. What comes next? They hit you with another question—and then another. On and on it goes. You're not leading them. They are leading you. And since there are countless negative turns they can take, they'll lead you away from the listing every time.

The Four Most Common Concerns and How to Handle Them

Let's address four questions you're likely to meet in any listing interview that you should porcupine back to the sellers.

1. "Can you have the home sold in 80 days?" If you answered, "Would you want the home sold in 80 days?" you'd be close. You porcupined it all right, but it sounded like a technique. That's why you learn to say these words: "Mr. Jones, would you be interested in giving possession of your home in 80 days?" Or, "Does 80 days best suit your time frame for having the home sold?"

2. "Will you put a sign on the property?"

"Would you like us to install one of our signs for you?" Or, "Do you have a preference of where the sign should be on the property?"

3. "Will you call before showing our home?" The obvious answer, "Would you like us to call before showing the home?" has the ring of rote learning and slick technique. That's why you should say, "Would you prefer that we call for an appointment before showing your home?"

If she says, "Please do," tell her that you're making a note of her decision. Where? On your friendly listing form.

By the way, while you're practicing, drilling, and rehearsing every word, gesture, and tone change, also work out exactly where you're going to make your notes on the listing form. Then develop a simple list of abbreviations, and get in the habit of writing small so you won't cover the listing with scribbles and have to copy it on a fresh form while they fidget.

Here's another pitfall for the untrained that's an opportunity for the skilled salesperson:

4. "Do we have to leave the draperies?" The professional wants the draperies to stay. Why? Because it'll help sell the home, which is what the sellers really want—far more than they want to keep their old furnishings. But they can't see the mountain from the basement. So professionals work very expertly here to get them to make the right decision for themselves—and for their chances of earning a fee. Here's how they do it:

"They certainly do enhance this room. Would you want to leave the draperies?" (Never say, "your draperies" because the word *your* reinforces their owning emotions.)

The pro knows that the wife doesn't want to leave the draperies or she wouldn't have asked the question. Maybe they were custom made to match the furniture. If so, you must tread lightly. The pro also knows better than to knock her answer in any way. She says, "No, we'd just as soon put the old ones back up. We just had the new draperies installed."

Here's how the pro works toward the goal of having them stay—especially if they truly enhance the room.

"Midge, the new draperies are lovely. They do enhance the room. In fact, I can see a buyer getting emotionally involved in this room because of them. May I ask, why did you replace the old ones?"

Now, what does she have to tell you? You've praised her choice of draperies, and you've put yourself on her side. So now lean forward and listen intently—without saying anything except to prompt her to keep on talking—while she tells you about how Junior used to play Tarzan on the draperies, about what the cat did to them, about the faded spots and the rips. Keep on listening and the husband will jump in and close her on leaving them. "Come on, honey. Leave the draperies if it'll help sell the house. They probably won't fit in our next home anyway."

When you're a trained pro, you wave the flag and then get out of the way. You never fight your clients. You never argue with them. The clients are always right. However, sometimes we have to show them what's right *for them*. That's what the reflexive listing technique is all about, because their best decision is to list with you at a salable figure and sell the home as quickly as possible. They will—if you make this material yours.

Learn all the closes, all the responses, all the leading questions word for word. I hope you're not telling yourself right now that you don't need to do that. When I first started taking training, I did that. I said, "Those words are not me," even when a great salesperson gave me a script that had been proven over and over again to work. Fortunately, I didn't fight him long. Instead, I learned his words so well that they became me. After you have total control of this material, after you fully understand the alternate of choice—let me make a note, tie down, feedback, porcupine, and all the other techniques in this book—you have the right to take my material and recast it in your own image.

You might not want to say, "Mrs. Jones, would you want us to call for an appointment, or shall we just stop by?" Maybe you'd rather say, "Mrs. Jones, we can do one of two things. Either just have real estate people stop by and see your home, or we can instruct the agents to give you a call before coming over. Which would you prefer?" When she replies, you might say, "Fine, I'll just jot that down." This is the same technique. Even though the words have been changed slightly, it still works. But beware. Slight changes can send the discussion off in unintended directions. So, before you tinker with the wording, learn the basic form given in these pages. Then use this basic form with several sets of clients until you fully grasp how this precise wording guides their responses.

This is where the practice, drill, and rehearsal come in. Don't short-cut it: You'll only be short-cutting yourself. Don't avoid acquiring the skills of your profession. Don't fight words that work until you have better ones.

Earlier in this book, we spoke about the game period of the listing.

Now that you're beginning to see the entire puzzle of taking a listing, are you beginning to realize the importance of charting out your entire performance in advance? Are you beginning to see that you need to practice, drill, and rehearse your complete presentation word for word?

A few weeks after I took my first sales training, I found myself in the cockpit of opportunity. I had achieved some success. I wasn't a failure anymore. But, though the negative-minded chair warmers at the office were blinking away their tears at my sudden turnaround, I still wasn't off the ground and soaring.

That's when I set out to learn my entire performance word for word and to coordinate every move and gesture in it. Long before I had achieved the perfection level of performance that I was seeking, I began setting new records. By that time I knew to the minute how long my listing performance would take. One hour and twenty-two minutes from the instant I sat down with the sellers, I would be heading for the door with the approved paperwork in my hand.

CHAPTER II

Getting Your Foot in the Door
with For-Sale-by-Owners

I love for-sale-by-owners.

Why? Because it's like owning oil wells when you know how to work with by-owners. Without a doubt, they are the easiest avenue to real estate success out there. Yet so many of us choke up whenever we have an opportunity to work with a by-owner. Somehow we always find reasons not to. It's true that by-owners rarely are easy or fun for people new to the business. Most newcomers who give the we're-selling-it-ourselves crowd a try get one good rejection, three at the outside, and they're done. Sure, some of them will keep making feeble attempts to list by-owners from time to time, but for all practical purposes they've joined the 95 percent who'd rather kick a beehive over than get into working contact with a by-owner.

That's right—95 percent of us won't accept the by-owner challenge. Take a random sample in any area and you'll discover that no more than five out of a hundred real estate agents really know how to tap the by-owner money tree. This is why for-sale-by-owners are the least worked gold mine in real estate.

Why do so many real estate people fail to tap the by-owner gold mine? Three reasons: lack of knowledge, fear of rejection, and no persistence.

Gaining knowledge of your market and inventory is up to you and your broker or manager. Chapter 29 will show you how to overcome your fear. That's two out of three. But you have to walk the last mile to the for-sale-by-owner gold mine alone. Persistence, the final element of every successful endeavor, isn't found in a book. You have to reach inside yourself to find that precious resource. However, I can give you a mantra that, if you'll live it, will put persistence in your action and success in your future: *I must do the most productive thing possible at every given moment.* We'll talk more about this vital concept later. Working with for-sale-by-owners means that you meet them, you qualify them, you bring down their defense barriers, and then you follow-up, follow-up, and follow-up until they list with you or die!

Follow my step-by-step process and you will find gold under by-owner signs. At this point, let me warn you about one thing: My process won't work overnight. You have to keep at it strongly for three weeks before you see the nuggets start to come out of your personal for-sale-by-owner gold mine. If you aren't willing to wait three weeks for a payoff, you're in the wrong career.

Some of the steps overlap a bit, but read them all before you do anything.

How to Tap the By-Owner Gold Mine

1. STAKE OUT YOUR CLAIM

Concentrate your efforts by choosing a clearly defined target area in which you'll work with all promising by-owners. This could be a geographical area, a type of home, or a certain price range of property. Before you begin, clear your plans with your manager. It's vital that you fully understand your office's policies and the rights of other agents.

Since you intend to dig deep enough to strike gold instead of skimming over the treetops, start with a smaller area than you expect to cover eventually. Sharpen your skills there. Then, as soon as you're working efficiently with by-owners, you'll be able to expand your area of saturation effort without losing power.

2. IDENTIFY THE PREFIXES YOU'RE INTERESTED IN

This is easily done in most places by checking the front information in your telephone directory. Or call your telephone company's business office.

3. MEMORIZE YOUR PREFIXES

They are the key to recognizing instantly ads for properties within your target area.

4. TRAIN YOURSELF TO LOOK AT THE PREFIX FIRST

When checking by-owner ads, make it a habit to ignore all of them from outside your target area. If you aren't going to work with those by-owners, why waste time reading their ads?

5. CUT OUT BY-OWNER ADS EVERY MORNING

Not once in a while—every morning. Of course, you do this only with ads that have your target prefixes. Paste each ad on a separate 3 × 5 card. Or enter the information into your computer's contact management software. You won't have all the information you need at first, but you're going to get it.

Once you start making some money in this business, you might want to subscribe to a service that does this step for you. There are companies online that will, for a fee, provide you with all the latest by-owner listings from your local newspapers.

6. DECIDE ON A PLAN OF ACTION FOR EACH AD

When will you call on them? What will you say? How will you get them to see that you're not the enemy, just someone providing a valuable service in the area? I give some examples of what to say later in the chapter, but want you to start thinking strategy the moment you lay eyes on each ad.

7. ACT ON YOUR PLANS EVERY DAY OF THE MONTH

Energy is the key element in getting started at listing for-sale-by-owners. One of the major reasons why they eventually go for professional service is that they get tired of giving up their free time evenings and weekends. By-owners look for workers, not players. If you call Monday on their Sunday ad, they'll think you watched the ponies run while they sweated through another open house. You won't become a champion lister on the forty-hours-a-week plan. Be sure to let the by-owners know that you're making things happen in real estate on the weekend.

There are two ways to get in to see a by-owner. You can phone them seeking a listing—only if their number does not appear on the National Do Not Call List. If you have a qualified buyer, you may call as the buyer's agent—even if the number listed is on the Do Not Call List.

Another way of contacting them is to stop by the home. If they're not on the Do Not Call List, always phone for permission to pop by and visit. The advantages are many. You can call earlier in the morning than you can knock. With the time that one unannounced visit will take, you can phone several by-owners. By phoning first, you won't waste so many precious minutes ringing doorbells at empty houses or interrupting people during their morning get-out-of-the-house routines. You can come on more softly. On the phone, you're more in control of the situation; you can use your sophisticated and well-rehearsed techniques to ease your way into their presence.

The primary disadvantage of calling for appointments first is that Harry Hottrotter may be sitting at their kitchen table writing up the listing before you can make a date to meet with them. If they were that "hot" to list, you'll have to have the integrity to congratulate Harry on getting there first—this time.

Many of the champions I've trained never telephone first; they simply go over to the by-owner's house. How do they get the address? They make it their business to have a way. For example, you can go on the Internet to a telephone directory site, enter the phone number and receive the name and address attached to the number.

I didn't use the dash-over method myself because it takes more time. At first, Hank, Mabel, and Pat often knocked on the door before I did. But I kept on using the phone because I believed it was the better strategy for the long term. As the weeks passed, I began closing for more and more appointments. And I began reaching the soft by-owners, the ones most likely to list, before anyone else did. Then, as my skills grew and I started working faster, I widened my territory. With every passing month, I heard less and less about the dash-over folks. Finally, one by one, they gave up. By spending my time wisely, I took over the by-owner business in Simi Valley, California, the little town where I started.

However, thousands of champion listers don't bother with the phone, and they continue to do well year after year. They know their areas. They know how to get the addresses quickly. So they move out fast to knock on every new by-owner's door. Even if no one's home, they have an opportunity to take stock of the property and leave their card, and perhaps a little gift that the by-owner will find as soon as they return.

There are several advantages to dashing over. Your appearance in the flesh makes a greater impression than a strange voice over the phone. You see the property. You can size it and the people up. You'll then form a better opinion of how promising your listing opportunity is than you would by only speaking to them on the phone. This better opinion will allow you to concentrate your follow-up on your best prospects. And, by being there early, you're in a better position to snap up the by-owners, who need nothing but a couple of hours with a highly skilled agent to see the advantages of listing today.

If you can minimize the chief disadvantage of this method, the time it takes, and if you feel good about charging over in person without an appointment—go for it. An impressive number of very successful champions are doing that every day.

Phraseology for That All-Important First Call to a By-Owner

Right after recording the ads, I'd start phoning people. By getting to the office early, I usually had all my new by-owners called before anyone else came in.

If a woman answered the phone, I opened the conversation like this: "Good morning, ma'am. My name is Tom Hopkins, representing Champions Unlimited. I noticed your ad in the paper this morning, and was wondering if you'd be offended if I stopped by to see your home."

Look at the power of that question. You're being very polite. If your tone matches the words—and you must carefully rehearse to make sure that it does—you'll sound very cordial and deferential. Not a whiff of pushiness. Yet, in this situation where they want to say no to whatever you ask, you've phrased your question so that a no answer actually means "yes, come on by." When you get a no here, go into your close for popping by.

Now let's work with the other response that a by-owner can make to my opening question. This time a man answers, and he turns out to be tough.

"Good morning, sir. My name is Tom Hopkins, representing Champions Unlimited. I noticed your ad in the paper this morning, and was wondering if you'd be offended if I stopped by to see your home."

"Yes, I would be."

"You would? Is the reason that you're intending to sell the home yourself?"

"That's right."

"Is that also because you'd like to avoid paying a brokerage fee?"

"You've got it."

"My reason for calling is that the first three digits of your phone number put you into my service area, and I wanted to ask you, if I'm driving by your home, and my buyer sees your sign, and I can't satisfy their needs with other homes I have listed, may I send them directly to you with no fee charged?"

"I don't have to pay a commission?"

"That's right, and you're probably wondering why I would do that, aren't you?"

"Yeah."

"You see, if I sent you some qualified purchasers, you probably wouldn't mind sending anyone back to me who didn't purchase your home, would you?"

"And I don't have to pay a commission?"

"If you sell it yourself, not at all. That makes sense, doesn't it?"

"You bet it does."

"To be more intelligent about your property, I would like to see it, and again, let me reiterate, I know you're selling the home yourself, and because of that, I just want to see it, so if I'm working with a buyer I can't find a home for, I can send them to you. Now, I am available this afternoon at around two, or would four be more convenient?"

"I'll be busy today."

"I better wait until tomorrow, then?"

"I'll be busy tomorrow too."

"Would you prefer the weekend? That's a better time for you then, isn't it?"

"Saturdays are okay."

"Fine. Morning or afternoon?"

"Morning."

"Good. I can pop by at ten, or should I wait until around eleven?"

"Ten."

Now I have their permission to visit their home. It's important that I confirm it by repeating the time that the by-owner has agreed to meet me. Also, I repeat my name, saying it slowly and distinctly, because he's probably forgotten it.

And I'm going to move forward now with getting his name and address. With someone as negative as this gentleman was at first, I would've failed to get anything by trying to learn his name and address before making the appointment.

Let's take up this telephone interview again. The by-owner has just said that he'd prefer a 10:00 A.M. meeting.

"Ten is fine. Again, my name is Tom Hopkins. May I ask your name, sir?"

"Dave Shaw."

"Awfully nice talking to you, Mr. Shaw. I'll look forward to seeing you. I'll be prompt. I'll be there at ten Saturday morning. In fact, what I'll do is . . . let me go ahead now and get your address."

Notice that my words ramble just a little. As you practice, drill, and rehearse your phraseology, don't aim for unnaturally precise speech. Deliberately put in—or rather, leave in—the slight imperfections of sentence structure that are present in everyone's normal conversation. In other words, rehearse so that you'll sound unrehearsed when you say the right things at the right times.

Dave Shaw gives me his address. As I write it down, I repeat the address out loud so that he can correct me if I get it wrong.

"What I'm also going to do, Mr. Shaw, is send you one of my cards so that when I arrive, you'll know that I'm the person who talked to you. Thank you again, Mr. Shaw. Good-bye."

It's all in the words. The next step would be to write up a quick thank-you note, telling him I'm looking forward to meeting him at 10:00 A.M. on Saturday, enclose my card, add the address and stamp, and drop it in the mail immediately.

Let's do another one, but this time we'll be calling people who've made it very clear in their ad that they don't want professional help.

Phraseology for Calling on Principals-Only Ads

Your competition doesn't know how to get around the "agents, stay away" admonition. Read on and you'll understand how it's done. Rehearse and practice the method, and you'll be able to do it successfully. Do it regularly and you'll make a lot of extra money.

Being in this business allows you to have an inside track on good investments in property. You are one of the first to learn about properties in the area that might be priced below market value, purchased, and resold for a tidy profit in a relatively short period of time. I know of real estate agents who have moved their families several times in a relatively small geographical area to take advantage of just such situations. They keep their kids in the same schools, but keep moving up in the properties they own because they find out early about good opportunities. This makes them not just real estate agents, but real estate investors. When you think about it, anyone who owns property could be called a real estate investor. You must have this mind-set in order to work the following method in an ethical manner.

Here's our study situation: It's about nine in the morning, and I'm ready to make my first phone call on a principals-only ad. Why am I beginning so late in the day? Because I've called all the help-me ads before starting to work on the principals-only ads. The help-mes are most likely to get calls from other agents, and I want to be the first one to call as many by-owners as possible. As usual, things are going well. I've made appointments with some of the help-mes; now I'm itching to get at the principals-only ads.

The first family I reach, although I don't find this out until later, consists of a husband who works outside the home, a wife who has a home-based business, and some young children. The husband has told the wife: "If any real estate people call, just say that we're not doing business with them." This is a situation that you'll encounter often. When I dial the number, the wife answers.

"Hello."

"Good morning, ma'am. My name is Tom Hopkins, representing Champions Unlimited."

"Are you a Realtor?"

"Yes, were you hoping one of us would call?" I say that warmly, as though I really think she was sitting there wishing a real estate agent would favor her with some attention. Please notice how I said it—no break at all between yes and were. If you pause after yes, some of them will jump in with a fast chop off, and all you'll hear is, "We're not interested," click.

But I don't pause.

My answer pitches the porcupine right back to her. After a second, she says, "No."

I don't give her time to gather her thoughts. Just as soon as she gets the no out, I come right back, speaking slowly and confidently, my tone warm and friendly. "Ma'am, I don't want you to think that I didn't read the ad. I realize that you only want principals to call, isn't that right?"

Now she's definitely off balance. What she wants to do, what she and her husband have agreed to, is to give real estate people nothing but negatives. But she has to agree with what I just asked her. So she contents herself with putting lots of ice in her voice.

"Yes, it is."

"And the reason for that is, you do not want to list the home—am I right in assuming that?"

"You are very definitely right."

"Good." I pause very briefly here because that's the last thing she expected me to say and I want it to sink in.

"Good, you see, I do also invest in real estate from time to time, and there's a possibility—of course, not without me seeing the home—that I could become a principal. Now if I were a principal, would you at least be interested in selling your home to me?"

"Yes, we would."

"Fine. Now I don't know if I would be interested, I do have to see the home first. So, I'm available this afternoon, or would you rather that I wait until this evening?"

"Well, I think you'd better call back when my husband is here."

"Fine, in fact, why don't I do this? What time does he get home?"

"Six."

"Tell you what. You probably eat dinner then, don't you?"

"Yes, we do."

"Well, it might be a better idea to let me wait until after dinner and on my way home, I'll just kind of stop by and give him a card, take a quick look, and see if I'm interested in being a principal. Now, would eight o'clock be convenient, or should I wait until around nine?"

"Eight o'clock."

"Fine. Now, my name is Tom Hopkins." I say it slowly and distinctly. If you have any but the most common of surnames, spell your last name out for her at this point. Then immediately say, "And your name, ma'am, is . . . ?"

"Rosetta Tines."

"And your husband's name?"

"Donald."

"Fine. Would you tell Mr. Tines that I promised you I'd stop by, and tell him I'll just drop off my card, take a quick look, and see if I'd like to become a principal. I'll look forward to seeing you at eight o'clock tonight. Thank you again. Good-bye."

Now, are you telling the truth when you say that you could become a principal?

Certainly. If their home is worth $180,000 and these people happen to be asking $136,950, you'd rapidly become a principal, wouldn't you? Probably, depending on their circumstances. You wouldn't take advantage of them, but if their situation dictates they must move immediately, this could be a wonderful opportunity for you. Perhaps they don't have the available cash to do the fixing up necessary to bring the home to market value. It's possible the home is being sold to avoid foreclosure or by an estate. In such cases, there are more reasons to move the home quickly than there are to go for market value. It does happen—more often than you might think.

So now you'll meet those principals-only by-owners. I hope you realize that all I've been teaching you in the preceding pages is to use your techniques just to meet the by-owners. When that's done, your aim is to find things in common, to establish rapport, to communicate on a warm, human level, and to create a basis for following up with them in a friendly fashion. You can't do any of those things unless you meet them.

As a side note: One of your personal goals should be to become an avid principal. The true wealth and tax benefits don't come from listing and selling real estate but from owning it. When you show up at the by-owner and the husband says, "Well, the wife said you may be interested in buying the home."

Your reply is, "Mr. _____, since I'm in the real estate business, I'm like most agents, only interested in personal real estate investments that could reflect an immediate profit, and thus are priced somewhat below the market. Most prospective homeowners want to become emotionally involved as an investor. I must remain somewhat objective. Let me step through and prepare a Comparable Market Analysis. At that point I can make a decision."

Trust me—these scripts work. I proved it years ago, and others are proving it daily in the current market. They will help you get permission to meet the sellers face to face. Once they see how professional you are, they'll open up to listening to your expert advice. Then, you'll move on to the next piece of the real estate puzzle—actually getting the listing.

By the way, I need to say something to you now. If you're sitting there thinking of reasons why none of this material will work for you, none of it will. And you'll be the loser. Don't look for ways to keep it from working, look for ways to make it work.

CHAPTER 12

What to Do and Say at the By-Owner Home

When approaching the by-owner's home for the first time, park across the street if at all possible. It's likely the homeowner will be watching for you. So, you must act professionally from the moment you and your car come into view of the property. I'm not saying you wouldn't act professionally when out of sight of the property, but be aware that it's likely someone is watching you. So, to begin with, keep your car clean.

Be on time or a few moments early to allow yourself the opportunity to survey the property from the exterior. Notice the homes of the neighbors on either side and across the street. Take note of the landscaping and exterior condition of the home—especially the roof.

Next, if you have a camera, take a photo of the property from that vantage point. Do you know how many people move in, move out, and never get a picture of their home with no one in front of it? All their pictures of the house have Uncle Horace or Aunt Olga standing there.

The camera doesn't have to be the most expensive model. You can work with the instant-print kind or a digital one—either a typical digital camera or the one in your wireless phone.

If you don't know much about photography, do some practice shots in your own neighborhood. Take photos of houses facing every direction and at different times of the day so you know what to look for in order to get a good one. For example, you probably wouldn't get a great shot of an east-facing home in the early evening.

Get in the habit of looking carefully at what you're shooting. It only takes a second to notice that you should move sideways before you press the button to eliminate a garbage can or to keep a tree from seeming to grow out of the chimney.

If the person you have an appointment with is watching you take the photograph, he or she is probably thinking, "What the heck is going on?" Once you have the shot you want, clear your mind of that detail and mentally prepare yourself to talk with someone who might not be overly happy that you're there.

If you used the techniques I taught you to close for the appointment, isn't it reasonable to think the woman you're about to meet might be a little upset with herself that she asked you to come by? In fact, if she and her husband had agreed not to even talk to any real estate people, the odds are good that she won't even be there when you arrive. Or she may make her mind up that, "All right, he can come by, but he's not coming in." This is the reason for our next technique.

Walk up to the door.

After you knock on it, step back, turn, and look up the street. When she opens the door, turn with a big smile to face her and say, "Good afternoon, Mrs. Bricker. We had an appointment at two o'clock. It's right at two. How do you do?"

Now, what did you just tell her by saying that? "I'm on time." What's that mean? "I do what I say I'll do." Then, without waiting for anything else, you move into your next phraseology:

"The longer I'm in real estate, the more I find that people live in a home and move without ever having a picture of it. In appreciation of your showing me your home, I took the liberty of taking a color photo." Hold the photo (or camera) up where she can see it and say, "It came out rather nicely, didn't it? I'll see that you receive this photo as my gift for allowing me to step through your home with you."

Keep a tight grip on the photo or your digital camera and start toward the crack in the door as you say, "May I step in?"

If you'll rehearse these words and use them confidently, you'll be delighted at how well they'll work. Here's this woman who was a bit agitated, and there you stand with a big smile on your face and a photo of her personal residence in your hand. If you'll do all this just as I've spelled it out, you'll get in even when she had decided in advance not to let you through the door just because you're so darn nice and professional.

The whole key is just to get in. By the way, the next thing you're going to do is stay in. Let me tell you a little story about the value of staying in.

When I went into management, my specialty for many years had been for-sale-by-owners. For a long time I had been taking most of them in our service area through the simple process of perfecting my techniques and applying them vigorously. Most of the salespeople in the area had stopped working by-owners. One who hadn't given up was a young man in our office named Les. After I accepted a managerial position, Les came to me and said, "Tom, I understand that you won't be competing with us from now on. I really want to be effective with by-owners. Will you teach me your secrets?"

I said, "Les, I'll teach you everything I did. But first, I want to see what you do. Find a by-owner." He did. Then, we jumped in the car, drove over to the home, and I said, "Now do what you normally do."

"Okay," Les said. We pulled right in front. He got out and I drove off. In the rear view mirror I saw Les staring after me with his mouth open. Then he turned and walked up to the by-owner's door. I went down the street and parked.

Thirty minutes later I drove back. As Les came running out of the house, he was all smiles. "Tom, I can't believe it. I think I'm going to get the listing. They have friends that we have too, and I know where they're from." He went on and on about how much he'd found in common with them and how well it was going until I said, "Les, what's so different about this time?"

"Usually, I go in, give them a card, walk through the home, tell them how great our company is, ask if we can serve them, and in five minutes, I'm out of there. But this time I couldn't leave because you left me, Tom."

I said, "What did you do?"

"We looked at each other for a few minutes." Les said. "Then I remembered what you'd told me, that the key to this entire business is to get people to like you and trust you by asking them the right questions."

Les went on, "I just started asking questions and I found out all this information. She likes me. I really think I'm going to get the listing."

What's the point of the story? That once you get in, you stay in. And your main goal is to have them like you and trust you. The next technique leads you naturally into that position of strength.

Touring the Home

Learn these words. "Mrs. Tines, would you please show me your home? In fact, why not pretend that I'm a buyer? This will give you some practice, and I'll give you some tips to demonstrate your property."

This is an ideal approach if you're the first salesperson they meet, which you will be if you check out the ads every morning. But it won't work for three weeks, remember, because you won't be getting the new ones. By filing your ads by phone number, you'll know when you hit a new one.

So here you are, walking through the front door, the first agent to get there. Of course, if it's a principals-only situation, you look at the house as a possible buyer, which you certainly could be if the home has everything it takes to qualify for your investment portfolio. And some by-owner houses won't qualify, will they? So you take advantage of the opportunity to hunt for common denominators and build the rapport that'll allow you to keep in touch. But whether it's a principals-only ad, or a help-me ad, follow these tips as you go through the house:

CARRY A PAD AND MAKE NOTES.

A true champion carries a notepad and is writing constantly while touring a by-owner's home. If you tell me something and I take the time to write that fact down, it's obvious to you that I'm really listening and sincerely interested. Make notes incessantly when you're on a by-owner home tour.

COMPLIMENT THEIR TASTE AND THE IMPROVEMENTS.

Some real estate people are very, very syrupy. Everything they see triggers an "oh, it's lovely; it's beautiful; I just love it." And the by-owners know they're being fed the old malarkey. Be sincere. And learn how to compliment people whose taste differs greatly from your own. The two ideas go together. When you have a professional attitude, whether or not you like some feature of a property won't matter. If just one buyer will like it, that's enough. Once you have this idea firmly lodged in your brain, you'll find that creating sincere compliments is a whole lot easier.

But it's not enough simply to be sincere. We can really believe that the lady's taste is terrific; we can love it all and still sound insincere when we tell her so. Why? Because we're not thinking. Instead of connecting our compliments with the value and uniqueness of her property, we merely let the tired old phrases roll out of our mouths. In other words, we're being mentally lazy—and she knows it. Will you believe that by-owners aren't interested in employing mentally lazy agents to market their homes?

Can compliments demonstrate that you're alert and energetic? Certainly. Can compliments build rapport? We know they can. But what gives them these powers? Thought.

There's the secret ingredient. It's found in every compliment that works. Unless you think, you'll repeat the worn out words that remind them you're there to make money. Unless you put your mind to work on fitting what you say to what they've done, you'll fall back on false-sounding flattery. Unless you build rapport with thoughtful compliments, you'll tear it down with thoughtless comments.

Now let's study eight samples of rapport-building praise for by-owners:

"The drapes certainly enhance your living room."

"I'm impressed with the way your color scheme pulls the whole house together. You've made a bold statement here and it really works." Use this approach when the floor coverings and walls are the same colors throughout.

"Your color scheme really gives the house a bright and peppy feeling. Just stepping in here raised my spirits. I'm sure that a lot of buyers will like it too." Use something along this line when the colors vary from room to room.

"The built-in bookcase lends an air of dignity to your family room. Was it professionally done, or is being a master woodworker your husband's hobby?"

"The mural creates a mood of warmth and comfort in this part of the house."

"Your treatment of that wall was the right touch to emphasize just how spacious this room really is."

"You've chosen an extraordinary wallpaper, and it certainly brings a sunny feeling inside, doesn't it?"

"I get a very good feeling in here but I can't pinpoint the cause. I wonder if it's the draperies, or the paneling, or that splendid fireplace? Ah, of course, it's the combination of all the elements. Everything here blends wonderfully. Well done, Mrs. McKiff." When you've learned the knack of thoughtful compliments, you can go through the entire house without dumping a single "It's beautiful" on them.

LOOK FOR COMMON DENOMINATORS

When a professional walks through a by-owner's house, he's very alert although his manner is casual. He's looking hard for anything that'll help him find common ground and build rapport. Here are five classes of things he's watching for:

1. TROPHIES.

If you see one, ask what the sport or event was and who in the family won it. You'll be able to talk a bit with them about that event.

2. SPORTS GEAR.

Look for golf bags, fishing poles, skiing posters. Anything of this sort gives you a chance to talk about things other than real estate.

3. EVIDENCE OF HOBBIES OR SPECIAL INTERESTS.

Be careful not to seem nosey as you do so, but notice what books and magazines are lying around, and whether or not any of the furniture is antique. Often they'll tell you what subjects and activities the by-owners are involved in. Enthusiasts and hobbyists are usually eager to talk about their special interests.

4. COLLECTIONS.

Do you know what's rare? A collector who doesn't want to show off his collection of beer cans, shark's teeth, or whatever. Bring a keen, intelligent, and sincere interest to his display and you're well on the way to writing up the listing. Even if you have to say, "I really don't know much about shark's teeth. Tell me what got you interested in collecting them," you're drawing the sellers out and opening them up.

5. PICTURES OF THEIR FAMILY.

When I saw photos displayed, I used to stop and say, "You've got three little ones, haven't you? What are their ages? They're really cute. What are their names? I have three as well. I have a Tim, a Lara, and a Tasha. Did you ever see Dr. Zhivago? We saw it twice."

I used these trifles to establish rapport, and to make them laugh a little. I'd mention one of my children and say something about my family. We all like people who are like us.

When there's no evidence of children past or present around, or if you're not comfortable talking about children, don't do it. And, if you're having problems with your own offspring, don't tell the by-owners about it. There's no surer way to destroy your chances of listing them than by dumping your troubles on their carpet.

COMPLIMENT ANY CREATIVITY

Many people have things in their homes that they've made and they're usually tremendously proud of their work. Check every room you see for handcrafted things, and for features they've built into the house. Also scan the garage if you get the chance. A quick look can tell you much about their interests and provide you with more openings for conversation. The same holds true of the outside. Many hobbies are carried on entirely in the backyard, and no evidence of them can be seen inside the house. Be sure to include a fast tour of the grounds in your first daytime visit. If you must return in the evening for your meeting with both of them, it's less likely that you'll have a chance to see the rear yard.

With so few families having someone at home during the day, you'll have to make some considerations. You might want to go for the first visit on a weekend. Or, the first visit could be in the evening, with a stipulation that you'd like to come back during the daytime to get a better view of the exterior of the home and landscaping. Either way, you've got a sound reason for a second visit, and the more time these potential clients spend with you, the better.

DISCOVER THEIR LIKES

Ask them, together or individually, what they like best about their home. These are safe questions that build rapport, give you valuable information, and keep them talking. The more they talk to you, the more they'll like and trust you and that's what you're there for, isn't it?

DON'T DISCUSS TWO ITEMS

Religion and politics? I don't recommend those subjects either unless you're absolutely certain that you and they share the same opinions. But what I'm referring to now are *price* and *policy.* If you get into a discussion of price with one spouse, you're dead. You're also dead if you talk about policy, that is, about what your manager requires in the way of fee, length, type of listing, and so on. And your reason for not talking about these things with her alone, or with him alone, had better not be that you want them both present in a closing situation before you get into the details. In other words, don't even hint anything like, "One of you can say no, but it takes two of you to say yes, so I don't want to risk getting into the sticky issues unless I'm in a position to close you both and get it in writing."

You had better prepare for this sharp-edged moment because it'll come up every time you start to make progress. Handle it badly and you're out; handle it well and you'll move a long way toward listing them. Let's work through one of these moments. The wife says, "Well, what do you think we can get for this place?" Here's how you respond:

"You know, I could pick a figure out of thin air, but I'm sure that's not what you want. However, since you've asked, I'll research the facts and compile a comparable market analysis. This will let us know exactly what the value of your property is at the present time. I can drop the comparable market analysis off this evening at six, or do you think it might be better if I wait until eight?"

There are two more ways in which the price question will come up. Here's one:

"We've set our price at $185,000 and that's firm."

Since she hasn't asked your opinion and you want to avoid all discussion of price, simply don't volunteer any comment. And that means, don't look shocked at how high her price is. But you must make it clear that you understood what she said or she'll probably bring money up again. So you say, "Yes, I remember seeing that figure in your ad. By the way, the chandelier adds so much to this room. I was wondering, are you planning to leave it?"

If the price wasn't stated in the ad, you need only say, "I'll make a note of that. By the way, the chandelier . . . ?"

The third way that price comes up is another opportunity wrapped in a hazard. This time she wants your opinion:

"We're asking $205,000. Do you think we should go higher?"

If you're knowledgeable about property values in her neighborhood, the odds are that you know their price already is 5 to 20 percent above market value. Maybe even more. But when she states the number, have your poker face on, or you've just kissed the listing good-bye. You can't gasp when you hear their wild price. You can't let your mouth fall open. You can't even lift an eyebrow or let the ghost of a smile play around the corners of your mouth. If you let any hint escape that you think their price is unrealistic, you'll become a casualty of your own carelessness. That means you lose your chance to list them. Here's how to dodge this danger and move ahead:

"We're asking $205,000. Do you think we should go higher?"

"Thank you for asking for my professional opinion. Of course, I could give you a snap judgment, but I'm sure that's not what you want. However, since you've asked, I'll research the facts and compile a comparable market analysis. This will let us know exactly what the value of your property is at the present time. I can drop the comparable market analysis off this evening at six, or do you think it might be better if I waited until eight?"

Now do you see why I call this moment sharp edged? It's sad how many unskilled agents cut themselves out of the business here. But you won't, will you? Instead of getting cut, you'll go for an evening appointment to see them both. And at that time, you'll be able to go into your full presentation with every prospect of walking out with the listing because you'll cope with the price at the right time in your listing sequence.

Of course, you won't always get the evening appointment.

But at the very least, you'll create respect for your knowledge and professionalism. When the sellers like you and trust your real estate competence, are they likely to list with anyone else?

When you're alone with one spouse, you must also avoid discussing your company's policies and the terms under which your company will market their home if you do get the listing. The one spouse you're talking with may throw out a number of cute ideas to see if they'll bounce or stick. Things like a 30-day open listing, or a ridiculously low fee arrangement. Don't allow yourself to be maneuvered into discussing such items. Instead, talk about the appointment you're aiming for: "Most of these things we'll discuss when I come back after I've done my research, and we'll go over that research very carefully so you both fully understand what validity it has. Of course at that time we'll thoroughly cover all the decisions that will need to be made."

To sum up, don't go cruising for the big no when you can't get the big yes.

CHAPTER 13

Be Ten Times More Successful Than Average with Effective Follow-Up

People have an enormous capacity to believe what they want to believe. By-owners want to believe that selling a house is easy: Just stick a sign in the lawn, run an ad in the paper, talk to a few people, fill out a form—zap, and it's done. If they're convinced they'll save thousands of dollars with little effort, you won't be able to puncture that idea before the ink dries on their ad.

When the by-owners' hopes are rising like a balloon, they're list-proof. The only thing that will change their minds is meeting reality. Until they feel the frustration of coping with the home-seeking public, until they experience the disappointments that are the by-owners' lot in life, until their patience is gone, and their time is running out, they can't understand why a real estate agent is a worthwhile investment. A pair of convinced by-owners can't be listed until some of the gas leaks out of their "we're gonna save a lot of money by selling ourselves" balloon and they become somewhat unconvinced that FSBO (for sale by owner) is the way to go. Knowing that, pros position themselves where they can see it happen. Then they're there when the FSBOs float back to earth. That's what follow-up does for you. It puts you there when they come down to reality.

And it's one thing more. It's using the time they're floating high on hope to build friendship, trust, and respect for your real estate expertise.

If you antagonize them while they're learning that they need professional help, they'll seek it elsewhere.

When first putting up the sign, three out of four by-owners are convinced they can successfully market their home in a very short period of time. As I've said, for all practical purposes they are not listable at that time. But not for long. Within three months, nine out of ten of those by-owners have either already listed with a real estate firm, or they've acquired so much respect for the trials and tribulations of by-ownership that they've become listable.

Lurking in those figures is a concept that can have a substantial impact on your future income. If you're active in real estate, you know that few agents are persistent about by-owner follow-up. They mostly find them, hit them a lick or two, and forget them. This means they stop working with each month's new by-owners before three-fourths of them can be listed. No wonder they're discouraged.

The persistent few, on the other hand, work through the time that 90 percent of all by-owners can be listed. No wonder the persistent few are making money. No wonder they're becoming more confident and more effective every day with the by-owners who list quickly as well as with the by-owners who hold out for long periods of time. The discouraged agents with little endurance think that by-owners are tough; what they don't realize is that the champions of persistence are tougher.

You can join the tougher group, the high-earning elite, simply by using the effective methods given in the rest of this chapter to follow up with your by-owners. But you have to keep at it day after day until you succeed. You can do it. To help yourself stay with it, keep in mind that an agent with strong follow-up is at least ten times as successful as the common run of quick-tiring salespeople.

You may doubt that. Yet, in truth, the advantages that effective follow-up will put in your hands are more likely to be greater than ten to one. Consider this: The average real estate agent doesn't write any by-owner listings that sell during his one year of "trying" real estate. During that same year, the champion lists at least one by-owner a month—and we're only counting the listings that sell and create income. I don't know how to put a meaningful multiple on twelve to nothing. Do you?

As we go through the detail of effective follow-up, please bear in mind that the timing given is aimed at the most common situation for home owners. That situation, of course, is the husband and wife both work outside the home during the day. Other circumstances, such as night shifts, will dictate a different follow-up schedule. Be alert for those opportunities, and remember that if they both work, their need for professional help is even greater and fewer agents will take the trouble to follow up with them simply because they may be difficult to reach at first.

When you do finally make a connection, here are the steps you'll need to follow:

1. MAIL A THANK-YOU NOTE IMMEDIATELY

Personalize it as much as possible. This means that you write it out in longhand. Speed is everything here because speed demonstrates energy. Your thank-you notes must be in the mail the same day that anything significant takes place: when you first contact them, when you first see their house, after any opportunity they allow you to give them service.

Keep all materials for writing and mailing thank-you notes in your car. When you leave a by-owner's house, pull over to the curb a few blocks away, write the note, and drop it in the first mailbox you pass. Do it now or you'll never do it.

2. CALL EVERY FRIDAY AFTERNOON

As your minimum program, call every by-owner you're working with every Friday between 6:00 and 8:00 P.M. Very few agents will do that because they don't know what to say to people. Or they just call now and then and bug the by-owners.

If you get an answering machine, leave a message like this: "Good evening, Mr. and Mrs. Proctor. This is Tom Hopkins with Champions Unlimited. I'm updating my inventory for what looks like a busy weekend and just wondered if your home is still available. If it's not, congratulations, you must be so excited. If you have not yet found the right buyer for your home, please let me know tonight and I'll keep your property in mind over the weekend."

If you find someone at home, you should use this script:

"Hello, Mrs. Putnam. Tom Hopkins with Champions Unlimited.

I'm updating my inventory for what looks like an unbelievable weekend. Is your home still available?"

"Yes, it is."

"Fine. Well, I'll keep it in mind and stop by to say hello before the weekend's over. Thanks. Nice talking to you."

You can make calls like that to a dozen by-owners in a few minutes, but your objective isn't to get through those calls in the shortest possible time. Pause briefly after each of their answers to give them a chance to volunteer information. Sooner or later, the strain of going it alone will begin to tell and, if you've been building rapport with each call instead of bugging them, you'll be all set to move in for the listing.

Let's go over the last vital bit of phraseology. Here's what you say:

"Hello, Mr., Mrs., Miss, or Ms. *whoever you're calling*. (No pause.) This is *(your name)* with *(your company)*. (Still no pause.) I'm calling to update my inventory for what looks like an excellent real estate weekend." (Use a different adjective each time. First, it might be an unbelievable real estate weekend, then it's terrific, exciting, tremendous, wonderful, and by that time you'll probably have them listed.) Again you don't pause for a discussion. Instead you go right into: "Is your home still available?"

Now you wait for their answer and, if they want to talk and especially if they show signs of beginning to realize how tough by-owner land really is, you make the appropriate move: You go for a listing appointment to give your full presentation.

However, they'll usually say something like, "Yes, it is, but we're still not ready to list."

"Oh, I know that, but, as I said before, if I have a buyer I can't satisfy, I want to be able to send them to you."

Then you say without pausing, "I'll be in the neighborhood Sunday, and may stop by just to answer any questions that you may have."

All of this must be said very warmly. You're always being nice. A lot of us don't realize something that I believe from the bottom of my heart: The average American is a nice person. A lot of us expect everyone to be nasty, but there are millions of wonderful people out there. Give them honest service; demonstrate integrity; help them and many of them will let you serve them.

Sunday afternoon is the best time to visit. It took me five hours to get home on Sundays and I only lived four miles from the office. Why?

I was always on my way home when I stopped in to see all my by-owners.

When they answer the door, the important thing is for you to act enthusiastic about how good your real estate weekend was. Let me give you the psychology of the situation. Most by-owners, like most real estate agents, aren't persistent. They only try to sell their home for a short time. After that sign goes up, they don't get in the recreational vehicle on the weekends anymore. They might not be able to play golf the way they used to all day Sunday. If one of them doesn't work, the chances are that they were home all week with the little sweethearts, their darling children, and they're ready to get *o-u-t*. The reality is that when people start thinking about selling their homes, they stop being able to really enjoy it.

If you knock on their door when the shadows are long on Sunday, and if you tell them how active your office is finding the real estate market, you'll score some psychological points. Your by-owners stayed home all weekend, keeping their home presentable for buyers, when they'd much rather have been elsewhere. And what did they accomplish? Zilch.

At such moments, people often have sudden flashes of insight—things like, "We're never going to sell this place by ourselves." So don't miss a single one of your by-owners "on your way home" Sunday afternoon. Here's what you say:

"Hi, Mrs. Putnam. Tom Hopkins—just stopping by to say hello. Did you have any luck this weekend?"

"No."

"Okay. Well, everybody's okay?"

"Yes."

"Well, here's another card. Call me if you have any questions."

That's a sample of tough conversation. Usually, you'll get an opening for a few minutes' discussion of the real estate market, during which time you'll have an opportunity to demonstrate your local knowledge.

Persistence pays plenty. So keep at it.

Here are some follow-up ideas that I try my best to get salespeople to use because I know they pay off. How do I know? Because the first two paid off for me, and I've seen the third pay off for people I've managed. The first is simple, doesn't cost much, and pays tremendous dividends.

Your Own For-Sale-by-Owner Signs

Committed by-owners spend money on fancy signs and large ads. The less committed use a piece of cardboard on a stick. This means that the by-owners who'll be the quickest to list with someone are the most likely to welcome your sign. Have three or four made up to begin with and rotate them among your by-owners. You'll find they work so well that you'll want to have more of them. The quality and appearance of these signs is important. You won't look professional unless they look professional.

Checklist for Signs to Help You List By-Owners

1. Size as specified by your board's rules.
2. Colors to match your office's regular FOR SALE signs.
3. Front legend in large block letters: FOR SALE BY OWNER
4. Blackboard or dry erase marker area below front legend to be large enough so that a by-owner's phone number can be written in and read from the street. (You can save a little money here by printing the phone numbers on white cards with a broad tip marker and taping them to the signs.)
5. Back legend (in small, cursive letters no more than an inch high):

    COMPLIMENTS OF YOUR NAME,
    YOUR PHONE NUMBER

The way you get them to take the sign is critical. Imagine that I'm talking with a nice young couple. They seem to like and trust me. Because their emotional responses are good, and because I'm with both of them, I decide to try the sign technique. As you can see from Mr.

Willis's comment, I'm not having it all my way. This phraseology, incidentally, should be memorized.

"Tom, we may call you later, but really, we're planning to sell it ourselves."

"Mr. and Mrs. Willis, one way of obtaining a buyer is having people stop when they see your sign. The color of our signs, for some reason, stops people. There's something I'd like to do for you. I'd like to let you use a for-sale-by-owner sign that I really feel will stop their eyes. Now you're probably wondering, Mr. Willis, why I would do that. I'm doing that, not so much to obligate you to give me the listing, more important, in hopes that if you sell your home yourself thanks to any of my efforts, you'll be kind enough to refer anyone else that I can serve to me."

Let's talk about this approach. You may be wondering: Is he telling me to help them sell it themselves? Does that make any sense?

The sign isn't going to make the sale. Don't worry about that. But if you can get your sign stuck in their yard, what will they see every time they leave the front door? COMPLIMENTS OF YOUR NAME. If you can get a sign in their front yard, they won't listen to anyone else. That's the whole reason you try to do it.

I kept my signs working. Yours won't do you any good holding up spider webs in your garage. After one of my signs was in someone's yard for a few days, I'd often hear something like this: "You know, Tom, we've had more people call and stop by since you gave us that sign, but still nothing's happened. Come on over and let's see what else you can do for us." You know what else I could do for them.

Using by-owner signs is great technique. Don't be afraid to try it. A sign will cost you less than a tank of gas, and it'll take you a whole lot farther.

For-Sale-by-Owner First Aid Kit

The results of this technique, if you'll learn it and use it, will thrill you. But you have to follow my instructions closely to make it work. Take one of the manila folders you put listings in and print the name of this technique in big black letters. You might want to print it out on your computer and glue the title onto the folder to look a bit more professional. Some of my students even went so far as to include the cross that's found on medical first aid kits on the outside of the folder.

The reason you want FOR-SALE-BY-OWNER FIRST AID KIT printed large is that the by-owner must be able to read it clearly when you hold the folder up. I used to make up twenty-five of these first aid kits all at once—that way I had them handy when I needed them.

Here's what you put in the kits: (All of the forms can be blanks or copies of actual documents on which you've blacked out the names and dates):

1. PURCHASE AGREEMENT

This document might be called the deposit receipt, the earnest money receipt, the binder—whatever it's called where you work, it's the original document expressing the buyer's agreement to buy. Don't use your office's form in the kit. Get a standard form from a title company or from a large stationery store.

2. ESCROW, SETTLEMENT, OR CLOSING INSTRUCTIONS

Again, they go by different names in different parts of the country but, whether the title company, an attorney, or an escrow officer does it, somebody has to get written instructions on how to complete the transaction. These instructions must be prepared by trained people. Get all the blank forms you can.

3. TITLE INSURANCE POLICY

In some states, it's called an abstract. Whatever it's called, get some blanks.

4. SETTLEMENT (OR CLOSING) STATEMENT

If VA, FHA, or other government-insured or guaranteed loans are common in your service area, use one of those forms in your kit. There's so much stuff on those forms—you'll love it. All you need, of course, is one form that you can run copies of.

5. DEEDS

You need four different kinds. Go to a large stationery store or go online to http://www.wolcottsforms.com/door/ and get Wolcotts forms.

There are other acceptable brands, but Wolcotts has good ones for this purpose. If you have a challenge finding their forms, call them at 1-800-421-2220 to find a vendor in your area.

You need four deeds for your kits:

General Warranty Deed
Special Warranty Deed
Bargain and Sale Deed
Quit-Claim Deed

Here's what you should do to put a high gloss on your ability to use this technique successfully: Talk to a representative of a title or abstract company and arrange for a tour of their office. When you're there, have one of the title people fully explain why title insurance is necessary, how it works, and who pays for it. Learn the difference between the different types of policies. When you've done that, you're ready to rehearse your phraseology.

Remember that it's important to give your first aid kit performance to all the decision makers at the same time. If you give it to only one of them, you'll lose almost all of the impact of this technique. Let's imagine this scene: You're talking with Jerry and Marge Ferris, a young couple trying to sell their home themselves and, as usual, having no success.

Hold up the folder as you begin to talk so they can see its name. As soon as you start talking about the first form, take it out and hand it to them. Work your way through the kit, handing them more and more forms as you continue to tell them about each of the documents. You need to have the words rehearsed so that they'll flow smoothly, as they should coming from a professional talking about his or her profession.

One set of names has been shown for the forms and procedures. If the names used in your area are different, say them instead. Here's the phraseology:

"Mr. and Mrs. Ferris, I've prepared something for you. This is what I call my for-sale-by-owner first aid kit. I find that if I give people service, they may not list with me, but they will refer other people to me. I'd like to go through the kit with you, and review the forms and the complexities that I, hopefully as your agent, will handle for you. But if not, this should make you much more aware of what you need to do if you handle the sale of your home yourselves.

"The first form, Mr. and Mrs. Ferris, is the purchase contract, and it's the first document you'll want your buyers to sign. It's also a receipt for their deposit, which is why it's often called the earnest money receipt, the deposit receipt, or the binder.

"I would suggest that you ask them for a large deposit. The larger the deposit you get, the firmer your sale. We always get the largest deposit possible.

"The second form I have in here is a standard escrow instruction to the third impartial party, that is, the attorney, the escrow company, or the title company. It will instruct them exactly what to do with all your money that's involved in the transaction.

"The third document is the standard title insurance policy. Now, there are different types of title insurance. First, there's the title insurance that you as the owner will obtain, under which you'll insure the title for the new purchaser. Then there's the mortgagee's policy. If a new loan is put on the property, the mortgagee, the lender, or, of course, the beneficiary, if a trust deed is used, will be the one who'll determine if you'll need the owner's and the mortgagee's policy. There are samples of the policies; you can kind of look through them.

"The next form is the standard closing statement, or the settlement statement. This is a copy of an actual transaction and, of course, to protect my clients' privacy, I've blocked out anything that could identify them. On this statement, you'll see two columns, the debits and the credits, representing the liabilities and the assets of the buyer and the sellers. I've made some notes here on the prorations of your interest and your taxes. Notice that this transaction involved what we call points, the loan discount fee, also known as the loan origination fee. And, as you can see, the charges were quite extensive.

"Last, let's talk about what in many ways is the most important document in any real estate transaction, the deed. Four different kinds are used, depending on the circumstances and to make sure we'd have the right one, I've obtained blank copies of all four deed forms for you. The deed is the document of conveyance whereby you two, as the grantors, convey your interest to the grantee, that is, to the buyer.

"Now, the most commonly used deed is the general warranty deed. The second deed is the special warranty deed. It has limited warranties and is very seldom used with title insurance, or when a new loan is obtained. The third deed is the bargain and sale deed. A bargain and sale deed is normally used only in a trust deed sale when there's a probate and it's handled through the courts. And then I have a deed here that is a dangerous kind of deed. It is known as the quit-claim deed. In a quit-claim deed, the grantor, which remember was you, is in no way warranting to the grantee any more than as stated on the deed, which may not be valid, and this is why very few people use it, and I would advise you to avoid it. There have been so many people, Mr. and Mrs. Ferris, who become involved in court proceedings because of the quit-claim deed. I would stay away from it.

"Now, do you have any questions?"

I know. It seems like a lot to learn. Maybe you think it's far too much. But before you decide that this isn't for you, listen while I tell you how easy it is to rehearse the first aid kit speech so that you can give a convincing performance with it every chance you get.

You only need to memorize the first three paragraphs, from "I've prepared something" through "largest deposit possible." After that, you just talk about the complexity and importance of each form, using the forms as cue cards. As a real estate professional, you already know enough (or soon will know enough if you're a determined beginner) to talk about the basic forms of your profession.

Begin your drill by copying what you'll say out of this book. Then sit down in front of a mirror with one of your first aid kits in hand, and give your performance to the face looking back at you. Run through that drill three times a day for a week, and your performance will be as smooth as Katie Couric's smile.

One final tip: Always have the forms arranged in the same order in your kit. Then introduce them with the same key words: first, second, third, fourth, or next, and fifth or last.

Your goal with this performance is to convince a for-sale-by-owner that the fee we earn is definitely not out of line. Real estate people sometimes don't realize it, but what they do is a very complicated thing. Focus on the difficulties in a positive way. How? By making your prospective clients aware of the legal, economic, and emotional complexities that must be overcome before any real estate transaction can be finalized.

For-Sale-by-Owner Squad

To make your life with by-owners easier and follow-up more efficient, you might want to team up with another agent. If you decide to use this technique, team up with a champion, a top producer, a highly-motivated individual. Otherwise it won't work. But when a pair of champions pull together with this technique, great things happen. Here's how it works and it must be done exactly like this:

1. Pick someone you feel you can work enthusiastically with, someone you like, someone who's a winner.
2. There are two roles in the squad technique: scout and cleanup. Maybe you'll switch roles back and forth, maybe you'll both prefer not to switch. The scout records the ads, makes the calls, gets the appointments, and sees the people first. When he's done everything in our program to list the by-owner, the scout notifies his partner to go in for the cleanup.
3. Let's say that you're running cleanup this week. Your partner, Bob Brophy, has been scouting. For example, at nine this morning, he was out to see the Johnsons. They are new by-owners, and Bob was the first agent to reach them.

Your partner performed eloquently. Now it's your turn. At five o'clock today, you knock on the Johnson's door. When Mrs. Johnson answers, here's what you say:

"Hello, Mrs. Johnson. Tom Hopkins with Champions Unlimited. I talked to a gentleman in our office who came by to see you earlier, Bob Brophy. Now, Bob and I work together."

Since you're splitting all brokerages received from converted by-owners, you must say, "Bob and I work together." Why? Most important, to be honest. Also, to build trust, to avoid disaster when friends compare notes, and to stay out of trouble with your board's ethics committee. "I only stopped by to let you know that you've really picked a winner in Bob. He'll do a great job for you. He's one of the top people in our company. You really don't need to look further for a salesperson if and when you ever decide to list your home. Bob will give you such great service. He's one of our top listers. Been in the business now for, let's see, more than five years. He's a veteran and he's full time, by the way. You'll like Bob. He's very involved in the community. And he's a very honest man as well. So, I wanted to let you know that. I, of course, will also be serving you along with Bob, and we both thank you so much."

Beware that you can only state truths about Bob's career. If you and Bob are both new to the business and working your way through this book together, that's fine. Invest some time in writing both your stories. Include points about your intention to serve. If you're new to the business, you may have to rely on the track record of your company until you can establish one of your own. Just tell the truth.

Here's the psychology: if you've praised the third party, they must be good. But you must let them know clearly that you're working together. You can say lots of good things about your partner and not sound as though you're bragging—but in effect, what you're saying is: We're both knowledgeable, energetic, and honest.

Summing Up

Close for the listing as soon as you have all of the decision makers together, and they're responding to your minor closes. Don't think that you have to go through every technique in this book with every by-owner. You don't have to hand them all a sign, become half of a for-sale-by-owner squad, or give them all the first aid kit. You only do those things if you're not getting the listing.

Many times I've gone over to see a couple on a Saturday morning. After an hour and a half, while chatting over a cup of coffee and acting like I don't want the listing, I've had them start to ask me questions. The questions made me take out one of my for-sale-by-owner first aid kits to help them. Then, after that, I've had some of them say, "You know, we were going to try it, but now we're not so sure. The only thing is, we've put the ad in the paper and it doesn't come out for a week."

Do you know what I'd say then? "Well, that's certainly no problem," and I'd give them the money for the ad just to show my good faith that I'll serve them well. I've done that. I've also written into the listing, "This listing has no effect until _____," the date their ad runs out. Or if they say, "We have two couples who're interested," I again tell them it's no problem. I get the names of those two couples and put in the listing, "No fee if sold to name number one or name number two."

You're going to have some people who wouldn't list with you no matter what you do. Working with by-owners will give you plenty of chances to say, "I never see failure as failure, but only as the opportunity to practice my technique and perfect my performance." With practice comes perfection through experience and fine tuning.

Working with by-owners will also give you plenty of chances to be paid well for performing well. But, again, how long will it take before this starts to happen?

Three weeks.

Expect no results for twenty-one days. Review every step. Practice, drill, and rehearse every technique. Then put them into effect vigorously, and watch what happens! You'll be more than delighted with the results you'll achieve.

CHAPTER 14

Real Estate's Royal Road to Riches
Is Called Prospecting

It's amazing, but the road to riches isn't crowded. There's plenty of room on it for you. And it runs right past your office's front door.

Before we get into the different prospecting methods, let's define what prospecting is all about. After all, it's the lifeblood of any real estate career. In general, prospecting means finding the right people to work with. In your case, people who want to sell or purchase homes. It involves two steps:

1. Meeting people with real estate needs.
2. Convincing those people of the benefits of working with *you*.

There are almost as many different ways to prospect as there are types of people who need your services. I'll be covering a lot of ideas in this chapter. Read them all and make a plan to work with those that sound right both for your personality and for the area in which you work. Do not add any new strategies until you've run the first ones through all their steps. Otherwise, your prospecting methods won't turn into the powerful income-generating system they can be for you. Let's begin at the beginning. You're new to the business or seeking a boost in your productivity. Since we're way past Chapter 2—What to Do When You're New—you've already compiled your list of everyone you know. You've mailed them each a letter or postcard telling them that you're ready, willing, and able to serve their needs. By the way, if you're not new, try mailing that postcard or letter to your contact list now. Follow up with key people on that list—folks you know to have a large base of friends, associates, and/or relatives.

Adopting Orphans

One good source of potential clients is right there in your office. I call it Orphan Adoption. Ask your manager about a salesperson who may have left the company in the last six months or so. Get permission to contact the people that agent worked with. In other words, adopt those folks who have been left orphans by the exodus of someone from your company. Send them a letter telling them that you're their new contact at the company. Thank them for their past business and offer to provide them with periodic information relevant to the community or specifically about home values in their neighborhood. Include a small item with your name and contact information as well as a "call to action."

A call to action is either a direction to send potential clients to your Web site, to e-mail you with their permission to stay in touch, or a return postcard that gives you permission to call them or otherwise contact them. If they give you permission to contact them and provide a phone number, you will not be violating Do Not Call restrictions.

Trading Up

Let's say you work in an area where there are a lot of new homes being built. Among your orphans or past clients you may have people who invested in what we call starter homes a few years ago. Today, a new development is going in a mile or so down the road with either larger homes or those with more amenities—perhaps a community center or higher end fixtures and appliances. Even though your clients may not have lived in their homes long enough to itch, they may be interested in moving up. Had these homes been available when they were seeking the home they live in now, they would likely have preferred them. Moving a short distance geographically doesn't usually affect the schools the children attend or call for selecting different areas in which to shop. Yet, moving up in status or quality can be a whole new world they wouldn't explore without your help. This is where knowing your clients' tastes, interests, likes, and dislikes come into play.

Expired Listings

In every area, there are bound to be people who listed their property with an agent. When nothing happened, they let the listing expire. What you need to focus on is the fact that these people did have a need and desire to sell their home at one time. Perhaps they listed it for too high an investment, based on market value. Perhaps their situation changed. Perhaps there is something wrong with the property that the previous agent wasn't bold enough to point out—something that kept it from selling. In any event, by contacting these people, you may be able to rekindle that old desire and help them to market their home professionally and at the right price to have it sell.

Note: If they had a bad past experience with an agent, you will have to tread lightly. Never knock the other agent. Just encourage the sellers to tell you everything they didn't like. Then, tell them that you're here to help them to never go through that again. Move into your presentation on your personal experience and talk about some creative ways you've helped others get happily moved.

Learning to Scratch an Itch

In the United States, the typical home owner gets the itch to move into a bigger home or a different neighborhood or to downsize to something smaller approximately every four to six years. To determine what the average itch cycle is for your area, look up information on folks who have used the services of your company more than once. If possible, talk with other, more experienced agents, as well. They should have a feel for the average turnover of homes in the area.

Once you know that number, start looking through both your personal files and the company orphan files to find those people who are approaching the beginning of their itch cycle. Contact them to open up a discussion about their current situation.

If there have been additions to the family, there may be a need for a larger home.

If the folks are getting on in years or have elders living with them, they may need a single-story home instead of their current split-level or two-story.

If the kids are going off to college, a smaller home might be in the picture.

In any case, if they've lived in the home for several years, they should have built up some pretty good equity. Your job will be to help them see the power of that equity to get them more of what they want in a home. Get them to open their minds to the possibilities. Then, show them homes that might be just right for them. If they get excited about something new, who is going to get the sale? And, the listing of their old home to sell? The agent who was there to scratch when they itched.

The Newspaper as a Lead Source

As a professional, you'll be reading the newspaper daily for FSBO advertising as we've already covered. However, there are other sections of the paper that are just as important. I'm referring here to the Announcements or Promotions or Business News sections of your local paper. Here is where you'll find people who have just opened new businesses; people who have just been promoted; people who are moving into the area. And those are just the people you want to serve, aren't they?

Become a client at the new business. Make sure the people who work there become familiar with your face. This works exceptionally well for businesses such as dry cleaners, hair salons, restaurants, gift shops, and bookstores. You need those items, right? Why not stake out those businesses as opportunities to serve their owners and staff? People like to work with people they know. Be a pleasant customer and a professional real estate person at the same time. Go into their businesses at their slowest times so they'll be sure to recognize you and remember you. Be sure they know what you do. You'll be amazed at how many of them will think of you when they need real estate assistance. Or, better yet, when they overhear another client mention their real estate needs. They can become excellent sources of referral business for you.

People who get promotions usually get nice raises as well—especially the people who will have their names and photos in the paper. Here's how you get to meet them: Cut out the announcement. Send it to them with a letter of congratulations. Mention in the letter that you are also in business in the community and offer your services should they also have an interest in promoting themselves to a new address.

If it's someone who's really up there in business in the community, you might want to take the announcement to a professional framing shop (another source of clients for you) and have it done up professionally before sending it out. Going the extra mile to demonstrate your professionalism and willingness to serve rarely goes unrewarded.

People who are being transferred to new business opportunities often need to sell their homes. I know of a real estate agent in the Phoenix area who sent an announcement news article to an NBA player who was being traded to the Phoenix Suns. She went so far as to offer to scout properties for him to save him time and effort when he visited. As you can guess, she saved him a lot of time in trying to get to know the area and select where he wanted to live by preparing information on several parts of town and the types of properties to be found there. When he came to town to look for his new home, the decision was made over a weekend. She got the sale *and* the listing when he was later traded to another team.

Baby and wedding announcements are another area to consider using as lead sources. Newlyweds buy homes sooner or later. Maybe you can catch them right after their engagement is announced. Babies need growing room and so do their families.

Don't limit your research to the local newspaper. Keep an eye on your local business journal as well.

Start a Swap Meet

This may also be called a lead group or lead club in your area. If you can find one that's already established and doesn't have a real estate agent in it, consider what the other occupations are that are covered and consider joining it. Ideally, you'd want to be in a group with people who provide other services to the people you work with. For example, people in the trades: heating, air conditioning, roofers, those who do home remodeling, plumbers, painters, cleaning services, and landscapers.

Other professionals that would make a good match for you are insurance agents, mortgage brokers, and even car salespeople. People who need to buy or sell homes often need those other services. Your past clients may also need services of qualified professionals in these areas. If you can easily see the two-way street with a particular group, by all means get involved.

A lead exchange group usually meets once a month for breakfast or lunch. Each member is charged with bringing leads for the others in exchange for those brought to them. If you find the group isn't providing you with qualified leads or enough leads, consider finding or starting a group that will.

Community Involvement

There are two areas of community involvement.

1. You can get involved in existing events or activities in your community.
2. You can create your own events within your community. By *your community* this could mean your town or region or your very own community of homes you serve.

I can't stress the value of community involvement enough. The more involved and active you are, the more people you will meet while doing good works. There is no down side to this.

Let's talk about your local area first. Here's a list of community programs where you could volunteer:

Senior center
Community center
Homeless shelter

Hospital
School
Blood drive
Library
Church
Charitable organizations
Police department

Every one of these places has a need for volunteers and provides valuable services within the community. Doing volunteer work is personally rewarding and I highly recommend it. While performing your duties, present yourself as a volunteer first, as a real estate professional second.

When getting to know people in these organizations, add them to your personal contact list. Send them notes of appreciation for their volunteer efforts. Keep them informed of your services when you send out business communications.

In your own *farm* community of homes you serve, you can organize events that help the greater community or the small group. Consider these:

Be the liason between the police department and the neighborhood for a Block Watch program.

Attend city council meetings to know what's going on in the community that might impact the neighborhood. Be the communicator of such news. Be the representative to speak up at such meetings on behalf of the home owners.

Organize a food drive. Notify everyone in your service area of what's needed and offer to pick up donations. Send every participant a thank-you note. Let them know how many pounds of food were donated. Or, consider matching their donations either with food or money so they're challenged to do more.

Do the same with Toys for Tots at Christmastime.

Or, adopt a U.S. service person or a family in dire straits. Send out a list of what's needed, when and how you will collect the items. Be sure to send every participant a thank-you note or small award of appreciation.

If there's a greenbelt or park area in your service area, reserve it for Easter egg hunts, Halloween costume contests, or neighborhood block parties. Be the one to get everyone together. People always enjoy such events but few will invest the time in planning and organizing them.

If your local area has a parade on July Fourth or for some other event, consider sponsoring a float. If it's too costly, try to get the company or several other real estate agents involved. Invite some of the children in your farm to ride on the float.

Another great idea for July Fourth is to have your local Boy Scout troop put American flags in the front yards of all the homes in your farm. Just be certain the flags are close to the street; that they are firmly planted so none touch the ground; and that the flags are Made in America. Nothing will ruin a good idea faster than a minor detail that could be perceived as offensive. Note: In today's world, we need to be aware of sensitivities of everyone in our community. If you have any doubts about whether or not the people in your area would enjoy having a flag in their yard, don't do it. Never presume that everyone else is as patriotic as you'd wish them to be.

Anything involving children is usually a good idea. Consider a coloring contest to give away circus tickets. Offer a pumpkin at Halloween to each child who comes into your office in costume. Better yet, have some teens help the children paint or carve their pumpkins.

To do something for the grown-ups in your farm area, consider giving away roses on Valentine's Day. Purchase several dozen from a local flower grower and have them in the entrance of your office. Consider enlisting the aid of a teenager who might be involved in floriculture at the local high school to add baby's breath, greenery, and a ribbon to each arrangement.

Being Remembered

On average, it takes six contacts with someone before they'll remember your name and face. These are six contacts in passing. If you meet someone and have an hour-long discussion with them, they'll remember you the next time they see you, but even then your name might not come to mind immediately. For that reason, I recommend that you set a goal to make a minimum of six contacts with the owners of each property in your farm within the first year.

You should mail them each a postcard or letter to let them know you are specializing in the residential market in their neighborhood. The post card must include your photo and contact information. Here's a sample letter:

Good afternoon, Mr. and Mrs. _____,
May I take this means of introducing myself to you? My name is _____, and I'm with (name of your company). I'll be representing home owners in your neighborhood, and will pop by in the next few days to meet you personally.

Sincerely,

You may also wish to offer a free market analysis for the neighborhood and tell them how to get one from you. This is a kind, professional, yet passive contact. Few people will read the entire letter. Some will toss the postcard in the garbage bin on their way back from the mailbox. Others will read it, yet not act. There may be a very small percentage who actually save the card or contact you. With such small result, you might be wondering why to send the card or letter at all. The reason is that you have to start somewhere, and an introductory letter or card is fairly economical.

Other ideas for items to send in the mail are:

A neighborhood newsletter. This would be sent out monthly. Be sure to include information on new homes listed; homes sold; local event information; and any charity drive you might be working on.

Once you get to know the people in your farm, you might want to include a Kid-of-the-Month recognition segment or Good Neighbor award. Some agents include recipes collected from others in the neighborhood. Get a large enough collection, and you can "publish" a neighborhood cookbook to give everyone at a later date.

Be sure to commend the local football team, soccer team, or marching band on their games and competitions. This is a great way to develop the community spirit.

There are companies that publish preprinted newsletters that you can purchase and personalize with your name and photo. If you're fairly good with the computer, you can draft your own newsletter at the beginning. Consider enlisting the aid of your children who might be learning how to create newsletters in their computer classes at school. Include simple clip art and maybe some photos to make the newsletter eye appealing.

Another type of mail device would be a flyer offering the free market analysis. Use an enticing headline like, "Do you know you could be living in a gold mine? Find out how much your home is worth in today's market! Call Mary Jones, today, for your free analysis. No obligation."

If there's a lot of activity in your farm and you don't want to wait for the next newsletter to go out, send a Just Listed or Just Sold flyer. At the very least, you'll want to specifically contact homes around one you've just listed.

Here's a tip that'll put a lot more power in notes like these that you send out. Use blank envelopes and have them hand addressed. Check with your broker. Unless local ordinances or your board's rules require it, don't use your company name on the return address. Don't even use the office address if it sounds commercial. Give your home address instead.

A pro uses hand-addressed, blank envelopes because they look like personal mail, and they get opened first. Do you know that many people never even open mail that looks commercial? Don't use the same envelopes all the time. Vary the size and color of your envelopes with each mailing.

Here's what you say in the mailing to those homes around a new listing:

Guess what? Your neighbor just selected us to sell their home. If you have a friend or relative looking for a nice home in this area, please give me a call. Or, if you're interested to know what your home is worth in the current market, contact me for a free analysis.

Be sure to include a free offer of that market analysis. Why? Because to do one, you need to see their home. To see their home, you must meet them in person and get inside the door. Once there, you'll help them to like you and trust you so you and no one else will be the recipient of their real estate questions and business.

I suggest you shoot for four contacts by mail or e-mail, if you can get the e-mail addresses, and two in-person contacts as part of your initial six.

Your community events are great ways to meet people in person. However, you will have to work hard to connect the person's name and face to their home. It's wise to find a reason to meet them at their home, even if it's just for a moment at the front door. If they've already received one or two items either in the mail or left at their doorstep that included your photo, they'll be more likely to open their door to your familiar face when you show up in person.

I am a firm believer in the power of thank-you notes. You might have guessed that by how many times I've already told you to send them. Thank-you notes are best when handwritten. If you have poor penmanship, consider having your spouse or someone else you know with nice handwriting help you out. If that's not feasible, go ahead and print them on your computer but be certain to sign them by hand.

Writing thank-you notes shouldn't take more than a few minutes each. They should be sent on store-bought note cards or your personal stationery, not on company letterhead or company note cards unless your broker requires it. The reason for this is that they won't look like junk mail. Also, be sure to use postage stamps on them rather than running them through a postal meter. It's a more personal touch that will get your note opened before that stack of bills that arrived with it.

When working for listings, there are many occasions you can thank people for. I worked hard to develop drafts for thank-you notes that demonstrate sincerity and professionalism. I'll include the wording here for you so you'll have no excuse for not sending them.

TELEPHONE CONTACT

Thank you for talking with me on the telephone. In today's world, time is precious. You can rest assured that I will always be respectful of the time you invest as we discuss the real estate opportunities available to you.

FSBO AFTER FIRST VISIT TO THEIR HOME

May I take a moment to thank you for showing me your lovely home. I sincerely wish you the best of luck in selling it. If you should find the need to employ a professional real estate agent, I would appreciate the opportunity to show you the excellent benefits we have to offer. Best of luck!

AFTER GIVING A LISTING PRESENTATION

Thank you for giving me the opportunity to discuss with you the benefits of allowing me and my company to serve your real estate needs. We believe that quality, blended with excellent service, is the foundation for a successful business relationship.

THANK YOU FOR THE LISTING

Thank you for listing with us. Now, we'll go to work in assisting you in getting happily moved. You can be assured that my company and I will do everything possible to consummate a successful sale for you.

AFTER NOT GETTING THE LISTING

Thank you for taking the time to analyze my service. I regret being unable at this time to prove to you the benefits we have to offer. We keep constantly informed of new developments and changes. So, I will keep in touch with the hope that in the years ahead, we will be able to do business.

TO ANYONE WHO GIVES YOU SERVICE

Thank you. It is gratifying to meet someone dedicated to doing a good job. Your efforts are sincerely appreciated. If my company or I can serve you in any way, please don't hesitate to call.

FOR A REFERRAL

Thank you for referring the Smiths to me. You can rest assured that I will do my best to help them and to justify your confidence in me.

Another way to be remembered is to give a little gift to each home owner. These can be as simple as a pen with your name and contact information on it. Some agents I know of give a cube of scratch paper. At the bottom of the cube, they insert a reminder that "It's time to call Jim Smith for a free refill of paper." Calendars are great at year-end. Check into what specialty items are available and find ones that you feel comfortable giving—both financially and by the meaning behind the gift.

Your gifts could be seasonal—an ice scraper in the winter if you live in cold country; flower seeds in the spring; a fly swatter or inflatable beach ball in the summer; and a small candle in the fall.

As a rule, I suggest staying away from giving gifts at major holidays. They get lumped in with other gifts and may not be appreciated individually. Send or give gifts at alternate times of the year.

If an interesting article comes your way about special mortgage offerings, new developments that will positively impact the value of residential real estate, or the latest hot items for remodeling to increase property value, have the article photocopied and send it to everyone in your farm. Include a little note about finding the information of interest and offering to get them additional information if they let you know they'd like it. Never send bad news—only good ideas or good news.

Another idea for contacting everyone in your farm would be to conduct a neighborhood survey. Ask what they like most. Get feedback on the schools, the shopping, the traffic flow, how safe the neighborhood is, favorite restaurants, which restaurants deliver to the neighborhood, the parks, etc. Ask if they'd be interested in having a neighborhood directory. If so, publish that as well. Then, send the survey results back to them. This is great information for you to have as a gift for new people who move into the neighborhood.

With every print contact you make, whether it's by e-mail, your newsletter, or a flyer, do your best to include at least one testimonial from someone in the neighborhood who had a positive experience with you listing their home. You're not the one doing the bragging about how great you are—the neighbors are doing it for you.

Speaking Engagements

You are an industry expert, unless you're new to the business. In that case, you're determined to become one, aren't you? To help people see the benefits of what you have to offer, consider teaching a class or offering a free seminar at the local community center or chamber of commerce. Many companies use this strategy effectively to get leads for new business. Your talk could be about "How to Get the Most for Your Home When Selling." Or, "Great Ideas to Make Your Home Marketable." Or, "What Every Home Owner Needs to Know."

Invite everyone in your farm or even the entire community if you want to post notices or place an ad. Guess who will show up? People who are wondering what they have to do to get the most from their home when they sell it. And they won't need that information unless they have an inkling of selling, will they? And which expert do you think they'll remember when they're ready? The one who taught the class because you're going to give them a handout, checklist, or some sort of take-home item that has your smiling face and contact information on it. And, you're going to follow up with them to see what other questions they might have about real estate.

Don't be overwhelmed by the ideas here. Just consider those that feel right for you and work with them until you achieve the success level you desire. When your desire grows even greater, come back and add some of the other ideas to your plan.

I hope you use them, or create exciting new promotions of your own, because specialized programs lift you far above the average. When you get these things rolling, you're not a peddler anymore, you're a celebrity. You're not out there begging for business, you're someone whose service is sought out. The secret is to keep in touch and to give, give, give.

CHAPTER 15

When Knocking on Doors Works

Door-knocking strategies were the foundation of success in real estate for many, many years. However, today, with so few people at home during the day and others not too happy about opening their doors to strangers, the success ratio for door-knocking isn't as high as it used to be. In fact, in some areas, there are ordinances against using door-to-door methods.

If you work in an area where it's acceptable to knock on doors to meet the people you wish to serve, my door-knocking strategy still works. If you don't know if it would work in your area, I strongly recommend you give it a shot because you'll be different. You'll stand out as a hardworking agent who doesn't rely on more passive means of communication. When you're new to the business, I suggest you try everything. Once you have some experience (defined *success*), you'll see which methods are most beneficial and make the best use of your time.

If you knock on doors, you'll have two kinds of results every day you do it. At some doors you'll have good conversations, you'll go away encouraged, and you'll approach the next door with increased enthusiasm. At other doors the opposite will happen. This brings us to the factor that will determine whether or not you'll succeed at this method of prospecting. That factor is how you control your thoughts about the results you get each day.

Which doors will you think about? The good ones or the bad ones? If you allow yourself to think only about the good doors, you'll soon be making lots of money through your canvasing contacts because you'll learn and use effective techniques. From every session of prospecting, you'll gain enthusiasm and confidence. But if you allow yourself to think mostly about the bad doors, you'll never make any money canvasing. And you won't do much of it either.

Turning doorbells into dollars is simple: Learn the easy methods of prospecting that follow, and then go out and do them.

I live by the belief that everything we want is behind a door. When you put down this book and go out to make your fortune in real estate, you'll walk out your front door, open your car door, and drive yourself to another door. Your life is punctuated by going through doors. When you come home, your loved ones are behind doors. Possibly you've heard someone in real estate say, "Knocking on doors is unprofessional." Whoever told you that is chicken. Knocking on doors is unprofessional only if it's done unprofessionally. When it's done professionally, it's fun. And people will often thank you for stopping by.

The Fundamentals

Let's begin our study of getting out there and meeting people with a quick look at the fundamental steps. Then we'll get into specific phraseology for two special situations. You can always go out and work on one of them. But, no matter what opportunity you're prospecting, success depends on sound fundamental technique.

1. WORK AROUND THE BLOCK

If you work up one side of the street and down the other, or cross over from side to side as you go, more people will see you. Many of them will phone one of their neighbors. The conversation will go like this:

"Who was that at your door?"

"Oh, just a real estate person."

That's one less door that'll open for you. Play the numbers. In today's world, you'll find less than half of them home anyway. Don't cut your percentages further. The pro works entirely around the block. It might open just three more doors a day for you, but that's enough to make a great difference.

2. WALK ENTHUSIASTICALLY

Do you know that successful people take five steps while the average person is taking only four? Do you know why? They always have somewhere to go. Walk like you have a purpose—somewhere to go, and a reason for getting there.

3. KNOCK ENTHUSIASTICALLY

Everyone rings the doorbell. You're different. So, you knock. You can't ring a doorbell enthusiastically. Every time, it'll give them the same old ding dong. When you walk up and knock on the door with excitement, you'll be amazed at how curious they get.

4. STAND BACK

After you knock, take a few steps back. If you're standing right on top of the door, they won't open it. So back up three or four paces.

5. FACE UP THE STREET

Turn your body and head so the person behind the door will see your profile as you look up the street. Your presence is less threatening if eye contact doesn't hit them the instant they open the door.

6. IF YOU'RE A MAN, WHISTLE

If you don't know how, learn. Always trill a few cheerful notes as you wait. If a woman is alone in the home when another woman knocks, there's not much fear. That's not the case when a man knocks. If you're whistling merrily, it lets her know that you're happy and harmless.

7. WAIT UNTIL THEY ACKNOWLEDGE YOU

Whether you're a man or a woman, don't turn to face the home owner until he or she speaks. You want the person inside to begin the conversation. They'll say, "Yes," "Hello," "What can I do for you," or whatever. When you hear that, go to the next step.

8. FACE THEM AND SMILE

Some salespeople have stopped smiling. They've forgotten how. Maybe you should practice. Stand in front of a mirror and smile until you've got the knack of it. Being able to put on a smile when you need one is a valuable prospecting skill. Although you can't prospect without interrupting people, you can certainly ease their shock by smiling.

9. BRING THEIR DEFENSE BARRIERS DOWN

Let's think about the feelings that the person behind the door will have. What goes through the mind of a lady who's alone at home during the day when there's an unexpected knock at the door?

She feels interrupted. She might feel some curiosity. She may even feel fear. Some people have such a negative image of salespeople that they won't open the door to one. If your company has clothing available with their logo on it, get it and wear it proudly when knocking on doors. It will help identify you, which should reduce some fear. It could be that your company's reputation in the community makes you a welcome visitor. Also, it's a good idea to wear a name badge with your photo. The print should be large enough to be seen from a few feet away. Everything you can do to ease their fears about strangers and demonstrate that you're a nonthreatening professional will open more doors for you and open them wider than those opened to the nonprofessionals.

I've had people who were afraid to talk to strangers open a little window and talk to me through it. You can give the same performance right through the window! Don't feel like they must open the door. Don't let their fear make you uncomfortable. You see, it's all a numbers game. The more people you meet, the luckier you get.

On the average, you have just thirty seconds after they first speak to bring their defense barriers down. When they realize you're in sales, many people decide, "I'm getting rid of you as fast as possible." Expect that whoever answers your knock will have some defense barriers up. Break through those barriers and catch a little of that person's interest quickly.

10. DON'T HESITATE TO USE CRUTCHES TO GET YOURSELF OUT OF THERE

There were days when I didn't want to go door knocking. I mean, I really didn't want to do it. So I'd sit in my office and act busy. Eventually, the guilt of my promise to myself to meet people would get to me. So I'd get up, shuffle out to my car, and drive someplace where I could prospect. By the time I came to the third or fourth door, I'd have my enthusiasm back. It never failed. I'd tell myself, "I did it again. I'm out here again. And I'm really glad I came."

Now let's study two special canvasing situations. In each one, we'll assume you've already run through the fundamentals. That is, we'll pick up the action right after the person at home has opened the door, said something, and you've turned, smiling easily, to face him or her.

The Warm Canvas Door

This can be the door of any property that doesn't have a sign on it. She says "Yes?" and I begin:

"Good afternoon. My name is Tom Hopkins representing Champions Unlimited. Real estate activity in this area has been unbelievable, and I was wondering if you'd thought of making a move in the near future?"

Notice the phraseology. Every word is important. "Real estate activity in this area has been unbelievable." Isn't that true of every area? The word "unbelievable" covers it whether it's bad or good.

"And I was wondering if you'd thought of making a move in the near future." I didn't say ". . . if you'd thought of selling the home." Use *making a move*. And when? Not now, but *in the near future*. Drill yourself on using these softer phrases that make you sound more likable and less pushy. Expect a no here. They'll follow their lines if you'll learn yours. But once in a while they'll say yes. So, pay attention. And don't lose your composure if she answers yes to any of your questions. You won't, if you've rehearsed what you'll say when you get a yes.

She says, "No." That first no is, psychologically, one rejection. She's rejected you. She knows it, and she feels it.

You keep smiling and say, "Do you know of anyone in the neighborhood who might be interested in moving?"

You'll usually get a nice big no here too. Then you warmly say, "Well, thanks so much for your time." That causes her to think you're about to leave. But you're not done yet. Then, with a cordial manner, you go on, "When I find a home today, would you know of any friends or relatives who might be interested in living here?"

Notice that you don't ask, "If I find someone who wants to sell." A pro operates with confidence: "*When* I find a home." It's as if there's no question about it at all.

"No," she says, giving you no number three. Back up so she's sure you're leaving. Then smile and say, "By the way, may I ask your name, please?"

Now you've let her reject you three times. If you're smiling as you ask for her name, she's going to give it to you. Why? Because she wants to show she's not a grouch.

"I'm Mrs. Johnson."

Repeat her name immediately, and speak pleasantly. "Mrs. Johnson, when *will* you be moving?"

Do you know what's exciting? If you let her reject you the three times, and if you've been radiating warmth and professionalism, many times they'll tell you the truth.

I've had the woman say, "Oh, we probably wouldn't be moving for at least three years."

Do you know what a pro says here? "May I keep in touch, and come back in three years?"

What'll she say? "Sure," because she doesn't believe you will. But you will, won't you?

If she mentions any reason for, or possibility of, moving within one year, start asking more questions. Let's suppose she says, "Well, uh, no, we've thought about moving. In fact, my husband's talked to the people on the job, but they don't think it's possible for at least a year."

"I see. Your husband . . . where does he work?"

"Well, he works at Northside."

"Oh, how long has he been there?"

"Seven years."

"Oh, really? So you'd kind of like to move—kind of like to transfer to another area? What kind of an area were you looking for?"

And you keep on asking her questions until she starts to get a little restless. What do you do now?

Three things. Smile. Warmly say, "Thank you so much." And then give her your card.

Please note that the home owner doesn't get your card until the end of your performance unless she asks for it sooner.

Some agents canvas like this: "Hi. I'm so-and-so. Here's my card." The prospect takes the card, looks at it while the agent goes on talking, and doesn't hear a word that's said. Give them the card last.

If you represent a company that uses realty in its name, I suggest you omit that word when you introduce yourself. In other words, if I'm with Champions Unlimited Realty, I would introduce myself as "Tom Hopkins, representing Champions Unlimited." Why? So that word doesn't trigger "He's a real estate salesperson" before I'm into my performance and she's listening to me. Of course, she'll realize what I am within a few seconds, but by that time I've had a chance to communicate with her as one human being to another. This is not a critical step. If your broker wants you to use the entire name, do so. Your broker is always right.

That's what I call a warm canvas door. You had no special reason to go there. You just said, "I'm going to work this neighborhood because I haven't seen any listings show up from here for a while."

After doing some effective work, you take a listing. What homes are most influenced when your sign goes up?

The five homes on either side and the ten homes facing them across the street.

Timing is vital on these doors. When should you knock on those twenty doors? Within forty-eight hours after you take the listing, and before you put your sign up on the listing you just took.

Now you can't always do that. Some people want your sign up the moment you take the listing. If so, don't fight it. Put your sign up. Other people will want you to hold off for a week or two.

I wanted to knock on those twenty doors fast before they heard the news on the front porch hotline. The morning after taking the new listing, if at all possible, I'd start hitting those twenty homes. If they were curious about what house was involved when I started talking, it went better. Stale news is not news. So be fast with the knocks. Then put up your sign.

Your approach to each door is exactly the same as to all the others— meaning that you run through all the fundamentals. Then, when you hear a hello, you begin with your usual warm smile:

"Good morning. My name is _____, representing (name of your company). A family in this area has employed us to help them sell their home."

Notice the exact phraseology. You don't say, "We just took a listing up the street." Doesn't that sound cold, commercial, and calculating? The pro says, "A family in this area has employed us. . . ." Most people don't know that the listing is an employment agreement, do they?

You then say, "We feel it's an excellent value." Why do you say that? And why do you pause when you do? So they can ask you how much their home is worth. Whenever that happens, go into your comparable market analysis appointment close.

"We feel it's an excellent value, so I stopped by to find out if you know anyone who'd be interested in living here."

Many people today would like to buy a single-family residence as a rental and hold it for appreciation. Not only that, many people have friends and relatives who've become interested in their area. These friends and relatives have told them, "Find us a place."

That's why you then say, "This home should definitely generate much activity." Doesn't everyone want something that's good, something that lots of other people will want?

I hope you realize that you must rehearse speaking these lines slowly, confidently, and with emphasis. If you say them too fast, or if you slur your words, they'll tune you out.

Make your next point by continuing the previous sentence.

We'll take it from the top: "This home should definitely generate much activity and produce a lot of qualified buyers." Go on in your warm and positive manner, "When we sell it, we'll have a surplus of people seeking homes. Would you happen to know of anyone who may be interested in moving in the near future?"

They say no.

"Well, I sure thank you for your time. By the way, when will you be moving?"

I hope you see the psychology in those words. It wasn't luck that permitted me to take an average of eighteen listings a month. It was words. My confident, rehearsed delivery of the right words to the right people at the right time did it.

Follow-up for the new-home-on-the-market door: Send a thank-you note to the nicest five people. You saw twenty of them. Choose the five who were the most pleasant to you; they get a little thank-you note.

Add those five people to your general file. Send them your newsletter, and keep in touch with an occasional visit.

The Most Productive Door in the World

Now you're going to canvas where the streets are paved with gold. When you sell a piece of real estate, please realize that you've put a big one in the record books. You've scored a victory for the sellers—and for the buyers too. You've done what you're paid for. You've come through. And people have respect for you. That's why the professional knows that her odds are best around the scene of her latest selling success.

When you canvas the twenty doors closest to your sale, carry your sold sign. Get out there fast. Do this within forty-eight hours too. If you don't, the neighbors will leak the fact that it's sold, and some other broker will get the listing next door.

Watch the phraseology on this one. I've got a little change in it, so watch closely. Of course, you go through the fundamental approach first.

"Good morning. My name is Tom Hopkins, and I represent Champions Unlimited. We just sold the home up the street to a lovely couple." (There are times when you don't say lovely.)

Hold up the sold sign so she can see that you're there to put it up. Had I just knocked on their door for the new-home-on-the-market canvas a week earlier, I'd change the phraseology, as I'll show you later. Let's do it now as though I hadn't knocked on their door before. Perhaps I've sold someone else's listing.

"We just sold the home up the street to a lovely couple. They have two children, about six and ten, and he's employed by the Salt River Project."

Before saying that, get the sellers' approval to talk about them. Never disclose personal information about anybody without permission. If you do, what might happen? You could get sued for invasion of privacy. That's why a pro doesn't divulge personal data unless she has their okay. But you can give this kind of information:

"While selling the home, we generated so much activity for the area that I wondered if you'd thought of making a move in the near future."

"No."

"Would you happen to know of anyone else in the neighborhood who might be thinking of moving?"

"No."

"Thank you again." Then give them your standard, "By the way, when *will* you be moving?" Of course, you wouldn't use this last question if, three days earlier, you'd been there doing the new-home-on-the-market routine.

Watch how I do it if the listing sold fast. When I show up at that door, believe me, I'll be radiating enthusiasm. Here's what I'd say:

"Good morning. Forgive me for not remembering your last name, but I was by three days ago, telling you about the property up the street—the exciting value."

Pause. Look at them. Then say, "Sold."

"And I'll tell you, we need inventory in this area, so I just came by to tell you that we at Champions Unlimited don't just list real estate, we get families moved. Have you folks thought of making a move? Please, I'd love to help you."

"Well, what are they going for?" is an answer that you're very likely to get.

"You know, I could pick a figure out of thin air. . . ." And you know the rest.

Isn't that fun?

But you have to follow your local board's rules, the code of ethics, and your broker's instructions. Some brokers have certain instructions about the canvasing. I'd also like you to realize that your city may not allow soliciting door to door. If you're new to real estate, or reading this book before you get your license, you may not know if there are ordinances about canvasing in your area. If I were in a city with a nonsolicitation law, I'd come up with phraseology so that I would not be soliciting. So if you live in one of those places and are sitting there thinking, "None of this canvasing applies to me," you're lazy. Because there's a way to create a method for seeing people. It's your obligation—to your company, to your family, and to yourself—to find it.

However, if you want to sit in the office all day, and if you're happy being average, then stay happy, won't you? Others want and will take the business you're not willing to go out and get.

One of the champions going after the business—and getting it—is Michael Fuller in Gresham, Oregon. Mike wrote:

> . . . over $1 million closed in my first year . . . over $3 million in my second year . . . on target now for my third-year goals. There's no way I would have done this without your help.
>
> The fact is, I did nothing but listen to Hopkins tapes my first year. . . . [and close over $1 million—T.H.] Practice, practice, practice has made the difference for me.
>
> One morning I knocked on a door and said, "Do you know of anyone in the neighborhood who might be interested in moving?"
>
> The lady said, "No, but I do know that Don and Millie up the street have four houses they're trying to sell, and they haven't had much luck. They're looking for a good Realtor to help them, but don't say I sent you." To make a long story short, I listed all four houses, and sold three within a month. Since then, I've sold two more of their homes and have had several profitable referrals from them. All from asking one question the way Tom told me to.

Mike said everything that needs to be heard about the value of using sound canvasing techniques, didn't he? So what are you waiting for?

CHAPTER 16

Developing Your Listing Bank
into an Income Gusher

Farming a listing bank is the next process that we're going to study. This is the queen of prospecting methods. It's the most gratifying and the most profitable system for creating brokerage fees that I know of. With it, my career went from average performance to outstanding results in a very short time.

Now I'm going to take you, step by step, through the entire program:

Step 1: Choose the Right Area

Don't think about the real estate. Think about the families. To become a champion at listing, you can't think about property. The people come first. With this system, you decide to become the family real estate agent for lots of people living in a certain area. If you think of the program this way, your listing bank will become something you'll be excited about building.

In my opinion, the ideal number for a listing bank is 500 families. But not everybody is a workaholic like I was. To take on 500 families demands strong commitment. Maybe you'll say, "I don't want to work that hard; I'm only going to work with 200 families."

Then 200 is right for you. One hundred? You can make money

working a 100-family listing bank if you do it thoroughly. Whatever number of families you choose to work with, you must teach them to think of you when they think of real estate. If it's farmed methodically, a 100-family listing bank will give you one listing a month on the average. Want two listings a month? Farm 200 families. Five listings a month? Then go for the 500-family farm.

Let's work out the numbers for a 500-family listing bank.

Nationally, we move once every 3.7 years. In our calculations, we'll use 5 years to give us a margin of safety. This means that 100 of your 500 families will move every year.

Let's say that 80 percent of them employ professional services to help them market their homes. That gives us 80 listings per year.

Can you get all 80 of those listings? Not likely. Some are committed to another agent. Others have friends or relatives in the business. Things happen. But if you do everything I tell you to do with enthusiasm, you'll get 80 percent of the listings that come out of the bank.

How many is that?

Sixty-four. In one year. That's more than 5 a month.

But those are unsold listings. With enough practice, drill, and rehearsal, how many of your 64 listings will sell per year?

Ninety percent. That's 58. But let's play safe again and say that only 80 percent of your listings sell. That gives you 50 sold listings a year from your 500-family listing bank.

Now, what is the average net fee that you'll put in your checking account for each listing sold?

If you're not in the business yet, you may not have a clue. Call a local broker. Tell him or her you're thinking of entering the business, and ask how an agent's compensation is calculated in their office.

Arrive at the figure for one average listing sold, and then multiply that amount by 50. This will be your yearly income from skillful and dedicated service to a 500-family listing bank.

Before we move on, let's give a thought to one additional idea. If you want to achieve the best results that you can reasonably expect to achieve, you won't spend all your time taking listings in your bank. Farming should require no more than a third of your time. And you should earn as much with the rest of your time as you do farming. In other words, your total real estate income should be three times what your listings-sold-in-farm income is. That's right. Multiply by three. It's fun to work that out on paper. It's even more fun to do it in reality. There's no reason why you can't.

Where will the other two incomes be earned? Besides farming for listings, you can sell your own listings, sell property outside your farm, and take listings outside your farm.

You can work for-sale-by-owners, open houses, expired listings, to name only a few of the techniques that you can specialize in to get additional business. And let's not forget the emperor of real estate income: referrals.

During my last year in real estate prior to going into management, I earned $52,000 just on listings sold in my listing bank. That doesn't sound terribly impressive now, but it was a record-setting performance in those days.

Now let me warn you about the greatest danger that faces the agent who is beginning to develop a listing bank. Many newcomers to this industry start off strong. They swiftly build up a following. They start to make some exciting money. And then they quit farming. Some of them think they've got it made; some keep themselves tied up with busywork; some simply forget about farming. Many of these agents know they should keep on farming. Maybe they worry about it now and then. But they just don't get out there. I hope you'll go all the way with this program. Only a few agents do, and those few, the strong listers and the champions, are very well paid for their persistence.

If you're a veteran of the business and have already built up a clientele, you may not want to start over with this program. You may be too active and successful with other techniques to take on a 500-family listing bank. Or you may already have a strong position, but not a dominant one, in your listing bank. If so, adapt parts of this program to your circumstances.

If you've been active in the business for less than six months, my advice is to make this program the cornerstone of your real estate success. Base your entire real estate career on your listing bank.

Now that you've decided how large a listing bank you can and will work, let's talk about what area to choose. The first consideration is that you must like the people who live there. If you don't like the families, you won't work them. Stay in your comfort zone. If you try to farm with people who make you uncomfortable, they'll sense your unease and return your dislike. You'll build rejection, not rapport, that way. And your listing bank will go bankrupt. Avoid all that pain by putting your energies into building your bank where you feel comfortable.

By the way, you may want to spread yourself around taking a hundred homes here, another hundred there. One fine champion I know decided that he'd be better off with plenty of variety. So he went for a four-part farm. He started off with a hundred of the nicer homes in the area. These were located in areas beyond where the other agents in his office had their listing banks. For low-priced property, he chose a group of blocks near an industrial park that contained a hundred homes. Another neighborhood, this one with two hundred homes, provides him with a wide selection of housing in the middle-price ranges. He completed his 500-family listing bank by selecting an area with a hundred executive homes. His farm gives him listings in every price range. He's a gregarious fellow with an unusually broad comfort zone who's doing very well with his diversified listing bank. It doesn't matter that his farm is scattered. He can't work it all in one day anyhow.

Step 2: Get Your Listing Bank Information Set Up

Use a computer software program like Act! or Goldmine that will allow you quick and easy access to the information on each family and details about their homes.

Step 3: Obtain the Owners' Names

The street address directory is your best place to start. This publication, often called the crisscross or by-street directory, gives you the addresses, names, and telephone numbers at the same time. Unfortunately, not all areas have one. Check with your local telephone company. Or, go on the Internet to http://www.whitepages.com. They have a reverse lookup feature that allows you to enter an address to get the name and phone number. Because of the changes that occur after printing or posting deadlines, the street address directory will be about 70 percent accurate. You may be tempted to organize your notes right out of it and skip going through your farm yourself to get the addresses as suggested in Step 1. Don't. You'll miss all the families that have unpublished phone numbers.

The tax rolls are another source for names. You can inspect these public records in your county courthouse. In some areas, this information is also available online.

In many areas, there's a more convenient way to get this information: title companies. If you find the right title representative, one who's eager to help a new champion start developing a lot of title business, that representative will supply you with the names and addresses you want on a complimentary basis.

When you complete this step, every family in your listing bank will have its information in your computer, complete with name, address, and phone number.

Step 4: Set Up a Visual Control Board

Use a map, an aerial photo, or a plot plan of your entire listing bank. Maps are available online at http://www.mapquest.com. You might be able to get aerial photos from http:// www.aerialsexpress.com or http:// www.landvoyage.com. If they don't have photos of your area, ask at your local zoning department. If you prefer, you might want to use plot plans from a title company.

Where do you put this control board?

That depends on whether or not you're committed to becoming the top lister in your farm. If you're serious about doing that, you'll put the control board on the wall opposite your bed. Why? So you'll see it first in the morning.

That's where I put the map of my listing bank in Simi Valley. It was the first thing I'd see when I woke up and the last before I went to sleep. My control board was a title company plot plan that I had a photo shop blow up to the size I wanted.

Now, this may go against decorating styles in most bedrooms, and your spouse may have some strong feelings about this but, at the very least, consider it for a minimum of ninety days.

I put colored pins in mine—red, for danger, highlighted other brokers' listings; black, for emphasis, gave the location of for-sale-by-owners; green, for money, showed my listings. There was no kidding myself with that map hitting me in the face every morning. I knew when someone else was making inroads on my area. Oh, the delight of sticking a green pin in. The pain of adding a red pin! The pin went in the map the first time I entered the bedroom after getting the news, whether it was good or bad.

If you'll use your visual control board this way, it'll be worth thousands of dollars a year to you. It was one of my main motivators; one of the important sources of my continuous drive to conquer my listing bank. You see the facts at a glance, and they don't lie. You always know where you stand.

Step 5: Use Letters of Introduction

Most salespeople don't plan ahead, and they won't commit themselves to an organized program. That's the entire reason why they're average. You want to be a strong lister. Maybe you plan to be a champion. Perhaps you even aspire to become a superchampion. You'll get where you want to go faster if you start off being different. Send a letter of introduction.

A sample letter of introduction is given in Chapter 14. Notice that it isn't fancy. The words are simple, friendly, and easily understood. Mail these letters in batches of twenty-five. Use blank envelopes, or envelopes with only your name on the return. No company envelopes. Why? Because it's more personal. And don't get overorganized with a label mailing system for your farm at first. If what you send looks like junk mail, it'll get ash-canned like junk mail. Hand-address everything you send to your listing bank until they get to know you and look forward to whatever you send.

If you have children old enough to write, get them involved in your business. Tim, my oldest, was too young when I started, but his babysitter was fifteen, and she had great handwriting. She loved to make extra money while being paid to babysit and watch TV.

Now let's integrate our letters of introduction into the farming concept. Six meetings per year is the means by which you reach your goal of becoming a family's real estate agent when they need service. But some people will move before you can see them six times. That's why you want to make as favorable an impression as you can with every meeting, especially the first. So you start with a letter of introduction.

What is the essence of that letter? That you, Mr. and Mrs. Homeowner, are important enough to be treated with respect, and I am a professional who is also worthy of respect.

Find out the mailing time lag. Ask at the post office, or mail a few sample letters to friends in the area. Know when your letters will be delivered. Your goal is to show up at the door right after your letter gets there.

Yon may learn that letters mailed by 5:00 P.M. Monday will be delivered on Tuesday about 2:00 P.M. Find out if some parts of your farm get their mail in the morning, and other parts in the afternoon. Then set your schedule so that you hit their door right after your letters are delivered. Doing that requires some planning and some attention to detail. In other words, it requires some professional-level work.

Step 6: Knock on the Door

It's Tuesday. You're getting next-day delivery. The twenty-five letters of introduction you mailed yesterday were just delivered a few minutes ago to the first twenty-five families in your listing bank. We'll start at house number one. The family's name is Wagner. Use all the fundamental door-knocking steps given in Chapter 15. Notice that you begin by addressing the home owner by name:

"Good afternoon, Mrs. Wagner. My name is Tom Hopkins. Did you receive my letter of introduction?"

It doesn't matter whether she's opened your letter or not. Just the fact that you say "Did you receive my letter of introduction" raises you to a level far above the average.

After she responds, continue with: "I just stopped by to make your acquaintance personally, as I plan on being the firm's representative in this area. I'm in the process of conducting a survey to establish market projections for the coming year. Would you please help me by answering a few quick questions on my survey?" Then immediately ask the first question.

This technique is beautifully effective when it's done right. If you're planning on becoming a champion, watch every detail carefully.

Unthreatening questions are the psychological foundation for the next technique that will take you twice around your entire farm. This one step allows you to go a full third of the way toward controlling it.

Let's go back to door number one, where we're using the survey technique with Mrs. Wagner:

". . . please help me by answering a few questions on my survey?" Hold up the survey form as you continue talking without waiting for a reply. "Do you feel the area is improving?"

Step 7: Use a Market Survey

Here's how you go about putting this technique to work:

1. Type the questions I'll give you on a sheet of plain paper. If you have access to a computer that allows you to create typeset-looking pieces, use it. If not, you might want to consider using a quick print company to create the form for you for a small investment. The more professional it looks the better. Make enough copies so you'll have one for each home you plan to survey.

2. Before you set out for a day's door knocking with the survey, write the name of each family you plan to see on one of the forms. Then, at Mrs. Wagner's doorstep, when you hold up the market survey, she sees her name written large there. What does that tell her? That you're organized. That you came there expressly to talk to her, Mrs. Wagner, not just to whomever answers whatever door you knock on. In other words, you have a serious reason for seeing her. All these details not only build impact and interest, they also break down fear and apathy.

The survey technique is a plan that gives you reasons for at least two of the six meetings you need. Always remember that it takes six meetings to fix yourself in their minds as a real estate expert with special knowledge of their neighborhood. With the survey, one call gathers the information, the second call passes the results back to them. What's more important, this technique puts flesh and blood on your skeleton wish to create a listing bank. Unless you set your sights on knocking on every door in your farm at least six times during the next year, you're not going to make farming pay.

Step 8: Put the Market Survey to Work

In Step 6, I showed you how to use the letter of introduction to swing right into your market survey. Now I'm going to give you information about every question on the survey.

Question 1: "Do you feel that the area is improving?"

If she's unhappy with the area, it means she probably wants to get out. That's good for listings, isn't it? If she likes the area, she'll probably encourage other people to live there. That's good for sales. So your purpose is to get her talking and to find out how she feels. You're not there to argue the area's merits. This is a pearl of a question. Nonthreatening. Flattering because it asks for an opinion. Not a bit personal. Always open with this one. And pay attention to the answers, because they'll tell you much about how this family fits into your farming future.

Don't let people flounder trying to come up with an answer. That'll make them feel stupid. If the question throws them for a loss, help them. Point to the yes or no. Mrs. Wagner might say, "I have no way of knowing." Or, "I don't know."

You could say, "Well, the homes sure have gone up in price recently. I guess we could say it really has improved. Let's mark yes." Now, you've got number one. Keep on moving to number two.

Question 2: "How long have you folks lived in this area?"

I used *folks* quite often. The word came naturally and seemed to help me establish rapport. It worked for me, and it'll work for you, if you like it. If not, don't say folks. Say whatever pleases you and your listeners.

This is the key question of the entire survey. You're using it to look for people who've lived there three years or more. Why? Because it's almost time for them to get the itch to move. Work a little harder with the over three. When you find a family that's been there five years or more, make a special effort to get close to them. They need help. They don't realize that it's time for them to be moving along.

If you can get an answer to Question 2, you've had a successful meeting. If you're running into short answers and hard looks, say, "Well, I see that you're busy. I won't take up any more of your time today. Thank you so much for your help. Bye."

But, if they're not too restless, press on with the survey.

Question 3: "Do you feel that the shopping facilities in this vicinity are adequate for your needs?"

You can ask this question in a variety of ways: "Are you satisfied with the stores in this community?" "Do you feel that the shopping facilities are adequate for the area?" "What do you think of the shopping here? Is there enough variety for you?" Use what suits your style, fits the neighborhood, and gets the best response. And you don't have to ask the questions with the exact words that are on the questionnaire. Your goal is to get the people to talk to you, so go with the wording that works for you.

One of the top champions we've trained is an energetic lady in the San Clemente area. She took this program all the way with spectacular results. Here's what happened: When she went through her farm for the first time, she used this market survey technique with enthusiasm. She didn't worry about rejection. She didn't waste energy wondering if it was necessary. She didn't tear herself down wishing she were back in the office chitchatting and twiddling her thumbs. She concentrated on working through her entire listing bank as quickly as she could without seeming hurried or uncaring to the people there.

By working straight through, she covered her entire farm in just eighteen days. That was a giant step toward achieving the dominance she came to enjoy there. Although she didn't think much about it at the time, the people in her new farm answered Question 3 with an emphatic no. Most of them thought the shopping facilities were miserable. Then some great luck occurred—the kind that keeps on coming to all alert, hardworking champions. A few days after she completed her survey, a firm of developers broke ground for a shopping mall on a huge vacant parcel of land bordering her farm.

So this lady went charging back through her farm for the second of her six meetings telling everyone the good news. People kept saying, "Thank you so much. We sure need that mall."

She just smiled and said, "You're welcome." And then she proceeded to talk some real estate.

That's not the end of the story. This lady knew that people forget very quickly. So she carried on with the entire plan—saw everybody six times—did all the other things. She locked up her farm, and few other real estate agents were ever able to penetrate it.

Question 4: "Where do you do most of your grocery shopping?"

I hope you realize that some of these questions are designed to keep the people moving with you. If you bore into real estate with every question you ask, they'll tighten up and turn you off. So the last two questions were throwaways. But the next one isn't.

Question 5: "How many are in your family?"

Before you ask this one, smile warmly. Question 5 is an important question. First, a major reason for moving is a change in family size. Growing families want more space; empty nesters want less upkeep. So this question can cause them to discuss one of the vital issues that bear on how long they'll live in their present house.

In addition, this question marks a psychological resistance point. Five questions are a lot to ask at one time. Make a decision here guided by this thought: They aren't likely to get more friendly today than they already are. They're probably getting restless and thinking of other things at this point. If you detect the slightest indication of that now, break off the interview before you erode the rapport you've already built. Tell the person, "I know I've kept you for several minutes now. I'll stop back at some future date and finish my survey. Thank you so much for your help."

You only proceed beyond this point during your first meeting if you've had clear go-ahead signals. The vibes are good. The woman feels like talking. Let's say that she answers this question with, "There are four of us."

Your response is, "Then you have two children?"

Here's the third reason why this question is important; you can make some real progress if she's relaxed as she answers, "Yes, that's right."

"What are their names?"

"Ricky and Susan."

"Ricky Wagner," you say, writing on your form. "And Susan Wagner. What are their ages?"

"Ricky's nine, and Susan will be seven next week."

"Oh, so Susan has a big day coming up. Wonderful."

You're going to review that information before you come walking up to the Wagner's home the next time, aren't you? You'll have more to talk about with Mrs. Wagner then. How did Susan's birthday party go? How's Ricky doing?

But if Mrs. Wagner was showing signs of getting restless when you asked Question 5, put her answer down, make your brief thank-you statement, and go.

Question 6: "Do you folks commute to work alone, or do you both use car pools?"

This one needs to be handled carefully. Women who work outside the home often resent it if you assume they aren't employed. And many homemakers are touchy about their status. In these days of two-income families, many areas can only be canvased successfully in the evening or on weekends; no one is home during the weekday. There's nothing wrong with canvasing in the evening. Some of our top champions are out in their farms between 7:30 and 8:30 nearly every night. That one hour is productive because they find a high percentage of both husbands and wives at home.

So you ask if they both commute to work alone or ride in a car pool. Most of them will say they drive their own cars. The purpose of Question 6 is to set up Question 7, which, had you sprung it without preparation, might not be well received.

Question 7: "Where are you and your husband employed?"

Never ask anyone where they work. That's a four-letter word. Everyone is employed.

The answer to this question is one of the most important facts that you can record about a family in your listing bank. It'll tell you a great deal about them and furnish you with many future conversational openings.

Question 8: "Do you believe the school system is providing the kind of education you want your children to have?"

In the sense that you don't have any direct use for the answers you'll get, this is another throwaway question. But it does serve four purposes:

It relieves the pressure built up by the last two personal questions. It encourages a little discussion of a safe subject. It establishes that your interests aren't limited to real estate and making money, that you're also concerned about community affairs. And it sets up Question 9.

That is, it may set up Question 9. Or your string may have run out. Be especially alert at this point, and don't ask the last question unless you've had an encouraging interview so far. If you feel yourself slipping, Question 9 won't pull you up. You'll have to save it for a future visit with this home owner.

Remember that you can't pound through this entire survey like an elephant heading for the river on a hot day. You've got to be responsive to the interviewee. That person is the whole point of the exercise. Be prepared to stop and head for the next door any time they get twitchy. Never forget that the first, last, and only purpose for the survey is to help you become a force in your farm. You can only do that by building rapport with the families who live there. The survey gives you a vehicle for gathering facts about people that will help you continue to build rapport. But it's counterproductive—it hurts you more than it helps you—if you use it to squeeze information from people when they don't want to spend time talking to you. In case of doubt, cut it short and keep moving. When impatient people learn that you don't linger long, they'll be more likely to talk to you for a few minutes the next time.

Question 9: "Do you have a full-time real estate agent serving your family's needs?"

Have an answer rehearsed for those who say, "Why should I? We're not selling."

"No one thinks they will—until they do. Lots of people suddenly find themselves with an exciting opportunity that involves moving or some other real estate transaction and they don't know where to get trustworthy information in strict confidence. I'm an expert in this area, and I can be your confidential source of accurate facts."

Some people answer Question 9 with, "Yes, we have a friend in the business." Don't let it bother you. Your answer is, "That's wonderful. I'm glad to hear that you appreciate the value of knowledgeable, professional service. Since I'm a specialist in this area, I'll keep in touch with you from time to time so I can be of help if needed."

After you finish with this question, close off the interview with these words:

"Thank you very much for your help. I'll let you know of any interesting developments I find out about our area."

That sets you up for meeting number two, doesn't it? The key to effective farming is to always look ahead. Always keep yourself moving toward stronger positions.

As you work through your farm with the market survey, you'll acquire a large collection of priceless information about the people living there. You've worked hard for this information, so treat it with respect. Every night, transfer the facts you've learned that day into your computer. Keep your notes current. The secret of not getting swamped is to do every day's work every day. Of course, if you're out until 3:00 A.M. with an offer one night, you'll have to play catch-up the next day. Start making your spare moments count. The budding champion expects to be busy. Time is precious; the champion doesn't waste it. The busier you get, the more ways you find to make one minute do the work of two. Keep going back to your listing bank. Every time you work there, you make a deposit.

Here are some of the facts you want to record in your listing bank notebook:

1. First and last names
2. Children's names—list surnames if different; ie., stepchildren, ages
3. Nicknames, if any, that they want used instead of their real names
4. Names of any pets they have and type of pets
5. Employment information
6. Length of time in the area

When you come back, you'll know so much about each family that they'll have to be impressed.

Step 9: Make Your First Sweep in 60 Days or Less

That's the test. If you can't knock on every door in two months, your farm is bigger than you have the drive to handle. This is the real world you're dealing with now, and in the real world, the only farming that pays is intense farming. You can make money farming a hundred houses intensely; you can only lose money by farming five hundred ineffectively. So be straight with your broker, be straight with yourself, and don't let wishful thinking lead you to disaster.

Step 10: Drive Your Listing Bank at Least Once Every Other Day

Your car and you must become part of the neighborhood's environment. Drive slowly in your farm, pulling over frequently. Keep your listing bank notebook or laptop on the seat to help you memorize names. You'll be able to do this with surprising ease, because you have a reason for learning these facts. Make it a challenge to learn everyone's name. A kid with a paper route knows all the people's names after about three months. You can bat in that league, can't you?

Some champions have their spouses drive so they can concentrate on looking at the homes and associating the names and the people with each house. Call each owner/couple to mind as you pass their house. Every trip you make through your farm will imprint more faces and names on your memory. Whenever you drive your farm, have your notes with you.

If you see a man out watering the lawn, the odds are good that he lives there, aren't they? Start flipping the pages when you see someone doing yard work. Before you pull up to the curb, you've found the information. Stacey Street, number 2856. Aha.

Down comes the window. "Hi, Mr. Jeffries," you call, giving him a friendly wave.

Mr. Jeffries will wave back. And he'll think, "There's that real estate agent again. Never too busy to say hello. And what a memory!"

It's fun. And it's effective.

Watch for activity in your listing bank. Don't get all the news from other agents. The competition will be taking a lot of listings in your bank for a while, but don't let that upset you. You won't become a force to be reckoned with in your listing bank until you've met the nicest 90 percent of the home owners there six times.

Are you thinking, "What if everyone does this?"

I wish you could sit down with any one of the top people I've trained and hear their answer to that question. They all say the same thing: Everyone goes out like gangbusters, but after three months only they—the champions—are still farming. The others just don't have the stamina and discipline to keep plugging until the listings start coming in. I hope you realize that you won't be getting fifteen listings out of your farm the first month. If you get one, you're very lucky, which means you worked smart and hard. After your third sweep through your farm, count on one a month. Quite possibly, you'll be doing much better than that. After six meetings, you'll be getting five listings a month from a 500-unit farm, if you've done everything I told you to do.

Step 11: Hand Out a Small Gift on Your Second Visit

Again, you make this second sweep in 60 days or less. This time you're reporting the results of the market survey, and you're also dropping off a small gift.

I hope that I can convince you of the value of giving. I believe in gifts as a sound business practice. You give them the gift for helping you with the survey. The gift doesn't have to be expensive, but it shouldn't be too cheap. In a service business, you have to spend money to make money.

Let me mention the Brown and Bigelow Company.

A young man with Brown and Bigelow walked into my office a month after my training with J. Douglas Edwards. I still had no money. I had lots of enthusiasm, but no money! But I saw that it was going to happen. Some of you reading this book know it's just a matter of time. If you know you'll make it, you're already halfway there.

This young man said, "Tom, I have lots of advertising specialties for handouts." He showed me all kinds of things. I really craved some of them. I said, "I'd love to take a few hundred of these two items out in the field and see what I could do with them. But I don't have the money."

Do you know what he did after an hour of talking? I didn't try to sell him on this idea because I didn't know what I was doing. I didn't have enough technique to do that. He finally said, "Tom, anyone who would sell real estate in a black and silver band uniform, anyone that makes $42.00 a month and is still here, needs help!"

I said, "I know."

This young man let me order my first little giveaways, and let me pay three months later. That's why I talk about Brown and Bigelow. I will never forget the people who helped me when I was on the bottom. To find a representative with Brown and Bigelow in your area, visit their Web site at http://www.brownandbigelow.com.

By the way, as you climb that ladder of success, don't forget to notice the people you pass. Because, if you miss a rung, you'll see them on the way down! And you may need their friendship badly.

So you give your potential sellers a gift the second time through and thank them for their help on the survey and let them know what you found out.

Let me show you what I mean. I knock on a door: "Hi, Mrs. Johnson, Tom Hopkins." I'd only use her first name if it felt right. "When I was by a few weeks ago, you were so kind to help me with my survey. And you know what? Ninety-eight percent of the people I surveyed said the area is improving. Seventy-six point one percent said the shopping facilities are adequate. And do you know that we have eighty-four children on your street?" Give her the information you learned on the survey.

"And here's a little something to thank you for the help. I'm really excited about serving the home owners in this area. I'll see you in a couple of months. Bye."

You notice there's one thing I'm not even mentioning—real estate. That's why, if you're in a nonsoliciting area, you have not solicited with this approach. You made a survey, and now you're giving a gift.

Step 12: Identify the Nicest 10 Percent

In a 500-house farm, you'll find 50 friendly families. Really nice people. Send them a special note the second time you sweep your farm.

Dear Ted and Maxine, Just wanted to drop you a quick note to thank you again for your help on my survey. I enjoyed seeing you. Hope the seeds grow beautiful flowers. Regards, Tom.

Cultivate these people with extra attention and they'll respond with all sorts of valuable information about real estate opportunities in your listing bank.

Step 13: Meet Everyone in Your Listing Bank Once Every Two Months for One Year

As I said earlier, if you're really hot, you'll have your six meetings in six months—but this is only for people who've decided to be super-champions.

Step 14: Organize a Specialized Program

This is a good idea for your third contact with people in your farm. It is a promotion program that's coordinated with a holiday or special event. Refer back to Chapter 14 for the list of ideas for your farm.

My first specialized program was pumpkins. I went to the source—the pumpkin farms of Ventura County—and bought 518 pumpkins at bargain prices out there. Then I arranged to haul them to my listing farm in a rented three-quarter ton truck.

But first, I did some advance work. Three weeks before Halloween, a letter went out to every home in my farm. It told them not to buy a pumpkin because I'd be bringing one. Then I painted a sign for the truck that read, HAPPY HALLOWEEN FROM TOM HOPKINS.

I recruited two little guys to help me, and right before Halloween, the three of us, dressed as ghosts, drove around the listing bank. My two helpers ran the pumpkins to the doors.

I didn't stop promoting, following up, and keeping in touch just because my pumpkin promotion was a tremendous success. But from that day on, I had that farm in my hip pocket. I didn't get every listing there—just most of them. You'll never get them all. You don't need them all. You don't even want them all. Some are run-down, overpriced turkeys dumped on the market by nasty people.

After my first year in the business, I decided that, once every 12 months, I'd try something in my farm that I'd never heard of anyone doing. Why not have a party for all my clients? That seemed like a great idea. I felt that I should do it right or not at all, so I mailed invitations engraved with gold leaf.

The first year, only thirty-five out of five hundred came to my party. That was fortunate, because I held it at my home. The second year, more than a hundred people came. By the time I put on my sixth annual Tom Hopkins Festival, it had become the yearly event in Simi Valley. No one had six hundred people to a party in Simi Valley— except me.

For my last one, I rented a large ballroom. My friends and family helped me decorate it with crepe paper, banners, and balloons. I always picked an evening between Christmas and New Year's for my reception in order to have it during party time but not be in conflict with everyone's holiday plans. I had two bands: ballroom first, rock second. There were two huge Christmas trees, food, and drinks. When I totaled up all the bills for my last year's gala, I had paid out $3,000.

But I never thought I was out $3,000 for that party. As a matter of fact, at least $6.00 came back for every dollar I invested in that promotion. Let me put a new word in your vocabulary: SALTMAL (Spend a Little to Make a Lot). You have to build up to it, of course, but be sure to spend a little of the money you make this year to make a lot more next year.

My last party was more than a financial success; it was a gratifying emotional experience too. More than once while it was going on, I remembered how I'd bought my farm's first little promotional gifts not seven years before, nervously, and on 90-day credit.

Who do people think of when they decide to move after coming to your party for five years since you helped them find their home? You see, after three years, the majority of the people at your party are getting the itch to move. Isn't that exciting?

I made the party formal. Made them all dress up! Here's a secret. Hire a sharp person, one who'll pay attention to your instructions to greet people warmly at the door and write their names on name tags in big, black letters. Don't let the people write their own names. Lots of them will write them too small for you to see. Remember, those name tags are there for the benefit of only one person: you. Pay attention to this detail. If the door person prints large and plain, you can see their names before they know you're looking. You can't remember them all.

This was really a big event. The mayor's office called because they knew the newspaper people were invited. The secretary said, "Mr. Hopkins, we understand you're having your big annual party this year. The mayor would like to stop by."

It would have been fun to say, "Would you advise the mayor that this party is for the people I've served. Luckily, we have two weeks before the party for him to get happily involved in some real estate!"

Step 15: Look for Two Special Types Your Fourth Time Through

By the time you go by to say hello for the fourth time, many wonderful things will have begun to happen. Lots of people will know you now. This time through, you're looking for two more special kinds of people. On Step 12, you spotted the nicest 10 percent. You've already marked these people for special attention.

This time through, look for the neighborhood snoops. Every street usually has one or two. Once they like and trust you, they'll be delighted to give you the latest update on who's getting divorced, who's having a baby, what's happening in each family.

And also, on your fourth sweep, decide who are the nastiest people in your listing bank. Then take them off your list. You don't need them. Why put up with the pain? Why fight the aggravation? You're a champion. You'll soon dominate your listing bank. You'll soon know more about the real estate there than anyone else does. It's their loss when you tear them out of your book.

They don't get a pumpkin! They don't get the gilded invitation to your annual party. Just walk right past their property. But don't put them in the nasty group the first time they're nasty unless the experience is really bad. Anyone can have a bad day. But if they get you two times running—out they go. Champions don't accept that kind of treatment.

There's an interesting phenomenon about the rottenest, nastiest people. They still want the best service. But I'll tell you something about many of that kind. The toughest to win over will often be your most loyal supporters once you've done it.

I remember a man I set a goal to list when he was a by-owner. It took me a year. Once I got that listing, I gave him such service that he was amazed. That man then moved out of state. For years afterward, when anyone he knew visited any part of California, they had to come all the way to Simi Valley to meet me. This is what happens.

Step 16: Ask for the Business

On your fifth sweep through, you're going to ask for their business. You've earned that right now. You're going to tell them that you have a lot of activity in the area. If they're thinking of moving in the near future, ask them to think of you. And do they know of any neighbors or friends who are planning to move?

What will make the difference in your career with this knowledge are the three Ds: desire, direction, and doing. You have the direction now, you have the desire, but two out of three doesn't close clients. You have to be out there doing. The doors to everything you want are in your listing bank. Go knock on them. Keep on knocking. You can have everything you knock for.

Your sixth visit may entail providing information specific to each home owner's needs as you have discovered them. It could be providing a market survey, telling them about a property like theirs or nearby that you just listed. It could be to thank them for a kindness or for letting you serve them. By this time, you should know enough about each property, home owner, and the community to select an appropriate reason for making contact.

CHAPTER 17

Listing Preparation Techniques That Will Build Your Fortune

As I travel the world talking with people in real estate, I often ask brokers, "Who made the most money in your office last year?"

The broker gives me a name.

"And who's your top lister?"

Nine times out of ten, the broker gives me the same name.

A piece of real estate that's listed right is as good as sold the night it's listed. When you know how to take good listings, you can figure out what your income will be a month in advance.

The key to this business is the listing. Put half your time and energy into listing and half into selling. When you have several realistically priced listings, you control the marketplace. When the going gets tough, it's the buyers-only associate who finds himself or herself looking for a time clock job to pay the rent.

Start by Being Prepared

Preparation is the lever that moves your work from slow futility to fast profit. You have to know the neighborhood. Real estate values can change dramatically in just a few blocks, sometimes in just a few yards. You have to know your business. If you think the ways of the real estate industry are mysterious, potential clients will have difficulty accepting you as a real estate expert. You have to know your technique. Many people hate to make decisions, and won't until someone comes along who's skilled at helping them do so. That's why my method concentrates on teaching you how to help people make decisions that are good for them.

So you need to have expertise in three areas: neighborhood knowledge, industry knowledge, and technique. Let's talk about a method that puts all three of those areas to work at once.

The Comparable Market Analysis

As I said before, you lose between 25 and 75 percent of your listing power unless you present a well-researched comparable market analysis during your listing performance.

Why is this technique so essential? Can't you just tell them what the prices are?

People don't believe the figures coming out of the mouth of the silver-tongued devil known as a salesperson. But when they see those same figures written in black and white on a printed form, they do believe them.

You see, when you present the facts, you're quoting lower sales prices than the sellers have heard from other sources. And they want to believe those other sources that justify a higher price for their property. So when they look at your comparable market analysis what hits them? Unpleasant facts.

First, your people see several comparable homes offered for less than they want for theirs. After discussing this with you, they begin to suspect that the price they had in mind is unrealistic.

As you draw their attention to the recent sales, they see what the home six doors up sold for a couple of months ago. That property, which has the same floor plan as theirs, never had a sign because it sold so fast. They didn't even know the people were leaving until they saw the moving van. Then they believed the first rumor that came around about the price the fast sellers got. Now they're shocked and angry to discover that those people sold for $15,000 less than what they've decided should be their own rock bottom figure.

COMPARABLE MARKET ANALYSIS

Property Address __12345 Success Circle_____ Date_____

FOR SALE NOW	BED RMS	BATH	DEN	SQ FT	1ST LOAN	LIST PRICE	DAYS ON MARKET	TERMS
12460 Happy Lane	3	2		same	85,000	158,300	141	VA
13601 Million Dollar Drive	3	2		same	85,000	157,090	42	VA
16104 Success Circle	3	2		same	85,000	157,750	80	FHA

SOLD PAST 12 MOS	BED RMS	BATH	DEN	SQ FT	1ST LOAN	LIST PRICE	DAYS ON MARKET	DATE SOLD	SALE PRICE	TERMS
12412 Dollar Drive	4	2		more	86,000	157,090	52		157,090	VA
16104 Success Circle	3	2		same	85,000	156,650	48		156,100	VA
12105 Happy Lane	3	2			85,000	157,750	71			VA

EXPIRED PAST 12 MOS	BED RMS	BATH	DEN	SQ FT	1ST LOAN	LIST PRICE	DAYS ON MARKET	TERMS
14106 Dollar Drive	3	2				156,090	120+	Cash to Loan
12104 Happy Lane	3	2				158,300	120+	10% + 2nd

F.H.A. — V.A. APPRAISALS

ADDRESS	APPRAISAL	ADDRESS	APPRAISAL
16401 Success Circle	156,650		
16201 Success Circle	157,200		
16201 Success Drive	157,090		

BUYER APPEAL   **MARKETING POSITION**

(Grade each item 0 to 20% on the basis of desirability or urgency.)

1. Fine location _____ %
2. Exciting extras _____ %
3. Extra special financing _____ %
4. Exceptional appeal _____ %
5. Under market price _____Yes_____ No_____%
                    Rating Total_____ %

1. Why are they selling _____ %
2. How soon must they sell _____ %
3. Will they help finance   Yes_____ No_____%
4. Will they list at
   competitive market value   Yes_____ No_____%
5. Will they pay for appraisal Yes_____ No_____%
                    Rating Total_____ %

Assets _____

Drawbacks_____

Area market conditions _____

_____

Recommended terms _____

_____

Top comparative market value $ _____

Probable final sales price $ _____

Yes, they're shocked to learn the truth. And they're angry, but not at you. The people you're trying to list see that Herman and Wilma Mildue actually sold for $248,000. That's another shock. They'd heard the "about $290,000" figure that Wilma tossed around in the bowling alley.

Then your sellers turn back to the houses currently for sale and notice that the Simpsons' home has been on the market for seven months. You discussed that point earlier, but they didn't seem to catch it. Their minds were on prices then. Now they give that time period some clear thought, knowing that a seven-month wait would spell disaster for them.

When you lead them into a discussion of the expired listing—of why it happens and how disruptive it is for the home owners involved—they begin to grasp your explanation of realistic value. They realize that you've brought a consistent price pattern to their attention with your carefully researched and well thought out comparable market analysis. Now that you've explained and *re*explained the meaning to them of the CMA's three sections, they see the reality of the market-value concept. Suddenly, they know that the facts you're presenting are the hard truth they'll have to live with. And now, for the first time, you have the opportunity to list their home at a price that will permit the property to be sold.

CMAs get easier as you go along. Beginning with my second year, I started filling out the top two sections mostly from memory because they were about my own sales and listings. Your first comparable market analysis might take you all day to complete. After that, you'll be doing them in much less time.

Once that we've put our CMA together, we're going to do what the pro does: analyze the area. The average salesperson looks up the comparables and lets it go at that. He doesn't go see the properties.

After a few months of alert and active work in your area, you'll know most of the properties that have sold or are on the market there, and you will have visited most of the expired listings. Are you beginning to see how it all fits together? If you've been farming your listing bank thoroughly, you'll have the whole CMA there in your head in a few months.

But you still write it down. They'll still believe the written data that you give them on the form far more than they'll believe or even remember what you say.

If your listing appointment is outside your farm, visit the area. Go see as many expired listings as you can find time for. At the least, you'll get information to help you with your listing appointment; at the best, you'll get another listing appointment with the people whose listing expired.

A high percentage of those appointments will lead to listings. Never rely only on the research that you dig out of the records in your office. Unless you at least drive by every property on your CMA, you're knocking on the door to disaster when you arrive for your listing appointment. Will you agree that the condition of those fifteen properties will vary? Just one example will show you how failing to see properties will kill your claim to real estate expertise.

Let's say that you're working on the price question with Keith and Wanda Lloyd. You've gone smoothly through your listing presentation up to this point. Keith Lloyd has already let it out that he thinks their home, which is immaculate and has lots of extras, is worth $292,750. It's a popular floor plan in your service area, and you're familiar with the general layout.

Your research at the office turned up three other properties of the identical floor plan that are for sale within a few blocks of the Lloyd home. One of them, you notice, has been on the market for nearly a year, the other two for several months. All three properties are priced in the high two-eighties. You don't find any recent sales of that model near the Lloyd home.

One sold on their street a year ago for $292,000. But the same contractor built a number of them in another neighborhood about a mile away, and you find three recent sales there in the $281,250, $282,500, and $283,950 range. Since you're pressed for time, you decide you've found all the information you need. "Obviously," you say to yourself, "that design won't sell for more than $284,000 anymore. I'll go with $285,000 as the top figure I'll take the Lloyd listing at. Just to make sure, I'll drive by the three identical houses that are for sale over there."

However, since the road to the infernal regions is paved with good intentions, you don't make time for the drive-by, find yourself running late, and hit the Lloyds' door without doing any field checking on your office research. But you're not worried. You don't see how all three houses can be much different from the Lloyds' pile of bricks and sticks. So, at the proper time during your performance, you close for the listing at a price of $285,000.

The sellers stare at you in amazement. After a moment, Keith Lloyd says, "Have you been in those three houses you say are our competition?"

"Ah, no. I haven't actually been inside. But they're all in this neighborhood and . . ."

Mr. Lloyd breaks in with, "Have you even driven by any of them?"

"Well, I . . ."

"Obviously, you haven't," Keith Lloyd says. "For your information, house number one on your list is a hippie heaven. Must be twenty people living there and it shows.

"House number two is a divorce situation. I guess they both just took off and let the place turn into a jungle. You can see the vandalism from the street.

"House number three is nice except that it backs up to the Interstate. I've met the people, and they know that highway noise is the reason their home hasn't sold.

"So now you walk in here—without even checking out those other properties—and tell us we'll never sell our house for more than $284,000. I'm not even going to mention the house up the street that sold for $292,000 last year. Frankly, I don't think you're the kind of real estate *expert* I want to do business with. Thanks for coming by and good night."

Things like that happen all the time to salespeople trying to earn a professional's income without bothering to do professional-quality work. Don't let it happen to you.

Now let's talk about what properties you select to put on the comparable market analysis form. The purpose of the form is to concentrate on the most important facts that bear on the price decision for the property you're trying to list. What are the most important facts? Those that pertain to the properties that are most like the one you're trying to list. In what way? In nearness, physical qualities, and time. The identical floor plan located on the same size lot a mile away may not be comparable at all: The second house may be downwind of a hog farm, reached only by a dirt road, and located in a different school district that's on the brink of bankruptcy.

In actual practice, you'll rarely have trouble knowing which properties to include after you've located all the facts. In case of doubt, it's quicker to use two forms and provide more facts to the sellers than it is to agonize over which ones to put on one form.

The properties you want on your CMA are those that the sellers will feel are comparable. You want them to rationalize: "If this property sold for that price, ours must be worth about the same."

Never underestimate the importance of location. In most cases, nearness is one of the most important aspects of comparability, and value differences between neighborhoods can be very difficult to get the sellers to agree on. However, when the two properties being compared are close enough to enjoy the same environment, adjustments can easily be made to reflect the value of a few hundred extra feet of floor space or a few extra amenities on one of the properties. Simply list all the items, place a value on each one, and total them up.

Packing Listing Power into the CMA

When you prepare a thorough CMA, you're almost certain to be presenting a lot of vital information the sellers have never had before. You'll be giving them data about properties they aren't familiar with, and also about properties they are aware of but may not really know. The longer they study your comparable market analysis, the more they'll realize that they're looking at the facts of record, not the fiction of rumor.

Here's what you should put on the comparable market analysis:

1. ALL ACTIVE, COMPARABLE, NEARBY PROPERTIES.

The CMAs for-sale section is your primary tool for showing what the competition is in their neighborhood today. When buyers wanting to live close by can choose among comparable properties offered in the high two-seventies, sincere sellers recognize that they can't sell in the high two-eighties.

Include every sign they'd see while out walking their dog. The only nearby homes you can safely omit are those a stranger to the area would know aren't comparable to the subject property simply by glancing at them from the street.

What's *nearby?* The answer to this question depends on whether you're selling ranches in Texas or condos in Connecticut.

2. ALL COMPARABLE PROPERTIES THAT HAVE SOLD WITHIN THE LAST SIX MONTHS.

This part of the CMA puts the most reliable floor possible under the value of the subject property by showing what real people spending real money have been willing to pay for comparable property in the most recent past.

The only action that establishes the market value of anything is an actual purchase. However, since there's no guarantee that another buyer who'll pay the same amount for the same thing will appear tomorrow, today's purchase becomes past history the moment it's made. All values change. Though past sales are not a perfect base for setting present value, they are the only base we have to work from.

3. ALL COMPARABLE LISTINGS IN THE VICINITY THAT HAVE EXPIRED WITHIN THE PAST SIX MONTHS.

The third section of the CMA puts a ceiling over the price that the subject property can command. This ceiling-over value is as reliable as the floor put under value by section two's record of recent sales. In other words, expired listings tell you how much you can't get for the subject property. Except in highly unusual circumstances, the record tells it like it is. And when that story's told, it's the market speaking, not you. Make that clear. Don't let the sellers blame you for what the market says it won't do.

When there are no highly unusual circumstances and you can show that you've found comparable listings, people who are sincere will accept the market's ceiling. Insincere sellers won't.

You can't make money working with insincere sellers because they won't sell for any price a sincere buyer would pay or a lender would risk money on. That's an obvious point, but I'm amazed at how many agents ignore it and go on trying to make money where there's no money to be made. Make a strong effort to find all the comparable listings that have expired. (Also, try not to take all of them from your own previous inventory.)

You may not be able to get inside all the comparable properties before your listing appointment but you should certainly make time to drive by them all. Unless you do that, you're not prepared. You don't deserve the listing. Or perhaps you deserve what you're likely to get—an overpriced turkey.

There's another reason why you must drive the area before completing your research. Comparable files are usually set up by number of bedrooms, with all two-bedroom homes listed together, all three-bedroom homes together, and so on. Let's say that you're getting ready for a listing appointment with Ed and Louise Kellner at their three-bedroom home outside your farm. You put all the three-bedroom homes for sale in the neighborhood on your CMA and swing past each of those houses on your way to the listing appointment. This gives you a nasty surprise: There are several properties for sale near the Kellner home that aren't on your CMA. From the street, you can't tell whether they have more than three bedrooms, which would explain why you didn't find them in your research. But there's no time left to check this out.

Later, at the Kellners, you reach the point in your listing presentation when you present the comparable market analysis. As you hand the form over to the Kellners, Ed pulls a piece of paper out of his shirt pocket and unfolds it. He has his own list of homes for sale to compare to yours. Right away, he's asking about three houses that aren't on your CMA.

"They've got to be four bedrooms, or I'd have them on the form," you say.

Staring at his list, Ed frowns. "I'm not sure they all are. Louise, didn't you say you've been in the house on Fig Street that's for sale?"

"That's right. And it's a lot like ours."

"Three bedrooms?"

"Definitely three bedrooms," Louise Kellner says.

Her husband leans back in his chair and says, "I'm sorry, but under the circumstances I don't see how we can make an intelligent price decision tonight."

A few minutes later, you find yourself in the street walking to your car. But you console yourself that all is not lost. You have another appointment with the Kellners for the following evening.

On checking the next morning, you discover why you didn't find the listing Louise Kellner spoke about: It's very recent and won't show up in the multiple yet. Had you driven the area early enough to have time to check out new developments, you would have known that the house on Fig has three bedrooms. While you're thinking about this, you get a call from another agent who says, "I'm afraid that I've got some bad news for you. You know the Kellners? Well, I met with them after you left, and they gave me the listing. Then they told me to give you a call and explain that there's no point in your going back over there."

An excess of enthusiastic attitude can't make up for a lack of preparation. But, the sad truth is that some people are all preparation and no attitude. They lose too. Some of the people in my office were professional appraisers. They had the expertise, but they radiated more negativity than any but the toughest of clients could handle. One by one they gave up trying to become high-earning real estate associates and went back to low-paying salaried jobs. No matter how our industry evolves, I promise you one thing: Human nature won't change. People will always prefer to be around positive people.

Inside Another Home

Whenever you inspect a by-owner home because you're compiling a CMA for someone else, do these three things:

1. MAKE NOTES OF THE COLORS.

You want to be able to identify the house by its exterior colors. And you want to be able to discuss the interior too. Knowing the color of the carpet or floor covering is vital. If there's anything about the walls or ceiling, note that too.

2. CONVERT TIME ON MARKET TO DAYS.

If the by-owners say, "We put our sign up three months ago," write down 89 days. Champions work with precise figures. Be articulate.

Speak in pointed numbers, not rounded ones. The more factual, accurate, and articulate you are, the more professional you are.

3. TRY TO GET THE HOME OWNERS TO ASK IF YOU CAN SELL THE PLACE.

You dress and act as professional as possible primarily in the hope that they'll say something like, "Hey, hot shot, do you think you can get my price?" "Can you sell the place?" "What do you think you can get for it?"

Then try for the appointment.

Whether or not you get an opportunity to do that, no matter how nasty, mean, and arrogant the by-owner was, send him a thank-you note for letting you see the home so that you could complete your comparable market analysis for your client.

Other Brokers' Listings

Whenever you go into another office's listing, follow the code of ethics. Respect the other broker's agency as you'd want them to respect your agency at your listings.

Sometimes you'll be sorely tempted to let the sellers know how much better off they'd be with you and your firm than with the one they listed with. But if you yield to that temptation—even with nothing more than a raised eyebrow at some strategic moment—you're not only being unethical and unprofessional, you're also being stupid. When you're in another agent's listing, keep your eyebrows straight and your thoughts pure. Let no criticism of the other firm, or praise of your own, escape your lips. Never forget that when you're there, you personify the entire profession. Anything you do that harms the other agent harms the entire profession, yourself included. Don't take this lightly. Unethical conduct, if allowed to feed on itself, can quickly take over in an area. Only you can stop that cancerous growth.

If any of this unprofessional conduct is directed at you, don't respond by lowering yourself to that level. Both in the short run and over the long haul, the way to beat the unprofessional agents is to be more professional yourself.

The rules and codes of ethics vary from one realty board to another. Find out what they are in your area and follow them exactly. In many cities, you are forbidden by the rules and ethics of your local professional organization to drive over and inspect a property listed in the multiple unless you call the listing agent first and obtain his or her permission.

Let's assume that you've done that, and now you're at the door of Pathetic Realty's listing. Again, you're carrying a legal pad so you can take plenty of notes. Here's what you say: "Good afternoon, Mrs. Simpson. My name is Tom Hopkins with Champions Unlimited. I called and obtained permission from Pathetic Realty to visit you. As you can see, I don't have a prospective buyer with me at this time."

If you're not working for that firm, you have to let them know why you're there: "I would appreciate seeing your home so when I am showing a buyer, I'll be aware of all the improvements you've made."

Notice the exact words. Did I say that I am going to show their home? No. Once inside the home, you say, "Mrs. Simpson, my purpose in stopping is twofold. First, to familiarize myself with your property and, second, to prepare a comparable market survey for a client in the area who's thinking of having me professionally market his home. May I measure a few rooms and make a list of your improvements?"

If you're dressed professionally, if you use this phraseology with practiced confidence, if you gather information about her property like an expert, is she going to see a difference between your action and that of Fred Blodgett, the full-time butcher and when-he-feels-like-it real estate person? This is the property that's been on the market for seven months. Nobody except Blodgett has shown it for 102 days, and Mrs. Simpson thinks there's always something strange about the people Fred brings through. Under these circumstances—and similar things happen far too often in most areas—do you suppose that Mr. and Mrs. Simpson are slightly unhappy they gave their listing to the butcher?

Now let's examine two common ways that sellers react to this situation. In both, Mrs. Simpson decides to come with me as I go through the home. I didn't ask her to, but she's a little curious. "Mrs. Simpson, that paneling certainly enhances the living room. Did you and Mr. Simpson put that in, or was it professionally done?"

"I chose the wood, and my husband installed it."

"A very tasteful choice, and your husband is a fine craftsman. The carpeting—it's one of the plushest weaves I've seen. It's new, isn't it?"

"Yes. We recarpeted a year ago."

"It gives your entire home an air of elegance."

I walk through the house with her, trying to establish rapport and making copious notes. I am professionally dressed and my manner is professional throughout the interview. Now, as I start to leave, what's very likely to take place? Remember that the lady has been waiting for action for seven months, and nothing's happened. Then I come in, open her eyes, and start to leave without including her in the bright world of professionalism I've just let her glimpse. Here's what I say as I'm leaving:

"Thank you again. I appreciate you showing me your home, and I wish you and Mr. Blodgett at Pathetic Realty the very best of luck in selling it, Mrs. Simpson."

"Mr. Hopkins, they're not calling. They're not showing our home. What is the problem?"

"Mrs. Simpson, I'd be happy to talk to you about your challenge. However, ethically, while your home is listed, I can't. We at Champions Unlimited believe that our company is founded on ethics. So I hope you'll respect me for that."

I want you to realize what I did with that phraseology. Her home is listed with another firm; ethically I have no right to discuss her challenges with that firm. Are you thinking, "But that part-timer isn't giving her any service." That doesn't alter the fact that the Simpsons entered into a written agreement with Pathetic Realty. It doesn't alter the fact that the ethics of our profession require—as they should and as they must—that you don't undermine another salesperson's agency. As long as it's listed, you can't discuss the price, the terms, the problems. Champions don't do it.

Do most people respect someone who is ethical? Yes, they do. If Mrs. Simpson sees that you're too ethical to take advantage of Fred Blodgett, she'll feel that you wouldn't try to take advantage of her either. And she also feels that you must have the ability to be as successful as she's seen you are from the way you dress, the way you conduct yourself, and perhaps in the car you drive. Your refusal to be unethical, though disappointing to her momentarily, is the final touch that pulls it all together. When her listing with Blodgett, the butcher at Pathetic Realty, runs out, Mrs. Simpson is very likely to call you. Or, if you work expired listings, perhaps you'll call her when you can ethically do so.

Here's the second direction that Mrs. Simpson might take as you're leaving. She might say, "Thanks for stopping by. They just turned my property over to Sally Thompson at Pathetic Realty. She works full time in real estate, and I hope she'll do better. I really like Sally, and I hope you'll call her when you have some buyers."

"So Sally seems to be giving you more service then?"

"Well, yes."

"I haven't met Sally yet. But I will, and when I do, I'm going to tell her you think she's doing a great job. And you're lucky to be doing business with a professional."

What I tried to show you in the above cases is that, if they knock their agent, you don't. But you do take note of their feelings and the fact that when their listing expires, they probably won't renew it with the same company. So if you show the Simpsons' home while you're showing your good listings and demonstrate that home as I recommend in my seminar, audio programs, and book, the odds are good that they'll call you when their current listing expires.

Find an REO While You're Knocking on Doors

REOs are Real Estate Orphans. Real estate orphans are people who are unhappy with the service their agent gave them when they bought their home. Do you know how many REOs are out there? Huge, uncountable numbers. What does finding real estate orphans have to do with compiling a thorough CMA? Everything. One of the best times to find yourself a promising REO is while you're visiting all the recently sold houses that are comparable to the property you're trying to list. Unless you see them, you can't know how comparable those houses really are, can you?

Here's the Hopkins rule for REO families: When you find them, adopt them. Finding a real estate orphan is another bonus that you get for working up a professional-level comparable market analysis.

Come with me as I knock on the Sweeney family's door. I'm not going there at random. I have reason to believe from my office research that the house the Sweeneys bought and moved into three weeks ago is the closest comparable to the Watt home I'm trying to list. So I'm knocking on that door for two reasons: to get vital information for my comparable market analysis for the Watts, and to find out if the Sweeneys are orphans.

My approach is based on the probability that the Sweeneys are like most people who've recently moved into a new neighborhood: They don't know all their neighbors yet, and they'd like to meet the nice ones. I go through all the fundamentals at the door. When Mrs. Sweeney speaks to me, I turn to face her and smile.

"Good afternoon. My name is Tom Hopkins, with Champions Un-limited. I understand that you recently moved in, and I wanted to welcome you to our area."

As a real estate person, where is our area? Everywhere we service. Perhaps your service area is a five-mile radius around your office, but when you say with a warm smile, "I want to welcome you to our area," what does Mrs. Sweeney think?

"Maybe this man and his family live real close. I'll be nice to him."

"Mrs. Sweeney, I'm in the process of preparing a comparable market analysis for a family near here who are employing me to professionally market their home. I'd certainly appreciate seeing your home for comparative value purposes. Would you mind taking a moment to show it to me?"

Do you know that, when you approach them this way, a lot of new people will take the time to do that?

Once you're inside and have asked a few questions, made a few notes, dropped a few fresh compliments, and built a little rapport, here's what you say to find out if they're orphans:

"I hope you were happy with the service rendered you by our industry." Avoid saying anything along the lines of "I hope your agent treated you right." Never assume there's a problem.

What are you in essence saying when you ask if they're satisfied with the service they received from our industry? The words really mean "Are you happy with the people who sold you your home?" But you wouldn't come right out and say that, would you? I thought not. However, Mrs.

Sweeney gets the point, even though you've used the diplomatic wording.

She says, "You know, I'm surprised I even let you in. We've never had problems like this before. They won't return our calls. Everything's different from what they told us it would be."

Clearly, based on what Mrs. Sweeney blurted out, she's telling you that they are real estate orphans. Whenever I met someone unhappy with real estate people, I used what I call putting the shoe on their foot. Smile and say, "So you were unhappy with these people. Obviously, they did not give you service."

They'll agree, won't they?

Then go on with, "If you were the president of a real estate company and a salesperson wasn't giving service to the clients, what would you do?"

What'll they say? Something like, "I'd fire them."

Smile and tell them, "If they're not giving good service, it's not likely they'll be in the business very long." Move right on to positive things by saying, "I'd love to serve you over the next twenty years. As a specialist in this area, I could better serve you, couldn't I?"

Then put their name and address on a card and mark it *orphan*. That same day send a thank-you note for letting you see their home. Within a year of keeping in touch with them, they'll be your people. If they move away, they'll list with you. If they decide to stay in the area for many years, what'll they soon want? A larger home. Then you'll have both a buyer and a seller in the Sweeneys—two transactions from one set of orphans. Or they may decide to buy an investment property. Aren't these multiple possibilities exciting?

Gathering Data Before Calculating Value

Use a legal pad to collect facts on all the properties that will appear on your comparable market analysis form. Call that pad your data sheet. Fill up as many pages as possible with written data about the important elements of value each property has. The more useful written data you have, the more professional and competent you'll be about arriving at true market value. Here are the basic items that you note about each property that belongs on your comparable market analysis:

1. NAMES OF PEOPLE.

A pro knows every property that has a sign on it by the names of its owners.

2. OUTSIDE COLOR.

A pro also knows every property with a sign on it by its outside color. If you're working in an area where most houses are the same color, find a distinguishing feature about each house to associate it with.

3. COLOR OF CARPETS.

A champion tries to find out the color of carpeting—or the type of flooring if the house isn't carpeted—for every property that's comparable to the one he's trying to list. I'll show you why in a moment.

4. PRICE AND TERMS.

Some sellers don't like to accept this truth, but the market for comparable properties is set by the best (for the buyer) combination of low price and good terms, without being influenced by the worst combination of high price and hard terms. An obvious point? Not to every seller. Many of them will try to tell you that value can be arrived at by some process of averaging the high priced with the low. Those same people would laugh at the idea when buying. The fact is, when comparable properties are offered at significantly different prices, the lowest priced will always sell first and highest priced will be ignored. Of course, the properties must be truly comparable in location, terms, prestige, availability, condition, and amenities. When you see a sale that seems to go against that rule, you can be sure the buyer found an important element of value in the higher-priced property.

5. TIME ON THE MARKET.

This is an important consideration. The pro knows that if a property has been on the market longer than the average selling time, there must be a reason. The pro also knows that, although the reason usually boils down to some combination of unrealistic price and unfavorable terms in the existing market for what's being offered, other factors may be involved. The only way to find out is to see the property inside and out.

6. URGE TO SELL.

When we're looking at other agents' listings, it's easy to overlook another vital factor: the motivation of the sellers. It varies widely, can change quickly, and is very emotional. Although it's often difficult to pin this factor down, probing for the reason and urgency behind their need to sell can give you valuable insights.

You've been compiling a comparable market analysis for your listing appointment this evening with Gloria and Jack Watt. Let's review a fraction of the information you've gathered.

For Sale Now

> Simpson home: White exterior, beige carpeting. $297,500.
>   214 days on market. Weak motivation.
> Bartlett home: Brown stucco, champagne carpeting. $259,500.
>   79 days on market. Weak motivation.
> Wenig home: Gray with rock trim, wheat carpeting. $254,000.
>   23 days on market. Strong motivation.
> Moyer home: White with brick trim, camel carpets. $251,995.
>   7 days on market. Strong motivation. Offer pending.

Sold Past 12 Months

> Jackson home: Sold for $247,000 in 5 days. This house is six doors
>   from the subject property.
> Sanchez home: Sold for $249,750 in 31 days.
> Mildue home: Sold for $248,000 in 168 days after being reduced
>   from $265,000.

Expired Past 12 Months

> Ripple home: $269,000 reduced from $279,000. 180 days on market.
> Grifz home: $262,500. 270 days on market.
> Pomeroy home: $289,950. 90 days on market.

Most of the CMAs you'll compile won't give as clear a message as this one does because you usually won't be able to find as many comparables to work with as the example has. The more real comparables you have, the easier it is to see what the market is doing and the more successful you'll be at convincing your sellers that you know what's realistic.

The message of the CMA you're taking to the Watts' house is that there's an active market for their property at just under $250,000, but the demand just isn't there for their floor plan at much above that price.

Now let's jump ahead to the situation you'll be working with when you are going over the comparable market analysis with the Watts. You know they were thinking about a price between $290,000 and $300,000. Mr. Watt is holding the form in his hand, and he looks down and sees the Jackson home sold for $247,000. That hits him hard. He thinks about it for a moment and then says, "What about the blue house on the corner?" "Oh, you mean the Smith home." Cross-reference your CMA properties in your head so you can show that you know all the houses well. When you've made that point, smile and answer his question about Smith's blue house with a question of your own:

"Have you been inside that property?"

They'll usually say no.

"As a professional, I stopped by today to inspect the property so I would be knowledgeable this evening. It's a nice home. They have green carpeting." And you talk about the home for a moment or two, concluding with something like this: "The Smiths are nice people. They've been trying to sell their home for about three years now."

"Three years?" Mr. Watt says.

"That's right." Give him a moment to think about it, and then go on presenting the truth about their property's market value to them. As you do so, frame your wording to constantly remind them that the knowledge you're passing on is fact, not opinion.

Then Mr. Watt says, "The property on Myrtle Street, is that the one with Pathetic Realty's sign on it?"

"Yes, it's white and has a picket fence all around it," you reply.

"Right," says Mr. Watt. "What's it like inside?"

"I visited Mrs. Simpson today," you say. "She was kind enough to show me through her home. It's a lovely place. They've lavished a great deal of thought and care on upgrading their home, just as you folks have. The carpeting is beige and very plush."

Mr. Watt is looking at the CMA form. "It says 214 days here. They've been trying to sell their house for more than six months?"

"You're right—for more than seven months. I think the reason why is shown by the comparable houses that did sell during that time. Of course, the Simpsons aren't my clients, so I can't ethically discuss their real estate challenges with them."

"But you think they're priced too high?"

"Mr. and Mrs. Watt, I've never asked a client to make a price decision based on what I think, and I never will. That's why I spend so much time and effort on research—to discover what the market's verdict is. After I've done all the office and field work that's necessary to develop a clear picture of what the market is saying about a specific property, what I think is irrelevant. The market speaks for itself." Smile and then continue, "The market said, 'No sale' to the Simpsons, but it said 'Sold' to six other families who offered comparable properties for less money. I've compiled those facts for you in the center section of the form."

Can you picture how devastating this knowledge is when it's used convincingly?

If you'll thoroughly research your comparable market analysis—including visits to all the properties on it—you'll be convincing because you'll know you're working with convincing facts.

What if none of the other home owners will let you through their doors? Just glance down and see what color the carpet is. Then look the property over carefully from the sidewalk, making copious notes as you do so. Do everything you properly can to be more prepared at the listing appointment than the sellers are.

Inspecting the Property

In the previous section we jumped ahead to the evening appointment. We'll do that again, but please remember that we're still preparing for that appointment. Let's talk about another important part of the preparation. You must inspect the subject property—the one you're trying to list—before your evening meeting with the husband and wife.

If they both work, you won't be able to get inside the house during the day, but you'll always be able to drive over to it. Whether or not you can get an afternoon appointment, do these four additional things when you visit the property during the day:

1. FIND THE MESSIEST HOUSE ON THE STREET.

On almost every street, there's a home that's outstandingly messy on the outside. Take the Smedleys. They live four doors from the Watts, and their home is a dump. The Smedleys have beat up old cars all over the property. What grass the oil spills haven't killed, the Smedleys never mow. And their front door has a poorly patched hole that looks like it was made by somebody's head. The place is the eyesore of the neighborhood, and everyone knows the Smedleys don't care.

Bear in mind that, even if the neighborhood eyesore isn't all that bad, it's still a very sore spot with your sellers. I always highlighted the messiest house on the street in my data sheet. Here's how the pro uses the eyesore during the listing presentation:

"Mr. and Mrs. Watt, I hope you realize that I in no way believe in knocking anyone. However, as your agent, I'm going to suggest that when people show your home, they bring them in off Baldwin Street instead of off Chamberlain. The reason is, there's a property four doors down that I really believe takes away from the loveliness of your home."

Do they know about that home? You can bet on it. Here again, you're pointing out another reason why you're worth your fee, and at the same time demonstrating your knowledge of their neighborhood and their situation.

2. INSPECT LANDSCAPING.

On the pad you're carrying to gather data about the subject property and the comparables, write a little story about the landscaping. I used to write something like this:

"Landscaping should be okay. However, might consider increasing the watering to green up the grass for better showing. Might consider pulling the weeds on the south side of the home."

What does that tell the Watts when I walk in after dark tonight with that information in my listing folder? That I've been there and done physical research. Do you see the power in this? I'm demonstrating competence.

You see, when I walk in many times they're thinking, "We have no intention of listing with anyone." But my efforts are obligating them to me emotionally in case they change their minds. Beyond that, I'm also giving them logical reasons for the emotional decision to list with me tonight by warmly demonstrating my expertise at the same time.

3. DETERMINE CONDITION OF PAINT.

This one works like magic. In your service area, how many homes do you think have been painted within the last five years—one out of three? If that's about right, the other two out of three homes—the ones that need repainting—are prime candidates for this technique. We're talking about average paint on average houses. An appraiser will agree that the home is suffering from deferred maintenance (lack of normal upkeep) if the house hasn't been repainted within the past five years. When your subject property is in this condition, the average seller is often thinking, "I'm saving by not having to paint the place—I'll put that money into our new home."

When the house you want to list needs repainting, scrape off a small amount of stucco or wood trim with a pen knife and put the paint chips in an envelope. Don't carve, just scrape. And do your scraping on the side of the house where it won't be noticed. Put the envelope of paint chips in your listing folder.

When you bring the envelope out that evening, here's what you don't say: "Mr. and Mrs. Watt, I've got to tell you that your home has to be painted before it'll sell for value." Do they like that? No. Will they paint the house because I told them to? No. Am I further from getting a market-price listing? Yes. My psychology was wrong. A champion turns the need for repainting into a listing tool with this phraseology:

"Mr. and Mrs. Watt, the buyer will probably want to repaint within the next year to put the home in top condition, don't you agree?"

If the sellers agree, they are also agreeing that their home is not in top condition. That's an important agreement to get because your listing performance succeeds only if you can get them down to within bargaining distance of market value.

Here's how you handle the paint chips envelope: Look at your listing folder and say, "I came by today and inspected the home." Pick up the envelope. "The landscaping should be fine. You might consider pulling that little patch of weeds on the south side. The paint condition, though . . ." Rip open the envelope and pour the contents in the middle of the table. Don't have a huge mound, enough chips to cover a half-dollar will do fine. As you talk, move these chips around with your finger. "Mr. and Mrs. Watt, the buyer will probably want to repaint the home during the next year to put it in top condition, don't you agree?"

"Well, yes, I suppose they might," Mr. Watt says.

"How long has it been since the exterior was painted?" you ask.

"Five years."

"I took some shavings here just in case you thought it would be a wise decision to paint the exterior. I could get some bids. If we matched the color as closely as possible, you could save some money. We could probably repaint the exterior for $1,800 to $2,000.

"On the other hand, you may want to wait and just let the buyer do the painting, and we could reflect that cost in the total investment that we arrive at."

Do you see the strategy here? I offered the service of getting bids and helping them decide on getting the painting done. However, if they don't want to do that, we can reflect the paint condition in the asking price that we agree on.

Perhaps you're sitting there thinking, "They won't come down $2,000 just for that." Only very highly motivated sellers will right away. But your attention to the paint condition detail is just one more lever to move the pricing decision of most sellers closer to market value.

By the way, when you present an offer that's a little below their asking price because they started above market, guess what you pour out on their kitchen table again? The paint scrapings in the envelope.

4. ASSESS CONDITION OF ROOF.

I'm not a roofer, but I can tell whether a roof will last through the closing. I'm sure you can too. Here's the dissertation you should write about the roof:

"Roof should be okay. However, if government financing used, may require roof certification."

Did I say that I must have a roof certification before the home can qualify for government-insured financing? No. I said it may require it. Imagine the scene as I discuss their roof with both the Watts that evening. From time to time during my listing presentation, I've flipped over a page of my legal pad. I have it out where they can see it at all times. Things like the dissertation are written legibly. Here's how you handle this aspect like a pro:

"Mr. and Mrs. Watt, when I was by today, I inspected the roof and it should be okay. However, if government financing were to be used, they may require a roof certification."

"What's that?"

"Let me explain. Both the Federal Housing Administration and the Veteran's Administration, the FHA and the VA, guarantee or insure home loans. Our best buyers may be people who can't or won't make the purchase unless they can obtain the favorable terms of government-backed loans. For that to happen, the buyers must qualify as good credit risks. Your home must also qualify as a good credit risk because it's the property that secures the loan. In order for a property to qualify, the appraisers must give it a certificate of reasonable value. Unless that document is in the file, the sale won't go through.

"In their appraisal processes, both the FHA and the VA pay close attention to a roof that's over five years old. Before issuing the certificate of reasonable value, they may require that a certified contractor inspect the roof and give them what's called a roof certification. Basically, it means that the expert says the roof is in good shape.

"However, today we have many sources of conventional home financing. So we may not be using a government-insured loan. Of course, as your agent I'll do my very best with the buyer or the buyer's agent to secure the type of financing that will save you as much money as possible. I guess what I'm really trying to say, Mr. and Mrs. Watt, is that when you do business with me, I won't let there be any surprises."

"Surprise" Is a Listing Word

The entire speech just given has two important goals. The first is to set up your discussion of the fact that home financing is complex, and you know your way around it. You have a complete understanding of the intricacies of FHA, VA, conventional, and creative financing. The sellers probably have never heard of a certificate of reasonable value before. Now, if they've had any thought of trying to sell themselves, they're beginning to realize just how involved real estate transactions really are.

The second reason for your roof performance is to set up the last sentence in the speech: "I guess what I'm really trying to say, Mr. and Mrs. Watt, is that when you do business with me, I won't let there be any surprises."

What is the one thing that everyone marketing a property is afraid of?

Surprise.

At the very least, you're anxious. You worry about the unexpected—and usually still unknown—costs and inconveniences of the latest surprise. And there's always the fear that the new challenge will bring your entire move to a halt.

"We have to get a termite inspection."

Surprise.

"There's dry rot around the shower."

Surprise.

"The appraisal came in low."

Surprise.

I hope you see the psychology behind your reassuring statement, "I won't let there be any surprises." Every surprise causes your sellers pain and costs them money. Another reason for your afternoon visit is to decide whether giving the roof performance is the best launching point for the financing and surprise discussions. If you decide it's not, devise another way to put these techniques into action for you this evening. They're too important to miss out on just because the house is new or government financing isn't available.

Roll Your Own Boilerplate

Professionals use it to help them do a better job in less time. What is a boilerplate? It's written material that can be used over and over. Attorneys put boilerplate paragraphs in wills, agreements, and court documents; doctors hand boilerplate diets and instructions to patients; architects write specifications in boilerplate format today so they won't have to work up the same specifications tomorrow for a similar job.

Nearer to what you're doing, the top people in commercial leasing and industrial site location use boilerplates to give their clients a large amount of information about a community's climate, population, facilities, and resources.

You must do the same. Gather information about your service area. Then write a story that highlights the local parks, schools, shopping, bus service, church locations, freeway or turnpike access, weather, cultural and economic opportunities, and any other features that contribute to the good life there.

The usefulness of boilerplates to inform possible buyers about your service area is obvious; its usefulness with sellers isn't. Let me explain how it will help you take listings.

People usually believe that they bought in a good part of town. If they try to go by-owner, they'll push the area hard to out-of-town prospects. Sellers know that buyers have to buy the area or it's no sale on the house, so they want to know that you'll promote the neighborhood enthusiastically and effectively. That's why you have the boilerplate in your listing presentation manual—it lets you quickly convince the sellers that you're an outstanding expert on, and booster of, the community they're leaving and you're staying in.

Put your boilerplate together in sections; each section covers only one subject. Let's say you start with religious organizations. Your local paper runs a special page on religious services every weekend; you can type up a complete list of the locations of the various houses of worship from that page, and have your first section done in a few minutes. Its heading could be Local Religious Groups.

At the bottom of every page of the boilerplate, type this line: "Compiled by _____." Keep the boilerplate originals in a folder and run copies as you need them.

A moment's thought will tell you where to get information on each category. Visit the city or county recreation department and get copies of their handouts and parks and recreational activities. You'll probably be able to make up a beautiful piece of boilerplate just by cutting out and pasting up the printed material that's available free from the school superintendent's office, the chamber of commerce, and the city hall.

Write your boilerplate about all the benefits and amenities of the area that you'll tell buyers about, and then make a list of the disadvantages, the detriments, the challenges that the neighborhood has. The sellers may be leaving, but you're staying—and you want to make clients of the buyers, not enemies. You want them to know the disadvantages before they make their decision. And some of those disadvantages may need to be reflected in the market value of the property. Let's list a few of the possible disadvantages:

1. Known flood or earthquake danger
2. Built on landfill, with danger of settling
3. Located on, or behind, a busy street
4. Tributary streets leading to the main highway are badly congested during rush hours
5. Industrial or aircraft noise
6. Downwind from the garbage dump, hog farm, pulp mill, or nuclear generating plant
7. No sewers
8. The elementary school is located on the other side of a major highway.

There are many other possibilities, and not every disadvantage is important to every buyer. Here's a good test. Does the seller want to conceal a particular disadvantage? If so, the buyer must be told about that disadvantage. How important the disadvantage is to a given buyer is for that buyer to decide. It's your obligation to represent the seller to the fullest extent possible without injuring the buyer. In other words, as a real estate professional who is or soon will be a champion, you're building a career based on honesty, service, and knowledge. You can't do that without being fair to buyers.

Many sellers fail to grasp what a dangerous position they put themselves in if they conceal challenges from the buyer. The next-to-worst thing that can happen occurs when the buyer discovers the concealed problem just before settlement and backs out at the last minute. The worst hits later, when a problem discovered after the closing winds up in court, and both the agent and seller have to pay damages. Think before concealing. Honesty is the best policy because it charges the lowest premiums.

Tell the buyers of any disadvantage or challenge that isn't obvious. They can see for themselves that there are no sidewalks, but they may never suspect that the basement floods until the rains come.

Listing in Two Steps

A professional lister always tries to do it in two steps. Many champions have told me that they get the listing 30 percent of the time using one step, and their average goes up to 70 percent when they do both steps. These figures parallel my own listing experience.

Step 1 is an afternoon appointment with one of the home owners. Step 2 is the actual listing presentation to both the husband and wife that usually takes place in the evening. I talked earlier about meeting with the wife in the afternoon, but sometimes it's the husband who's at home during the day while the wife is out pursuing her career.

Since half a couple isn't likely to list without the other spouse's approval, why do I want to see one of them in the home during the day?

To learn how to take the listing.

Let's pick up the phraseology after you've made the evening appointment. This all occurs during your morning phone conversation with Gloria Watt.

"Mrs. Watt, I'd like to stop by for a few minutes this afternoon if that's at all possible. You see, it'll help me do a better job this evening when Mr. Watt is there if I can see the home first. I have a considerable amount of research to do before this evening, and the more I know about your home, the more accurate and valuable my research will be to you and your husband. Would one o'clock this afternoon be convenient, or should I make it around two?"

When you go over to the Watts' home at two this afternoon, be professional. Go through all the fundamental steps just as you've done every other time you've knocked on a door. And be on time. You're there not only to learn how to take the listing, you're also there to demonstrate expertise and reliability so that you'll have his wife on your side tonight. Being late won't help.

As you walk through the door (notice that I'm suggesting you address her by surname at this point), use this phraseology:

"Mrs. Watt, it would be a great help to me, and enable me to do a more professional job this evening, if you'd be kind enough to show me all the things you've enjoyed in your home."

You have your legal pad with you, of course. And you'll make lots of notes. These notes are invaluable. Sometimes I knew exactly how to work with a couple before I was halfway through Step 1, but more often it wasn't until I'd taken my notes back to the office and worked over them that it dawned on me how to best handle the upcoming listing appointment.

The next three techniques will be a tremendous help in getting set for that appointment.

1. TAKING THE MEASUREMENTS.

Walking through the home in the afternoon with Gloria Watt, you have a hundred-foot cloth measuring tape inside your legal binder. You say, "Mrs. Watt, the paneling gives this room a very cozy feeling. It looks like it was professionally done—or did you do that yourselves?"

"We had a contractor put it in."

"Very nice."

Have you noticed that I ask about the paneling in every mythical house we visit? I do that for good reasons. The question is designed to let you compliment their taste without sounding insincere. Also, since it's an alternate of choice, the question is an effective way to get her talking on safe subjects. You can use a similar question about a skylight, the french doors, whatever. Look for an off-sized room, a family room or a den, that the home owner probably doesn't know the dimensions of. "Oh, this is a nice large room, Mrs. Watt. Do you know its exact size?"

"I'm not sure."

Look at the room as if you're gauging its size, and pull out the end of the tape. Then warmly smile and say, "I'd like to check. Would you help me measure it, please?"

"Oh. I'm not sure we're going to sell." She's beginning to realize that you're taking her call seriously—that you're a professional who means business.

"I understand that, Mrs. Watt. Your husband would want a professional job this evening wouldn't he?"

"Yes."

"I don't mind the extra effort. May we?"

She can't say no when you're so nice and when you want to work harder to serve them better. So you measure the room and note down the dimensions. Then start rolling the tape up and say:

"Mrs. Watt, the longer I'm in real estate, the more I find that people really demand accuracy from the professionals who represent them. This is why I measure everything to the inch, because, I'm sure you'll agree, accuracy today is important, isn't it?"

"Yes, it is." What else can she say? What you do now depends on how she reacts to measuring the first room. If she isn't comfortable helping you do it, stop after the first room. But if she's going along with you, measure every room in the house.

2. WARMING YOUR LISTING CHANCES AT THE WATER HEATER.

You don't have to know anything about plumbing to use this powerful technique. All you need to learn is the phraseology and two words, galvanic corrosion. A number of processes go under that name but we're interested only in one: the corrosion that takes place when two different metals are in contact around the hot water heater.

The most common situation involves copper pipes connected to a galvanized steel water heater. Unless the two metals are insulated from each other, an amazing thing takes place: a type of electricity literally rots the galvanized steel out. That's a quick and simple definition of galvanic corrosion.

Maybe you're not interested in plumbing school. But you are interested in becoming a strong lister. Let me show you how to put this little bit of knowledge to work. At an opportune moment, use this phraseology:

"Mrs. Watt, would you mind showing me your water heater?"

"The hot water heater?" The odds are good that she's hardly given it a thought since they moved in.

"Yes. I'd like to check three things: the gallonage, the recovery rate, and the condition of the pipes. Would you mind?"

"No." Usually she's puzzled by this move of yours. Gloria Watt doesn't know whether she should be annoyed or impressed, but she's beginning to suspect that you're a very thorough and knowledgeable pro.

You walk down the hall with her and she shows you where the water heater is. I used to get down so I could check the gallonage and recovery rate on the label, and check for corrosion. I'd make my notes and then look carefully at the pipes. While I was doing that, the home owner would be watching closely. Then (unless I'd discovered a water heater that was about to blow) I'd say, "Well, it looks fine. What I was really checking for is a thing we in the industry call galvanic corrosion."

Did you notice that I slid one other little item into my water heater technique? I mentioned recovery rate. Lots of people might expect a real estate expert to know the gallonage of a water heater just by looking at it. But you can't tell the recovery capacity without looking at the label. What is recovery capacity? Let's compare two 50-gallon water heaters. The recovery capacity for Brand A is 20 gallons an hour, and for Brand B it's 40 gallons an hour. This means that Brand B heats water twice as fast as Brand A does, which can be very important to a family that uses lots of hot water in a short period of time.

3. COOLING YOUR LISTING CHALLENGE WITH THEIR AIR CONDITIONER.

Again, we demonstrate knowledge through a practiced technique. For this one, ask the tonnage of their air conditioning unit, convert that into British thermal units, and give it back to them. It's really very simple. Here's how I do it. As I walk down the hall with the wife on the afternoon scouting trip, I notice on the thermostat whether they have air conditioning. The Watts do. So I say, "Mrs. Watt, I notice that you have refrigerated air conditioning. Do you know the tonnage of the unit?"

Of course, if it's nice and cool inside and 105 degrees outside, that's another clue. In that case you'd say something like, "It's delightful to come into this cool air on a day like this. You must have the right-sized unit. Do you know its tonnage?"

"Three tons."

"Oh, then you have 36,000 British thermal units. That should be more than sufficient, based on the square footage. Excellent."

There are 12,000 British thermal units per ton. A pro never talks in terms of tonnage—it's British thermal units, or BTUs, all the way. Many people have heard of BTUs, but they don't know what they are.

A British thermal unit is equal to 1 degree of Fahrenheit in 1 pound of water. Let's say you have 1 pound of water boiling at 212 degrees. Take away 180 BTUs from that pound of water and you'll have a pound of soft ice. Pump another 32 BTUs out. That pound of ice now is solidly frozen at zero degrees Fahrenheit. Put 105 British thermal units back in the pound of ice and you'll have a pound of water ready for your hot tub. Simple, isn't it? Each ton of air conditioning represents the capacity to remove 12,000 British thermal units of heat in an hour. When they mention tons, give them British thermal units.

All these little things are important. You may be wondering if you can make them work for you. You can. Make yourself practice them. When you've done one once with a seller, that technique is yours from then on. It becomes a permanent part of your performance.

The Main Reason You're There

The main reason for your step one meeting during the day is to find the answer to this question: How can I list these people?

You'll get the answer to that question if you'll ask the right leading questions in an unthreatening way. This means that your manner and tone are casual as you do so. And you put a lot of spacer material between the leading questions, meaning that you don't keep pounding in to get the vital information zap, zap, zap. Instead, you talk on safe subjects for a while, slip in a leading question, and go back to talking easy stuff for another few minutes. Then, as though it just occurred to you, ask another leading question.

As you go through the house with her, keep looking for things to compliment, for things to talk about, for things you have in common. Be sure that you don't give away that you're using technique. She can't know that you're there to ask specific questions; she can't know that you even know what you're going to ask her. If you're new, until you've memorized this material and used it repeatedly with sellers, write these questions where you can hide them in your legal pad. Then you can check what questions you should ask when she's not looking. Here are the leading questions:

1. PAST SELLING EXPERIENCE.

If they've sold seventeen homes themselves in the past ten years, it's a fair bet that they aren't listing with anyone now. So you casually ask, "Have you folks sold another home before?"

2. PAST CHALLENGES.

This one can put the listing right in your hand. If I know what challenges they've had with real estate sales and agents in the past, I can figure out how to show them in my performance this evening that they won't face those same issues with me. So, after you've discussed the previous sales they've made, you ask: "Did you have any difficulties?" You'd probably add, ". . . with the house you sold in Minneapolis?" or ". . . with any of the three homes you sold before you moved here?"

3. NEED TO SELL.

When you're taking a listing, the most powerful tool in the world is to know why they need to sell. And by that I mean knowing the real reason, not what you might guess. Here's how you ask this question, and notice how well it'll fit in after you've complimented something they've done to the house: "You've done a nice job on the home. After all this work, why would you ever consider moving?"

By setting this question up right and then asking it sympathetically, I usually got the results I wanted: The owner usually told me the real reason they were selling. Had I come right out with a blunt, "Why are you selling your place?" she might not tell me the whole story.

4. THEIR VALUE.

What are they thinking about price? I want to know before I go in for the big showdown tonight. Don't rush into this one. You'll often find that the normal flow of conversation will give you a beautiful opening for it. But don't wait until she's starting to fidget either, because it's one of the most important questions you're there to find the answer to. You should ask it in these exact words:

"To do a better job this evening, Mrs. Watt, do you have an approximate idea of what you would like from the home?" Practice saying this with the attitude that whatever she says has no bearing on your chances of getting an at-market listing tonight. You must keep a poker face here. Let's say you know the home is worth about $275,000, and she looks you right in the eye and says, "We want $290,000." If you choke up or break out laughing, you're finished. Show no emotion no matter what she says about price.

5. HER LIKES.

Ask her the things she likes about the home. As she warms up to you, ask for permission to use her first name and ask her to call you by yours. I used to say, "Gloria, pretend that I'm a buyer. What are the things you like most about this house that you think I'll like best, too?" Many of the things she'll mention will be features her husband likes also. By finding them out, you can make sure that you let the husband know you appreciate those things this evening.

6. LOAN INFORMATION.

If she's been nice and warm and helpful, go with this question; if she hasn't been, pass it up because you can hurt yourself with it.

Ask for their loan or mortgage information. "I'd like to try to ascertain information about your loan for this evening. Now, it would help me do that if I could get the mortgage number. Most people have all the papers to the house in one box or file. Do you have a place like that?"

If she says, "Oh, no, all the papers are in a safe deposit box at the bank," tell her, "I'll try my best without them." But she may say, "Oh yes, we have a file with all the papers in it; I'll go get it."

Now the odds are good that she won't let you have those papers. But if she doesn't give you the papers, what'll she let you have? The information from those papers.

7. TONIGHT'S TABLE.

Early in my career I discovered that it's very difficult to take a listing while you're all sitting in easy chairs in their living room. The mood is all wrong. When you speak some truth that doesn't delight the husband, he'll exchange looks with the wife. She doesn't know what the look means except that it's not a yes-let's-go-ahead-tonight kind of look. They can give signals while you're writing, and before you know it, you've lost them. If that happens, suddenly they have to sleep on it; they have to think about it; they have to talk to their real estate adviser friend.

You want them sitting across from you at the table—either the kitchen or the dining room table. The kitchen table is best because it's usually cozier and more intimate. If you're not controlling them, they'll try to control you. So set it up with the wife to have your meeting at the kitchen table if possible, at the dining room table if not. Toward the end of your Step 1 interview in the afternoon, do this by saying,

"Gloria, tonight I'll be presenting the results of my research to you and your husband. I don't know what conclusion it will point to yet, but I'm confident both of you will want to give it careful consideration. To help you do that, and to keep us all from shuffling papers around, I'd like to ask for your help on one small but very important thing."

"What's that?"

"Could we meet at the kitchen table instead of in the living room? I know it doesn't sound like it's worth mentioning, but if I'm moving back and forth with papers, I can't do a professional job for you and your husband."

She'll rarely turn you down when you sincerely ask for her help with those words.

"Okay, sure," Gloria says.

Rope it down tight with, "I'd really appreciate you having the table ready for our meeting with Jack, Gloria."

As you're leaving, confirm the time of your appointment this evening. Unless you remind her, she may forget. Here's how I'd make it seem very real. When I was ready to leave, I'd look at my watch and say, "Well, it's after three already, which means I have less than five hours to finish my research and get back here for our eight o'clock appointment this evening. Thank you so much, Gloria. I'll see you and Jack at eight o'clock sharp. Good-bye."

Preparation Back at the Office

Please, before you do anything else, get ready for your evening appointment. This is particularly important when you're new in the business or new to using champion techniques. Don't get sidetracked by any of the other things you could be doing, run out of time, and have to rush this final and most important phase of your listing-taking routine. It helps enormously to work to a plan. Mine follows:

START UP YOUR PSYCHE

The first move on this vital process is to set up an assumptive listing folder. You're not going there tonight to chitchat, you're going there to take the listing. So start your psyching up process as soon as you get back to the office. Write their name and address on the assumptive listing folder. You've done your field and office research on comparables; now you're in the final stages of taking the listing. So you start assuming that you're going to take the listing because that puts positive forces to work in your mind. I'm not saying you should tell yourself, "It's in the bag. I'm going to walk in there tonight and sign 'em up in a hurry. No sweat." What I'm urging you to dwell on is almost the opposite:

"By the time I get there tonight, I'll be the best prepared agent in the world to handle their listing. They're going to give it to me because I'll eliminate every doubt that the wisest thing they can do is to let me serve them. I've paid the price to own this one. I'm going to go in there tonight and give my greatest performance ever."

Here's what should be in the assumptive listing folder you'll carry with you tonight:

1. A listing form. Please, try never to go out on a listing presentation without the form. I've done it. I've been busy and have forgotten to take a listing form with me. Suddenly I'm at the point where I want to start writing on the form and I don't have one. Put one listing form in the assumptive listing folder. And put a dozen extras in the trunk of your car, sealed in an envelope so they'll stay clean just in case you need another copy.
2. A comparable analysis form.

3. A sellers' proceeds form.
4. A picture of their home. Take one when you're there on your afternoon appointment or drive-by.

DEVELOP YOUR DATA

At this point you have a lot of rough notes and maybe some ideas about how to work with these people. Now study the data and develop your plan for taking that specific listing. Start with the listing form. Fill in the following information:

1. Lot size. You can get this from the title company or, in many areas, online at your local county records office.
2. Legal description. Do you realize that most of them don't know that their home is Lot 76 of Tract 9876 of the Happy Homes Subdivision? Show them that you know.
3. Taxes. Few people know what their annual property tax is. In many areas it's included in their monthly investment and they've lost track of the amount. If you call the tax assessor's office with the parcel number and legal description, they'll give you the annual taxes. Put that information on the form. It's impressive.
4. Room sizes. If she wouldn't let you measure, don't guess. Never guess at any fact in real estate or you'll learn the hard way that guessing will cost you big money. Let no listing go in the book unless the taxes, legal description, loan balance, room sizes, and all the other factual information is accurate.
5. Write a description of the home. Do you know that the remarks are one of the most critical parts of the listing? If you enjoyed good rapport with the wife in the Step 1 meeting, you'll usually be able to write a set of remarks that'll help you get the listing. Keep in mind what's important to them. And don't write three hundred words when there's only room in the book for fifty. When I wasn't sure about what remarks they'd want, I wrote a trial version on a separate piece of paper.

SIT BACK AND THINK

Most agents don't do this, and it's one of the most important phases of preparing for a successful listing presentation. The more listings you take, the quicker you'll see the way to go when you sit back and think. But even when I reached the eighteen listings a month stage, I found that I still needed to take a few minutes to quietly reflect and review the information I'd obtained. It always helped me to do it systematically, step by step.

1. How long in the property? Have they lived there five years, or only six months? In the first case, they've probably built up a considerable equity. In the second case, their net proceeds from an at-the-market sale may give them less cash than they put into the home.

2. What did they pay? Get this information from your county records office if it's not available through your office.

3. Think about their employment or income situation. If the husband is the family's only breadwinner, what's happening with his job? Does the wife have a business career? Review what you've learned, and you'll understand more about what emotions are dictating the logic of their decisions. Then you'll know more about how to influence those decisions, won't you?

4. Why are they selling? A pro always wants to know why they're selling. Have they been transferred? Has he lost his job? Are they planning to finance a business venture with their home equity?

5. The urgency. Probably no other factor is more important to know than this one. What is the real urgency behind the sale? Are they about to lose the home through foreclosure, or are they eager to move on to the new job he or she has been promoted to? Maybe they'll never tell you the real reason, and you'll never know it unless you figure it out for yourself. Reflect on everything you've learned and been told. Does it all fit together?

6. Will I enjoy working with these people? Granted, maybe you've only met one of them, but you can get a good feel as to the kind of people they are from that. I had a philosophy. If she gave me a lot of hassle, I'd still give my entire performance that evening, but I wouldn't be upset if I didn't get it. Maybe they just weren't my kind of people. It happens.

ARRIVE AT VALUE

This is another thing that most agents don't do. My job now is to establish the actual price that this home is worth in today's market. Here's how we do it:

1. How well do the comparables really compare? How close in value are the homes on your list of comparables? Are they in the same neighborhood so that all the off-site factors are the same? Are they similar in age, condition, size, construction, number of bedrooms, amenities, and landscaping?

Did Mrs. Watt let you know that she doesn't care for Mrs. Mildue? Then if you come in tonight and tell her that the Mildue home is just like hers, you've created a problem for yourself, haven't you?

2. Is the home sharp, average, or poor? Because of the emotional appeal of a beautifully maintained home, you can increase the value if it's sharp. If the home is in average condition, you have to bring it in at close to market value or it won't sell. If the home has been poorly maintained, you must work the price down below the normal market value before it'll excite a buyer.

3. In today's market, given all the comparable properties that are available, the number of buyers coming in, the financing situation on that particular property, what must be done to make the property sell? Maybe they have to change their crimson and blue color scheme. Maybe the house is too packed with furniture.

What can you do to interest other agents in the area in showing this property to their buyers? Unless you ask yourself these questions and find good answers to them, I don't know why they should list with you.

4. How do I tell the sellers? Think about and rehearse how you'll tell them the things you'll have to get across if you're going to take an at-market listing. Very few home owners are planning to sell a beautiful property for less than market price; most are planning to sell a less-than-beautiful property for far more than market value. The crux of your job is to inject reality into their thinking. Doing that effectively takes planning.

Don't attack the people, attack the problem. Think about the best way to motivate them to do what has to be done to increase the emotional appeal their house will have to a buyer. Then practice saying that in the best way.

By the way, I'd let someone else have the pleasure of listing families like the one I've called Smedley in this chapter. As a champion, you can afford to avoid the aggravation.

5. If the property is overimproved, depreciate the improvements.

The appraiser for the lender will depreciate overimprovements in arriving at value. Before you go in, list the appraisal value of the overimprovements in this manner:

**Estimated Cost of Estimated Lender's
Overimprovements Appraisal Value**

Swimming Pool	$20,000	$8,000
Patio	$ 4,000	$1,000
Carpet $20 per yard, 1800 sq. ft. $5 per yard 200 yards	$4,000	$1,000

When you present the facts in this manner, it isn't you who's quoting bad news, it's the professional appraiser.

6. What is the demand? There are some areas where every broker in the city is panting for listings. If you have an opportunity to give your performance for such a listing, you might have to compete with a bidding situation to begin with, but there's a top market value in that area too. Get it at market value if at all possible because you and your office need that inventory.

What if the property is in an area where the demand is average, low, or even nonexistent? Don't let some other agent, one who hasn't done his homework, pull you into a bidding competition in such areas. What you never need is an overpriced turkey where there's little or no demand.

7. Set your maximum price. Setting a maximum price that you'll take a listing at before you go in for the appointment is one of the greatest tools I know of. First, if you'll stick to your top price through thick or thin, and if you know you will, that knowledge makes you work harder to get the listing at your maximum price or less. Second, it will eliminate the enormous loss of time, money, energy, and enthusiasm that every overpriced turkey you list costs you.

8. Prepare and rehearse your final game plan. As you go over all the data you've collected, plan your listing presentation in detail. You know what points are important. Plan how you'll emphasize those points. Plan how you'll give them the facts they have to understand before they can arrive at an intelligent decision. Work out exactly what you need to say, and rehearse how you'll say it. When you've done that, there's only

one more item in your afternoon preparation for an effective listing performance that evening.

9. Schedule your final psyche-up time. This is one of the greatest moneymaking edges that the big winner has. If you read the sports pages at all, what theme is repeated over and over? The loser wasn't mentally prepared. It's the same in the real estate business. But psyche-up doesn't happen automatically. You have to make time and solitude for it. Psyche-up has to have a regular place in your schedule. It must be an honored part of your I'm-going-to-take-a-listing ritual.

The Final Psyche-Up

You'll be a little bit psyched up because of all the research, preparation, and review that you've done, but don't steam yourself up hours before the appointment or you'll be emotionally worn out by the time you get there. Hold off on the psyche-up until just before you get in your car to go over to see them.

It goes best if you have a routine for psyching up. After you've done it a few dozen times, you'll perfect your own system and be able to use it for anything on short notice. Let me suggest a program for every listing appointment psyche-up.

1. Run quickly through all the papers you've written preparing for this listing. Tell yourself that nobody else has done that much, that you deserve the listing. Double-check any math that you have done.

2. Stare at the top-price commitment you've made to yourself for listing that property. Repeat how much they need to sell and how they won't be able to sell unless they list with you at the market price.

3. Close your eyes. Then picture yourself taking the listing. Look through your own eyes as you do so. See the clients as you say and do what must be said and done before you'll get the listing. And feel your pleasure at writing another listing at market value.

4. Write down the reasons why they will list with you. Write the reasons out every time.

> Gloria and Jack Watt will list with me because I know more about their property than any other agent in the world.

Gloria and Jack will list with me because I specialize in their area.

Gloria and Jack will list with me because I'm honest and ethical.

Gloria and Jack will list with me because my company gives great service. Spell out the reasons why your company gives exceptional benefits to its clients.

Gloria and Jack will list with me because I'm the hardest working agent in town.

If you can't come up with at least a dozen reasons why Gloria and Jack should list with you, maybe they shouldn't. Any great salesperson will tell you that it's a hundred times easier to sell something you believe in, and if you don't believe in yourself, how can you sell yourself? That's what listing is: selling yourself, your knowledge, and your skills. Make sure you have something worthwhile to sell.

5. Use body language in your psyche-up. Maybe you want to sit at a desk and silently psyche up. Maybe you'll do it better walking around waving your arms and shouting. Do whatever works for you, but get the adrenaline pounding.

6. Write out a series of psyche-up slogans that you go over and over before every listing appointment.

I will take their listing at market value.

I will have my sign in their yard.

I will get a key to their property.

I WILL WIN! WHY? Because I have faith, courage, and enthusiasm.

Now, get out there and make that listing presentation!

CHAPTER 18

The Mood of the Move

Many times we do things without really knowing why or how we're doing them. It's not enough simply to cope with your own emotions—mostly fear in the beginning. To be successful in real estate, you must also have a practical understanding of the emotions churning through your clients.

Let's look at the makeup of a strong listing presentation from an emotional standpoint. We've analyzed the area, we've seen all the comparables, and we've gathered other data. Now we're in the process of preparing our performance. From here on out, we're getting ready to put the spotlight on ourselves. Our purpose is to perform so well that the sellers will want to trust us with the marketing of their largest and most emotional asset, their home.

Having empathy for your clients and knowing their situation is crucial. We have to become skillful at synchronizing our moves with a wide variety of client emotions. How well we do this has a powerful effect on our incomes as salespeople. In fact, I can't think of anything that will have more to do with how much you make than your ability to feel empathy toward your clients. Without this ability, your knowledge of inventory and technique won't be more than 50 percent effective.

True, there'll be days when it seems that there's no empathy left in your being. You'll feel that somebody—anybody—has to pour about a ton of empathy on your head before you can give even one more ounce of sympathetic understanding to another client. We're human too; our wells of empathy can run dry just like anyone else's.

But if we're going to be champion listers, we have to organize our feelings. We have to discipline our emotions. We have to increase our inner strength. We have to do all these things until we have an ample supply of empathy every day for the people we're working with professionally. That's our job.

We often work with people who are suffering severe pain from the major upheavals that are taking place in their lives. Always keep this firmly in mind: What we do in real estate symbolizes what is happening in our clients' lives. We are the people who pull the levers that move them in and move them out.

Selling a cherished home; facing the personal turmoil of moving to a new area; worrying about making far greater financial decisions than they as home owners are accustomed to; coping with whatever situation—sometimes a family tragedy—that has forced their home on the market; all these are intense forms of change that are painful to bear.

What does the average salesperson who's struggling to survive in this business have for those people? A vacant smile and a breezy, what's-in-it-for-me manner that pounds home his ignorance of, and indifference to, their emotional pain. Champions know more about techniques and real estate, but that's not the only reason they list more. They care more about the people.

Start asking yourself, "How do I feel about how they feel?" If your attitude is, "I couldn't care less," don't be surprised if they couldn't care less about listing with you. Most people know when you can't stop thinking about yourself long enough to feel for them. There probably aren't two clients in a hundred who'll admit it, but one of the main reasons people pay real estate fees is to get attention and sympathy while a matter that's of great importance to them is being resolved.

With many people, you'll never hear anything about emotion. But if you could dig deeply into their eventual decision, you'd see some familiar stories behind this move, and realize that the decisions they made were dictated by emotion too. You'd discover that people secure enough to let their pain show aren't the only ones who hurt.

What I'm concerned about is that maybe you're only listing the homes of people you relate to easily and without thinking. If that's the case, you have a challenge: You'll work at listing all kinds of people, but you've cut yourself off from listing many, and probably most, of them by not being emotionally in tune with their needs. To be a strong lister, you have to relate to many kinds of people. The way you relate to people is to consciously imagine yourself in their circumstances. As with all skills, the more often you do this, the better you'll be at it.

If I were talking to a wife and husband who are being transferred again, I'd be more concerned with relating to her than him. He's excited; he has his promotion; his ego has just received a big boost. And this is happening to a man who's ambitious, successful, and engrossed in his work. It's his life. In this family, the wife is concerned about her career as well, but more concerned with the children and their needs. So, when you talk to this couple, you can't be overly excited about the husband's promotion or you'll turn the wife off by being insensitive to other factors involved.

Now let's look at another listing situation that a change in the husband's job creates. Here's a man who, instead of getting the promotion he's worked for and thinks he's earned, is making a lateral move. Maybe he's being moved because the company needs him somewhere that he doesn't think will further his career. As he sits in their living room waiting for you to come over, he's mad at his company. But he's also mad at himself for failing to get a better promotion, and for not having the confidence to quit. So he's going to move again, and there's no joy in it for him.

When you walk in there, you're part of the company he's mad at because you're the vehicle that's going to move him. And he's especially afraid of making a mistake in listing his house because of his insecure position at this point. When people are excited and happy about the move, they'll be more in line with your research on market value than people who are unhappy about the move.

When your clients are looking forward to a bright future, they're more willing to cut their roots with the past. But if they don't want to leave, and it's a fearful move toward an uncertain future, they want more security when they sell the home. What does that mean? They'll want more money. In this situation, you may have to take the property higher than market to begin with.

You will frequently run into cases where it's a change in the woman's career that puts the couple's house on the market. When you walk into a home you want to list, quit thinking about yourself. Start asking questions so you can understand why they are doing what they're doing. There's a reason for the move. Until you know that reason, you can't start feeling their feelings and relating to them properly in order to serve their needs.

Let's talk about taking the listing where the reason for moving isn't exciting and up, or even horizontal. It's definitely down and discouraging. Although these situations are touchy to work with, they're more likely to give you the opportunity to render great service to someone who really needs it. The focus of this book is on making money in this business, but do you know something that's very important? You'll make more if you believe very strongly in yourself and in what you're doing. Though you won't get much praise in public for helping people through these troubled situations, in the place that counts—the privacy of your own mind—you'll know. Few things will help you get through the tough spots more than being genuinely and quietly proud of the service you render your fellow human beings.

In very few divorce situations can the listing be taken and held until the sale of the property closes unless the agent exercises great tact and understanding. Don't take sides. This is crucial. The husband is quick to resent another woman; the wife is quick to resent another man. You have to play it very professionally with both of them. Keep it constantly in mind that if either person suspects you of making moral judgements about their marital affairs, you're not going to be their agent. You're working now with highly emotional people; the great pain they're feeling makes them turn to anger, resentment, and noncooperation at the slightest hint of provocation.

Imagine a couple who have been married fifteen years. Suddenly the husband, who is now forty, started to grow in new areas of his life. From the beginning of their marriage, he had been the dominant figure and, though his wife also worked outside the home, she earned less. He's getting promoted to such an extent that they can live a different lifestyle. She's not ready for the change. She's happy where they are. They both gave the marriage all those good years, but now he's changed a lot and she hasn't. He wants out. She doesn't want to stay in the house with all those memories. Sound familiar? It probably does, unfortunately.

When you go into that kind of emotionally supercharged situation, you're as much an undertaker as you are a real estate agent. You're working with grief—a marriage has died. You're there to help bury it. As quickly as possible, the husband wants to get rid of this hurt he knows he's putting his wife through. The wife, on the other hand, is afraid to list the property because she subconsciously knows that the moment the sign goes up, her feelings of insecurity are going off the chart. She's losing her husband, her home, her roots, maybe even her occupation. When the sign goes up, she'll have to face up to making her own way in the world and with a lifestyle changing in the opposite direction to that of her soon-to-be ex-husband. But we're not there as marriage counselors; we can't reengineer society. All we can do to help is to get them the most money for their home in the shortest possible time. To earn that chance, you must handle both those people so very carefully.

If you're a man, you must also just sit there and think, "How would I feel if this was happening to me? How would I feel, after fifteen years of memories, and of having the security of this marriage, if I suddenly learned that I'm going to be on my own? What am I going to do?"

If you're a woman, your challenge might be to make sure you don't display so much empathy for the wife that the husband decides you're adding to his already heavy load of guilt. If he comes to that decision, they won't list with you because they both have to approve the listing agreement.

Build a performance that relates to their needs.

How would you handle this listing situation: The family is selling because someone in it has passed away.

Or this: The husband is a successful entrepreneur who's been in business for himself all his adult life; he's a good family man with a solid image in the community. For years, his favorite recreation has been golf at the country club. He thought he was in fairly good health. Then, in one minute, the doctor tells him it's all over for him in that town. A lung problem. He has to move to a drier climate.

His motivation to move is health, but he's saying to himself, "I've never been knocked down. I won't be now. If we don't get the money I want, I don't care. I'll stay. We sacrificed for twenty years to get my business on a firm footing, and now, after ten years in this house I expected to live out my life in, well, I'm just not giving it away."

Look at his wife. She loves him. And because it might mean three or five more years together, she wants to get the move over with.

If you go in there and run a standard routine off on them without connecting your emotional level to theirs, you're not going to reach them, and you're not going to list them. First, you must gain their attention; second, you must gain their liking and trust; only then do you have the opportunity to gain their business. Think about financial crisis, another common reason for moving. Have you ever known people who were about to have their home repossessed? It's a terribly painful position to be in, and you will have to be exceptionally considerate and aware of how these people feel about their difficult circumstances.

As a real estate professional, you have more than a job; you have an absolute obligation to do everything in your power to feel like your clients feel.

CHAPTER 19

Creating a High-Scoring Listing Presentation

We've done all the preparation and all the grunt work. Now it's time to put it all together. It's time to go over there and take the listing.

But beware. Just because you've impressed the lady of the house doesn't mean you're going to have an easy time with her husband. She's told him that you're hot stuff.

"He measured the whole house, and he even inspected the water heater. He told me we've got 36,000 BTUs and not one bit of galvanic corrosion. Honey, I think he's our man."

Is that good or bad? At first, it's bad. The husband doesn't want you there for your reason; he wants you there for his reason—to check prices and get all the information he can from you to help him sell it himself. So the more his wife brags about how great the agent she found is, the more he's thinking, "Maybe she's sold, but I'm not. I'll show this agent what's what in a hurry."

Then you drive up. He looks out of the window as you walk up to their door. You're radiating enthusiasm, confidence, and energy. What does the husband see? A fee of several thousand dollars strolling up his driveway.

Your first goal is to prove you're worth it.

What is he feeling? Fear. He's afraid of losing money. He's afraid of being lied to, taken advantage of, made to feel stupid. He's afraid you'll tie up the home and then do nothing. He's afraid of committing himself, of giving up his options, of putting his family's destiny in a stranger's hands.

How to Take Control

The process is quite simple. You work to a plan that keeps you one jump ahead of your sellers throughout the evening, a plan that allows you to guide the entire meeting from one reasonable step to another until you take the listing. They'll fight you. But after you've practiced, drilled, and rehearsed your plan based on this book's principles and phraseology, you'll be working your plan so smoothly and nicely that they'll never think of fighting you. Here's how to raise the curtain on Act One of a successful listing play:

1. Be a pro all the way. Dress professionally. Go through Chapter 15's fundamental steps at their door, and introduce yourself with warmth and enthusiasm when you meet the husband. Another professional touch is to hand your card to the husband when you enter the home.

2. Refer to the wife formally in the beginning. Start off calling her Mrs. Watt, not Gloria. Do this even if you were on a first name basis with her that afternoon. Let the husband know you respect the fact that you're in his castle; show him plenty of deference so he won't feel obliged to defend his authority and position. Whether you're a woman or a man, this is vital. A husband can think two women are ganging up on him and resent that as much as he'd resent a strange man's familiar manner toward his wife.

3. Boost his ego. It's crucial at this point to make him feel that he's the key element in the listing process so he won't fight the idea of working with this person (you) that his wife brought in. Here's what you say to accomplish that:

"I saw the home earlier today with Mrs. Watt. However, to establish the highest possible market value, I think it's important that you show me all the improvements you've made and express your feelings regarding the home."

4. Keep him on his feet. You're in trouble unless you tour the house right now. Why? Because if you let him sit you down, you'll be in the living room, and you'll go straight to talking money. Never sit down

and start negotiating money a few seconds after meeting someone. That's the fast track to failure. Slow the process down. Give yourself time to learn a little bit about him; give him time to get over feeling that you're a stranger.

5. Clinch the best possible negotiating arena. You worked with the wife this afternoon about having your meeting at the kitchen table, but you can lose what you've gained during the first few minutes of your evening appointment. Avoid that by taking the first opportunity to confirm where you'll meet and negotiate. As soon as you're near the kitchen, say this: "May I put my briefcase down?" Then head for the kitchen, set your briefcase on or by the table, grab your note pad, and go on with the tour. When that's over with, you'll all naturally come back to where you want to be—at the kitchen table.

6. Build rapport as you tour the home with the husband. Keep looking for common denominators. Ask friendly questions. Talk about his interests. Discuss his employment—but approach this carefully and with empathy; maybe they're selling because he's out of work. Hopefully, you've learned the reason they're selling from Mrs. Watt earlier in the day so you know what the mood might be this evening.

7. Slant your vocabulary toward him. Top-flight salespeople speak many different levels of language. You can, too. All it takes is a flexible attitude and an open ear. You don't have to use phony accents, but you can talk a little more down home with a carpenter, a bit more uptown with an attorney.

8. Praise their housekeeping, if you sincerely can. If the home is a cluttered mess, avoid the topic until after the listing agreement is approved. Then, give them pointers on how to make the home show well.

9. Stay away from price until it's time. You haven't made your presentation yet. Your carefully researched comparable market analysis is still in your briefcase. So it's disaster city to talk money now. But they'll try. You're walking down the hall with the sellers and the husband says, "You were by today. What do you think we can get for this place?"

"Mr. Watt, I want to make sure I didn't miss anything this afternoon that might affect the value of your home. I'll know in just a moment."

"You're the professional. Can't you just give me some idea?"

If you do, you'll be galloping off on a full-blown price discussion standing there in the hall, out of reach of your CMA. Be nice but firm.

"Mr. Watt, I could pick a figure out of thin air, but I'd rather rely on facts. Please, may we wait until we get to the table?"

"Well, I don't want to waste a lot of time tonight, so how about coming up with a ballpark figure?"

I used to smile and say, "Mr. Watt, I consider myself as professional as any doctor. If you were sick, you wouldn't want your doctor to diagnose what's causing you pain after one quick look, would you?"

The pressure for talking price too soon can get very heavy. If you crack under that pressure, you're gone. Nine times out of ten, the sellers want more than your top figure. Talking price before getting the weight of your research and your presentation behind you is like trying to pour concrete without cement. So, until the tour with the husband is over and you've reached the proper moment in Act Two of the listing play, you must hold off all discussion of price.

Act Two takes place at the kitchen table. This is when successful agents put their visual aid books to work—a technique that's second only to the CMA in listing effectiveness. I'll tell you about it in the next section, but before I do that, let me ask you a question. Since the visual aid book and the comparable market analysis are easily the two most effective listing methods known, why not use both?

Creating Listing Power with a Visual Aid Book

Many companies spend thousands of dollars developing visual aid books because their new salespeople need all the help they can get. Yet when management looks at results, they find that most of the people using the expensive new visual aids aren't beginners. They're veteran agents with long records of superior performance. It's easy to get the top producers to use a fine new visual aid; they know that prospects need more than an agent's face to look at, more than an agent's voice to learn from.

The finest script for Act Two of your listing performance is a visual aid book that you've personalized. If your company supplies one, start with that. If not, develop your own. Either way, a little effort creates a visual aid book you'll soon realize is worth far more than its weight in gold to you.

Build this priceless listing tool in a flip chart or three-ring binder that holds the standard 8 1/2-inch by 11-inch paper. Get a stand-up model. They come in both styles: flip chart with the long edge of the paper on the bottom and binder with the long edge of the paper on the side. Use plastic sheet protectors. The nonglare type is best.

Between the time when you called Gloria Watt this morning and now, as you're sitting down with both of them at their kitchen table, you've been in control, haven't you? They aren't fighting you because you've been so reasonable, professional, and confident, and because you've been so very nice. Without realizing it, the Watts have fallen into the habit of letting you take the lead because you're leading them where they want to go. At the kitchen table you must maintain that control or they'll sleep on it instead of giving you the listing.

The tour with the husband gave you a last chance to confirm or change the conclusions you reached during your afternoon think session. You've asked yourself these three questions:

1. Are they sincere about selling? Whether or not they're realistic about price at this moment, do they feel they have to sell before they can do something else they want to do?

Unless the answer to this question is a firm yes, what you're doing there is practicing your technique and perfecting your performance. That's wonderful—really. Full dress rehearsals are hard to come by, so don't waste one. Give it all you've got. Just don't be disappointed when you walk out without the listing.

2. Have they already decided to use professional help in marketing their home?

It's a serious mistake to see a by-owner hiding inside every seller's shirt. And it's an even more serious mistake to spend any of their short attention span talking sellers out of something they've already decided not to do.

If you believe the answers to the two questions are yes, you can concentrate on the big one:

3. Why should these sellers list with me instead of with some other agent?

Answering that question so convincingly that they'll give you the listing is the sole purpose of the visual aid book. It won't get you the listing at market price. Your professional technique with the comparable market analysis form does that. But first you have to sell them on your expertise, energy, and honesty.

How can you do that without bragging, which so often turns people off? Somehow these three blunt questions must be satisfactorily answered or you won't get many listings:

Who are you?
What have you done?
What will you do for us?

The visual aid book can give the right answers for you in a powerful, graphic way that minimizes the bragging hazard. But if you're new to real estate, the plain truth is simple: You haven't done much yet. Are you wondering how the three blunt questions can be answered honestly without destroying yourself?

Don't worry. Here's a list of fifteen convincing items for your book that you can start gathering on your first day in the business:

1. Certificates you've earned at the professional seminars you've attended. While you wait for your license to come in the mail, go to seminars and learn all you can about how to earn a professional's income with that license. Put all your attendance certificates (or a printed list of the seminars you've gone to) in your visual aid book. Then open every presentation, from the very first one, by pointing to the evidence of your professional training and saying, "A reputation for professionalism is important, isn't it?"

2. A crisp, 8-inch by 10-inch color photograph of your office, with the entire sales force standing in front of it. Suggested phraseology: "I'm proud to be associated with this strong team of professionals because, collectively, our office has over _____ years of experience at serving, with honesty and integrity, the real estate needs of this community. The point I want to make is this: When you employ me as your professional representative, you're also employing all the benefits that only a dedicated and proven local organization can provide. These include instant name recognition, a vast amount of community goodwill, a reputation for professionalism and integrity, and the assurance that we'll be doing business here when you or the buyers want us a week—or ten years—from now."

3. A photo of the president of your company. Early in my career, I put one in my book. I was proud of our company's president and, in bragging about his accomplishments, I built up the whole company and basked in the reflected glory without sounding like I was bragging about myself.

4. Plenty of boilerplate. In the last chapter you learned how to develop this material quickly. Put your name on every page so they'll know you created the boilerplate yourself. If you have the professional tools—and if you use them with confidence and skill—they'll never suspect you're new and inexperienced.

5. Cartoons, graphs, pictures. Be alert for arguments that'll strike with more impact—and cause less backlash—when you show instead of tell. Keep it simple. One idea to a page. If they don't get the message instantly, it's too complicated. One of the most effective pages in my book was a cartoon showing a 9-foot Frankenstein peering down at a tiny woman and her two small children. The three of them clung together as they stared up at the monster with expressions of panic on their faces. Frankenstein had ripped up their by-owner sign and was holding it over them like a club. Under the cartoon I wrote this caption, "Do you really know who'll come into your home?" A cartoon puts ideas like this across better than a thousand words. If cartooning isn't one of your talents, find a picture of Frankenstein and write the caption under it. That's all you really need.

6. Photograph of your office's for-sale sign in front of a home with your name rider on it. Here's what you say: "There's something about the colors and size of our company's sign that sure does the trick. Buyers are always calling to ask us about the properties we have our signs on. A sign that generates lots of calls is a great help, isn't it?"

7. Photo of a happy family shaking your hand under a sold sign on the front lawn of a house. The people can be any family—even your own friends or relatives—because you're not going to say you moved these people. Here's what you do say: "It would be convenient to move as a family, wouldn't it?" Then you flip right along to the next page of your visual aid book.

8. Photo of a moving van. Call up one of the major moving companies, and they'll be happy to send you this picture for your book. The

phraseology is: "Lots of people aren't fortunate enough to sell within their time limits. Don't you agree that double moves are expensive?"

Do you see how the visual aid book is used to start the yeses coming? Keep that yes momentum going right through to the approval of the listing agreement.

9. Typed list of all the transactions your office has had in the past month, year, or three years. Select whatever period gives you an impressive-looking document. All you need for each transaction is the property address, the sale amount, and the sale date.

10. A map of your service area. Don't stretch this out to the furthest limits you'd go to under any circumstances—what you want here is the compact area you're planning to cover thoroughly. Use these words: "As a specialist in this area, I could better serve you, couldn't I?"

11. Map of your listing bank. Leave this page out of your book whenever you go outside your farm to make a listing presentation. But when you're working in it, pass over item 10 and go directly to this map. "As a specialist on these 500 homes, I could serve you better, couldn't I?"

12. A copy of the ad you placed in a local paper when you joined your firm.

13. A color photo of you promoting a listing at your local realty board meeting. To get this photo, show up a little early at your local realty board meeting with a commercial photographer. Dress professionally, of course. Just before the meeting begins, while everyone is still getting seated, jump up on the stage and act like you're pushing a listing hard. Practice your gestures and intense expressions beforehand, and tell the photographer exactly what you want: a dramatic photo of you in action before an audience. Give the photographer a few moments to shoot several pictures so you can choose the best print among several.

Here's what I wrote under my best print: "I will expose your property to the top salespeople in the multiple."

14. Photos of your first transactions. In the foreground, beside your office's sign with your name rider on it, you and the sellers are exchanging big grins and a handshake. At first, when you need all the help you can get, spend a little to get a lot of emotional impact: Have a commercial photographer give you prints that'll fill the page the way your

book is turned. When you have five or six of these large "I-did-it" pictures, you've reached the point of diminishing returns. Switch to small snapshots—a friend can take them for you—and start putting four happily-moved families on a page. When your list of transactions builds, only keep photos of the eight most recent transactions in the binder.

15. Photo of you getting an award for being your office's top lister or top seller of the month. If you've earned one but your office doesn't give awards, buy your own. Any trophy shop can supply a plaque made to your specifications. Then have someone hand it to you while a commercial photographer records the event.

Be careful here to show what's true. Don't go making up any award that you haven't truly earned. If you've learned nothing else from me in this book, I certainly hope you learn that integrity and ethics *must* be at the foundation of your real estate career.

Arrange your book carefully. A professional presentation—one that inspires confidence and makes people want to list with you—moves quickly and smoothly from point to point without backtracking or leaving anything important out. Role-play in front of a mirror with it. Practice, drill, and rehearse your words, gestures, and movements. Keep in mind that your phraseology, and the techniques you use to showcase the book, are as important as its contents.

Four Easy Ways to Polish Your Performance Using the Visual Aid Book

1. Sit across from the husband and wife. Place yourself where you can see both of them at the same time. Avoid any seating arrangement that'll make you swing your head from side to side to look them both in the eyes because that situation robs you of control.

2. Look at the page you're talking about. Their eyes will follow yours. When you look at them they'll look back at you; when you look at the page, they'll look at it too.

3. Hold their interest with variety. Change the pace constantly. After a cartoon or two, show them a graph. Follow the graph with a map, and then turn to a few pages of text (boilerplate) that you flip through

before switching to a photo. Never drone on and on—tell them something, ask a question, and tell them something else.

4. Use tie-downs. In Chapter 9 you'll find lots of examples of tie-downs: "As a specialist in this area, I could better serve you, couldn't I?"

"Don't you agree that double moves are expensive?"

"A reputation for professionalism is important, isn't it?"

As you develop phraseology for your visual aid book, be sure to work in tie-downs so you'll get agreement on the most important points.

After the Tour

Let's continue with our evening meeting. After touring the house with Jack, you're just sitting down at the kitchen table across from them. Here's how to begin your listing presentation:

"Mr. and Mrs. Watt, many people feel that all real estate companies and salespeople are the same. Before making a decision on a company or its representative, I think it's important that you are aware of what the company will do for you. I'm very proud of my firm, and I'd like to show you the benefits we have to offer."

Don't wait for their permission. Launch right into your listing presentation. Keep it moving. One of the advantages of a well-organized, visual aid book—one that's not cluttered with material you don't need or use—is that they can see how much of it is left. If you're moving through it quickly, they're more likely to sit still and pay attention since they can see it's not going to take all night or be boring.

The final part of your presentation introduces the comparable market analysis. If you're new, lead into it with:

"Mr. and Mrs. Watt, I'd like to begin by thanking you for allowing me to be here tonight. In appreciation, I've taken a color photo of your home." Hand it to them. "It came out rather nicely, didn't it?" Then go on with:

"Most of my work today consisted of formulating this comparative market analysis. One of the basic factors that determines whether a property will sell is the establishment of a fair market value price. As you can see, this form shows the properties that did not sell during their exposure to the marketplace. Let's go over the form together."

If you're a practiced veteran, open with:

"Mr. and Mrs. Watt, I spent most of today researching data and compiling a comparative market analysis on your property. Would you take a moment and verify my accuracy on these details?" Hand them the partially filled out listing form that you worked on at the office.

Jack Watt will probably say, "We haven't decided to list with anyone yet."

Smile. "Oh, I'm certainly aware of that, but I'm also confident that when you see the benefits we have to offer and the service I'll give you, you'll agree that (your company's name) is the firm you'll wish to have represent you."

Champions get their listing form on the table at this point. Then they pick up the previous phraseology from the second sentence: "One of the basic factors that determines whether . . . let's go over the form together."

Hand each of them a copy of your comparable market analysis, and retain one for yourself. Having two copies of the CMA for them is critical; you need a response from both the wife and the husband. If one of them doesn't get a copy, that person is going to feel slighted and will probably start fighting you.

As they look at the form, watch their expressions. Remember Wilma Mildue? Gloria, who used to bowl with her, doesn't really like Wilma all that much. But after the Mildues' house sold, Jack talked Gloria into calling her. Now Gloria tells you, "I spoke to the owners of this one, and they said they got a lot more for it than you show here."

Expect to be challenged every time you present a CMA. When it happens, a pro smiles warmly, and calmly says, "We find this happens quite often. People who have had their home on the market, when asked by a neighbor what they sold it for, often reply with, 'We got what we wanted.' The inquisitor assumes they received much more than they actually did. It's a common problem, but I can assure you that these figures are facts of record."

Emphasize the words given above. You've just called their friends—or at least their informants—liars. But you've done it in a pleasant, professional manner. That is, you've brought the facts of record to their attention that they need to know before they can make an intelligent decision.

Gloria Watt is a little upset that Wilma lied to her, so she says: "Our home is nicer than these places. Well, I haven't seen them all, but our place is certainly lots nicer than Wilma's." Always agree. Do not fall on the floor roaring with laughter. Here's the proven response to the often heard "Our home is nicer" statement:

"Indeed it is. Your home is one of the nicest in the area. Quality improvements and pride of ownership are so important in selling a home.

"However, it's a proven fact that the improvements primarily enhance the property's ability to sell faster but don't always increase the value in proportion to the costs of those improvements."

Isn't that smooth and effective? And it's true.

Then Jack Watt says, in the same tone he'd use to tell you where to jump, "We wouldn't sell our home for these prices."

You should be delighted when you hear that. Why? Because they are telling you that they do know what they would sell it for. Establishing that figure is one of your preliminary goals, isn't it?

This next sentence is important. Practice until you can say it slowly, sincerely, and word for word: "Well, based on that statement, you obviously have some idea of what you'd want. What do you feel the price should be?"

No matter how much smooth empathy you put into asking that question, you'll often get an answer like this from Jack: "You're the professional—you tell us."

When anyone says that to you, what have they done? By calling you a professional they've complimented you, haven't they. So thank them, repeat what they've decided about you, and then tie it all down: "Thank you." Smile. If you haven't already used this phrase, say, "And a reputation for professionalism is important, isn't it?"

Charge right into the rest of your rehearsed speech for smoothly fielding his fly at overpricing: "The sales price of a property is flexible, depending upon the terms and the length of exposure to the market. You would like to move in the next (quote the period you know is their need-to-move time), wouldn't you?"

The words are important; your tone and manner are even more so. If you ask that question in a smart-alecky way, you can destroy yourself with it, just as you can by misusing any other technique. Jack Watt says yes, so you move into your next planned step: "Well, I think it's important that we keep as close to market value as possible. So do you have some idea of what you would want?"

He's studied your CMA and can't punch any holes in it. So now Jack knows that he isn't going to get what he wants, which is $290,000 for a house that should go on the market in the low $250s if it's going to sell as quickly as they need it to sell. This means they have gut wrenching decisions to wrestle with. Jack may not be prepared to admit in front of Gloria that they're not going to get as much money as he'd told her they would, based on the garbage information we saw him collect in Chapter 7. And Gloria may be in shock because she's afraid that, if they have to sell in the low $250s, they won't be able to buy the new house they want.

In most listing situations, you'll have some version of these emotional situations to contend with. Often there'll be another difficulty: Your sellers have already made a commitment to a house they can't qualify for unless they sell theirs at an impossibly high price. Here are some questions you should be asking yourself at this point:

How heavily are they committed, emotionally and financially, to their unrealistic price?
Can they adjust to realistic pricing?
If they can adjust, how long will it take them to get realistic?
Even at the risk of alienating them, should I go all out to list them at market price tonight?
Or, should I take the listing high, with the understanding that we'll bring the price down to a realistic level in an agreed time if we don't get action at their price?
Or, should I give them a few hours to adjust to reality, and schedule another meeting tomorrow night with both of them?

You'll usually have to answer these questions in the heat of the listing interview, but you'll make better decisions if you've given them thorough analysis during your afternoon think session.

The ball is still in the Watts' court: ". . . so do you have some idea of what you would want?"

By now, Jack has acquired a grudging respect for you, and he doesn't want to appear stupid. So, after grinding his teeth, after looking again at the line on your CMA showing the Bartlett home on the market for 79 days at $259,500, after making some agonizing reappraisals of their financial situation, Mr. Watt says, "Well, we wanted a whole lot more, but I guess our rock bottom figure would be about $265,000, wouldn't it, honey?" He's closer, but he's still not realistic.

Gloria swallows hard and says, "Well, that's all right with me."

But it isn't all right with you. At that price you know their house won't sell fast enough to let them move in the time period they have indicated they need.

But you don't look shocked. Your expression shows puzzlement, nothing more. No struggle to keep from saying something sarcastic— just puzzlement. Then, you say sympathetically: "Mr. and Mrs. Watt, maybe I missed something in the property." This has to be said very warmly—and with great empathy—or they'll blow you out of the water. "Could you take a moment and tell me why you feel that way?"

When you say that, you must sound like you've made a mistake. Now it's their turn. Let them pour it on: "Okay, Tom, I'll tell you why. This is the finest location in the state. We have upgraded light fixtures and switches, awnings on every window, and the paint is guaranteed to outlast the house. Our ceiling has 14 inches of insulation, every bush in the yard is individually drip irrigated, and we've installed an industrial grade trash compactor."

Don't interrupt. Listen to the whole story. And pay attention. When it's your turn, you'll need to come back, strongly, smoothly, and professionally. To do that, use:

Powerful Turnaround Phrases

Practice the phrases that follow. They are among the most powerful short combinations of words that you can put to work in selling. The system is simple and devastatingly effective.

First, agree with them. Then state your own contrary point.

"Your point is certainly valid, although . . ."
"Looking at it from your view, that's true, but . . ."
"I can certainly see your point, except . . ."

"I understand how you feel, but we should also consider . . ."

"There's no question about it, your comments make sense. However . . ."

"I agree with what you're saying, and I'd like to take that reasoning a bit further. In this case . . ."

"Beyond a doubt, that's true. Still . . ."

You warmly agree. Then, you disagree with friendly warmth. First, you make sure that the person you're persuading knows that you heard what he or she just said. If you fail to do this, that person won't be persuaded at all by your argument, he'll just be thinking about making his points all over again the first chance he gets.

Handling the "We Can Rent It" Balloon

"We can always rent. We don't really have to sell now." If they say that, have they ever been a landlord before? Nine times out of ten, they haven't, or they'd never do it again with a single-family residence. The entire reason for this objection often is simply to slow things down in which case you can ignore it. At other times, it'll become their justification for taking no action tonight unless you get this objection out of the way. Do that with a similar situation close: "It's certainly true that owning rentals has been a good investment for many people. However, it's definitely a fact that very few tenants take the pride in the property that the owner does."

Is that true? You bet it is.

"By holding the property for two or three years, any appreciation could be offset by what we call deferred maintenance—necessary repairs. Have you ever rented or managed a home before?"

They'll usually say they haven't.

"It can be a rude awakening."

I tell my seminar students to say this: "Recently I heard a speaker who had been in real estate for fourteen years. He decided to rent the home he was leaving." (I did when I moved from California to Arizona. Renting that house was the biggest mistake of my life.)

"This trainer thought he had carefully selected his tenants, but he soon found out he was working with professional renters. After six months of not collecting rent and eviction attempts, he finally got his property back. Refurbishing it to its former condition cost him $2,000, and he was out the cost of carrying the property all that time, too."

If you haven't heard me speak, you won't want to say it that way. Perhaps your manager, or someone else you know, has had a similar experience. They're not rare. Ask around and you'll hear some horror stories about renters in single-family residences. Research this point and be ready for his objection with a similar situation close that's effective and true. The point you want to convey is this: If people experienced in real estate can't protect themselves against rip-off renters, what chance do amateur landlords have, especially if they have moved far away from their rental?

Working the Price Down to Market

On many listings, you'll need all your skill and knowledge to cajole the price within bargaining distance of market value. It's a hard, thankless task, which is why so few agents do it. As a result, an enormous number of overpriced listings are written every year. These listings hurt everyone. Least hurt are the agents who won't take them. They'll get a second chance when the wishful thinking expires. More hurt are the agents who win the bidding contests and write the overpriced listings. Their only reward will be expense and trouble. But the real hurt falls on the owners. Instead of moving when it's convenient, they wind up selling when they're emotionally—and sometimes financially—desperate.

So, as you work at getting a price that's near market, bear in mind that you're doing it primarily for the sellers' benefit. All you have to lose is a few hours work. You can list another home in a fraction of the time you'd waste trying to sell a $250,000 value for $265,000, or even more. Work hard at helping the owners see where their best interests are—in getting a selling price, not a sale-killing price. Use this three-step program to set yourself up for closing on market price:

1. Go over your estimated seller's proceeds form and explain all the costs. Your purpose is to find out what they must net after the sale, what their net walk-away cash needs are. Many people aren't interested in

what you sell the place for as long as they get that specific amount of cash out of it.

2. Mentally compute how far off you are. "Mr. and Mrs. Watt, forgetting price for a moment, if I were to write you a check right now, how much would you want for your property after all the charges, including the mortgage, are paid?"

"We couldn't take less than $40,000."

"We definitely need that much," Gloria Watt says. When you hear that, it almost always means they've already spent that much, mentally if not actually. So they're not going to find it easy to look at price logically (no one ever does) because a lower price doesn't just come through to them as an abstract reduction of a number. It hits them as the loss of their vacation to Mexico, the postponement of buying their new furniture, and no new entertainment system.

Sometimes "We definitely need that much" means another broker has verbally "guaranteed" them that price. What value do verbal guarantees have? Try to deposit one in your bank account and you'll find out.

Do you have a challenge with math? I did. So I learned some quick mental formulas for arriving at approximate net figures. Do you realize that almost all real estate decisions are made on the basis of rough figures? When the choice is being made, quick and roughly accurate figures work; slow, penny perfect figures don't. (As with most rules, there are exceptions to this one. Don't hesitate to pull out the calculator and work everything out to the last cent if they make it plain that quick estimates make them uncomfortable.)

But if quick estimates make you uncomfortable, you need to study this section and change your thinking. Most people can only be held at the point of decision for a very short time. Let them dangle and they'll fall off. Learn to be as quick with approximate figures as you are with your practiced words. It's the only way you can stay in control and lead them to the decision you want them to make.

Let's work the example out. The Watts need to net $40,000, and you know their mortgage balance is $182,046.79 ($180,000 for fast figures) making the total $220,000. Add closing costs. For quick estimates, I used 10 percent. Not only was it close enough, it's wonderfully easy to figure—just drop a zero. You've got to keep it simple or the tension and pressure will mess you up. Now, we're at $242,000.

But I'm not done yet, because I left $2,000 out when I rounded their $182,046.79 mortgage to $180,000. Add that back for a grand total of $244,000—a price that's within bargaining distance of market value. Hurrah, I'm working on a live situation. The Watts don't need to sell for $265,000.

You can make quick estimates like that in your head, can't you? Drill yourself on it. Practice until you can come up with the total price as quick as you, or the friend you're practicing with, can come up with hypothetical mortgage and walk-away figures. A pro can do this very quickly without touching a calculator or pencil. But sometimes you can hurt yourself here by being too slick. Guard against having them suspect that you know what they're thinking; it worries some people and makes others feel stupid—and they'll start fighting you.

3. Use a legal pad for your price calculations, but don't let them see the figures. If they don't see them—and if you keep nodding reassuringly as you work—they'll think you've agreed to their value.

Close for the Price

Never forget for an instant that an overpriced listing is nothing but a dead weight that'll pull you down. You don't want it. So keep focusing on your goal. Your goal for the price was $254,950 and your top figure is $259,995 but only with the understanding that the price will be reconsidered after 30 days.

But they're thinking in terms of starting at $265,000 on the theory that they'll probably have to come down. Study these words carefully. They work beautifully:

"Mr. and Mrs. Watt, I'm trying my best to put myself in your shoes this evening. Many salespeople are mainly concerned with taking listings and will tell the sellers anything they want to hear. I don't think this is fair because your main concern is selling the property, isn't it?" (Don't pause. You must jump on the next sentence.) "That's why I spent all day preparing facts to substantiate fair market value. I've seen salespeople take a listing at any price and then, six months later, the property is still sitting there. The advantage of first-time exposure is gone. In many instances, the sellers even receive less than they would have, had they started at a realistic figure."

Use an alternate of choice to arrive at value. They're feeling hurt to get down to $265,000, and you know the market is $250,000. Here's the next step: "Based on the facts, Mr. and Mrs. Watt, I feel we should start between $252,500 and $257,500."

Why do I use two figures? I feel certain that I'm not going to get it at $250,000. An important point to remember here is that if they had not been so far off in their thinking, I would have set my range a thousand or two under market.

Suppose I'm working with clients who want $285,000 for a house with a market value of $275,000. I'd probably suggest this: "Based on the facts, Mr. and Mrs. Johnson, I feel we should start at a figure between $272,500 and $277,500."

If I have to go as high as $285,000, I'd only do it if they gave me the listing for six months and agreed to reconsider the price after thirty days.

Operating on the Price with the DOM Study

In Chapter 6, we introduced the DOM (days on market) study. When they're weighing the question of price, use this report to pile more counters on the side of reality. Here's how:

"Mr. and Mrs. Watt, this is a days on market study that covers all nearby sales in our price category for the past (month, six months, year—whatever you have). I wanted you both to see this information because it tells us a lot about the relationship between market price and speed of selling. I know that speed isn't as important to you as price, but it's at least possible that your attitude on this will change. Or that the situation will change—making the timing a crucial rather than a minor consideration for you."

Again, you have copies for both of them.

"Notice the home at 2020 Country Club Drive. It's very comparable to yours except that the grounds are huge and they front on the golf course pond. This property came on the market more than a year ago at $299,995 and, after several reductions, it finally sold last month for $263,000. It was on the market for 391 days.

"Compare that to 220 Concord, where there's a pool and only three bedrooms. So it's not comparable to your four bedroom—but what's interesting is that it went on the market at $257,500 and sold just three days later at $256,500."

Do you see how you work with the DOM study?

Without saying so, you're telling them that for less money than they're asking, people can buy a home that offers more in location or amenities. And at the same time, you're making vivid points about how overpricing will take them over their time limit.

This method doesn't take the place of the comparable market analysis; it simply gives you more persuasive power—and often all you need is just a little bit more power to take the listing.

Listing the House by Its Barbecue

Lots of people are strange about making decisions. They'll never come right out with a big one. With these people, if you force them to say yes or no, they'll always say no. So you don't put them in that position. Many times I've spent half an hour discussing what personal property they're going to leave. They had never said they were going to list with me, but after that half-hour, they approved the listing. Never force them to make a big decision. Just work with them on lots of little decisions. "Do you want to leave the fireplace equipment, the barbecue, the draperies?"

Discuss the pros and cons of these little items with great interest and put every decision they make on the listing form. The moment you put your pen to the listing form at their kitchen table, you're halfway to writing a good listing.

After you've covered all the personal property and led them through all those decisions with friendly interest, what do you do? It's simple. "Have we covered everything? Fine." Turn the form around. Place your pen on it. Slide the form to their side of the table, lean back, smile, and say, "Well, Mr. and Mrs. Watt, with your approval here, I can start getting you happily moved."

Now, to read the form, what must they do? Pick up the pen. Mr. Watt does that, looks at the form, and sees the time you've put on it.

"This is a listing for six months," he says, bristling a little.

Do you see the psychology here? Instead of talking about whether or not you're going to get the listing, they're talking about how long they're going to give it to you for. Sometimes the way to get the listing is to let them say no to the length of time you've put on it.

Here's your answer to Jack Watt: "We could go longer, of course. However, I feel this will be enough time." You don't know if it's too long or too short, do you? When you say that, they'll probably come back with, "Oh, no, we'd never tie our home up that long."

If you go in there committed to getting a 180-day listing, you may have to settle for 90 days. If you shoot for 90 in the beginning, you'll often get knocked back to 30.

How to Turn Down a Turkey

If you have to turn the listing down because they won't budge from a price that's so high it only spells trouble, you'll be glad you did after you do. I always referred an overpriced listing to another broker.

When you're turning a listing down because you've determined that it can't be obtained on a reasonable basis, says these words: "Mr. and Mrs. _____, I sincerely am interested in representing you and marketing your home. In good conscience, though, I can't honestly put a sign on the property and list it at a price that is too out of line with the market. Maybe I've missed something and I might possibly be wrong. Many real estate firms will take a listing just for the sake of putting up a sign and hoping the property will sell. I can't do that. May I suggest that you feel out the market and give the listing to another firm, at your price, for thirty days and see what happens?"

Set Up the Sellers for Future Events

Once you have the listing approved, it's time to brief them on what to expect in the selling process. Cover these points with your new clients before you leave:

Prepare them for the property preview by the agents from your office. "Mrs. _____, I will be bringing salespeople by on _____ to preview your home. This is a very important day. If the salespeople are impressed with your property, they will be much more apt to show it to their prospects. The more showings we receive, the greater our chances are for a sale. So, let's have the home looking its very best by _____. Okay?"

2. Instruct them on how to make their house look the most presentable: lights bright, draperies open, stereo low. Explain why they should go through a clean-up, freshen-up, turn-on routine whenever the house is to be shown.

3. Cover yourself on the damage that incompetent agents will do so they won't blame you. There are salespeople in almost every office who never think about the clients or their profession's reputation. They don't care whether they call a seller or not before showing the property. They'd just as soon knock on the door without warning.

Explain to your sellers that you can't control everyone in the industry but, if they'll make a note of everyone who shows the property or calls, you'll follow up. Then if the clients have any complaints, you can call the agent responsible and with great politeness ask that person to please help upgrade the profession's image.

"As we discussed earlier, Mr. and Mrs. _____, we will stipulate that each salesperson call for an appointment to show the home. However, sometimes after showing a buyer another home in the area, a salesperson may think of your home, and in the excitement of telling the buyer about it, forget to phone. If this happens, please understand. If you are too inconvenienced at the time, ask them to return but, if it's possible, let them see your home, for they may be good, qualified buyers and purchase it that day."

4. Tell the sellers not to approve anything about the listing or the sale that doesn't come through you. I always asked them to make sure they notified me, before approving anything. You should be advised of everything relating to the sale of that property. Sometimes an amendment can be sent to them directly without your knowledge. That document may not be to your sellers' advantage, but you can't protect them if you don't know about it. That's your main job: to protect them. You're their agent, their representative. Let them know that they can rely on you.

"Bob and Mary, my job is to represent your interests. Because of this, I'd appreciate your not signing a contract unless I approve it. If a salesperson or broker wants to present an offer to you, please make sure I'm notified, so I can protect your position."

5. Have them remove any personal property that is not staying if buyers would expect it to stay. I've lost sales because of a chandelier the buyers wanted to take with them to their new home. I've lost sales because of a unique throw. I've lost sales because of fireplace equipment that should have been put in storage. You see, a lot of buyers get to the point where they think that if they lose the chandelier, they've lost a good buy; the sellers get emotional and stand on principle—or whatever they call it—and a $200,000 sale goes down the drain over a $1000 chandelier. If you encounter a situation where any fixtures will not stay in the home, have your sellers replace them before showing the property.

Here's how to tell them about the affects of their personal items: "Mr. and Mrs. _____, since you've definitely decided against leaving the (name the personal property involved), let me suggest something that could head off a challenge. The (chandeliers or whatever) enhance your home so much that anyone making an offer will probably fall in love with them. Then we all have a challenge. I've lost sales over a throw rug. Please, let's not have that kind of problem here. We won't if you'll put those beautiful things in storage. It would be a shame to lose a sale over one of them, wouldn't it?"

6. Set them up for a low offer. Make sure they understand that the price of property is set by the most willing sellers getting together with the most willing buyers. In other words, it's set by the market. You don't set it. And remind them that you're obliged to present all offers. "Finally, I think it's important that we realize that buyers establish value by what they actually pay for property. We're of course, shooting for $————. However, if a lower price is offered, we will carefully go over it to see if it's feasible and, at that point, discuss the plan of action to take. Thank you again for your confidence in listing your home with me. I'll do my very best to justify your trust. Good night."

7. Prepare them for a fast offer. If they don't expect one and aren't mentally prepared to handle it, they'll hate you instead of being happy if one comes in. Suppose that after two hours of negotiating with Steve

and Millie Renaski, during which time you maintained that the market price is $275,000, you finally list it at $287,500 with the understanding that they'll reconsider the price after 30 days if there's no action.

When you post the listing in your office, another agent says it's just what his buyers are looking for and tomorrow night you have an offer for $285,000. What will Steve and Millie Renaski think? That you were trying to give their home away for $275,000 and beat them out of ten big ones. That is, they'll think that unless you set them up. Say these words: "I think it's important that you realize that most of our sales staff are working with about five prospects at all times. They may have a buyer waiting for this type of property, so maybe we'll be lucky enough to obtain a deposit in the next few days. That would be great, wouldn't it?"

Twelve Tricks of the Top Producer

Actually, I'm going to give you thirteen, and the extra one is as important as anything in this book. Here it is: don't depend on memory for details. You've put yourself on the fast track to championship status and the big money, which means that you'll soon have more business than you can handle unless you're highly organized. Even in the beginning, you don't need to waste time cleaning up the big mess that forgetting to handle a small detail will cause.

I'll give you many helpful forms throughout the rest of the book; and we'll cover time planning in Chapter 28; but take time now to create a checklist for all the after-I-take-a-listing details. This checklist will get you off to a fast, professional start at marketing your new listing. Run off some copies of your checklist, staple one inside each of your listing folders, and mark off each item as you complete it. Ask your broker about items 4 through 7; procedures vary from office to office.

1. Get your broker's approval of the listing.
2. Send a thank-you note to your new clients. Do this immediately. It reassures them when things happen right away. This note should be handwritten. You'll find the wording in Chapter 14.
3. Send the "Guess what your neighbors just did" card to at least ten

homes across the street from your new listing and the five homes on each side of it. (Get the sellers' permission, of course.) The wording for this "New-on-the-market" card is also given in Chapter 14.

4. Get your listing in to the multiple office immediately for the hot sheet and MLS book.

5. Arrange for the sign and install the lock box.

6. Put your listing in your office's inventory.

7. Set up your office's file of the listing.

8. Schedule your follow-up with the client.

9. Develop your marketing plan for the listing and put it into high gear.

10. Call the sellers at least once every week. Unless you keep in close touch with them, little challenges will become bigger than you can cure before you know you have any.

11. See the sellers in person at least once every month.

12. Reduce the price and extend the listing until it sells.

Part Two

Your Selling Real Estate Career

Chapter 20

How to Handle the Telephone Effectively

Some people in real estate believe that their job is to sell real estate when they answer the telephone. It isn't. The first thing you must realize is that people don't "invest" in real estate over the telephone. You can't get your pen through the phone for their approval on the paperwork. And very few callers will say, "Here's my credit card number. Just charge this home listed in the paper to it. I know it's right for me."

Do you realize how many people in the field of real estate operate as if that's what will happen when they answer the phone? They're not properly prepared, mentally or physically, for the job they're supposed to do.

When you talk with potential clients on that telephone you want to sell them only one thing—a face-to-face meeting. Ads are only written to make the phone ring so you can meet the caller. Forget everything else when you answer that telephone.

So, how do you make the phone ring? With good ads.

Ingredients of a Good Ad

Let me give you a successful advertising formula to make the phone ring. Whether he realizes it or not, the average buyer uses the same formula to decide what ads he or she will respond to. In fact, most major advertising companies use this formula as their basis for creating ad calls.

Attention. The first thing an ad must do is attract attention. Most people don't read every word of any ad; they just scan when they're looking at the paper. That's why good ad writers use eye-catching headings. They know they must stop the buyer's eye on their ad.

Interest. Once you've gotten a buyer's attention, you must then build their interest. This has to be done in the first two lines because they're still scanning.

Desire. The desire to see a property is created in the body of the ad. This is where you get a buyer emotionally involved.

Action. You need to call for action on their part at the end of the ad, in your closing line.

This is what motivates a person to call. They see a heading that looks pretty good; they build their interest, develop the desire to see the home, and pick up the phone to call you. Now, all this is wasted unless you meet the caller.

I can't tell you what properties make the best ads. You must figure out what works in your area. Perhaps people there are looking for new homes, and in another area it's used homes, fixer-uppers. I don't know. You have to be the expert in your own area to know what people are looking for so you can write the ad to get them to call you.

One thing I can tell you is when you should write an ad. I'll tell you a little secret: The more attention your ads get, the more likely your owner or manager is to run them. The more they're run, the better your percentage of getting calls, showings, and sales. So it makes sense to write a good ad. But when should it be done? At a predetermined time.

Professionals set appointments with themselves to get the job done long before the deadline imposed by your office or local newspaper.

Now, the average salesperson will wait until fifteen minutes before the deadline, write up something haphazardly, and wonder why their ads aren't run. Or, if they do get run, why they don't get any response. Those same average salespeople, when they do get a call, give out enough information so the caller doesn't need to see the home. They literally eliminate the prospect.

It's almost like a contest. The caller is trying to find out everything you know and give you nothing. You're trying to get all the information

you can on them—and an appointment—without giving them anything. The problem the average salesperson encounters is that some
callers are better at this contest than he or she is. You can't let the callers
beat you at this game!

Now, which prospects represent the toughest ad call? It's not the unqualified people with no money and no credit. They have all the time
in the world to look at homes. They're not in any hurry and not particular about the area the home is in. It's the qualified ones, the ones
with both money and credit that are the difficult ones. In fact, the more
qualified they are, the tougher they are. Which type of people would
you prefer to work with, unqualified or qualified? Qualified, of course.
And you can't know which type they are until you meet them.

Preparation for Taking a Call

Your main goal when you answer an ad call is to:

1. Get their name. You can't close a voice.
2. Get a phone number. You can't call them back if you don't have their
   number.
3. Make the appointment. If you don't have an appointment to meet
   them, who are you kidding?

Now that you know what your goal is, let's see if you're properly prepared to take that call. The main thing you must know before you answer that telephone is all of the properties that are being advertised.
How can you help them "own" the property they're calling about if you
don't know it?

There are people in this field, maybe in your very office, who will
answer the phone not knowing any of the properties being advertised.
You must know what is being advertised! The next thing you must do
is to pick out five of your favorite homes in various price ranges. Professionals have five homes in mind at all times that they think are the
best in the marketplace. These are homes that can easily be suggested to
the buyer if, in qualifying, the agent determines that the home the
buyer called about is not for them.

You must also have a call card or your computer ready to record the information you're going to get. A call card is nothing more than a prospect card or a 3-by-5 card on which you write everything down. Don't rely on your memory. You may get twenty-five calls in one day. Don't expect to remember each person and his or her needs. Take good notes that will help you get them to like you and trust you when you meet.

If you have a good contact management program on your computer, by all means use it for entering all of this information. Some people can't type as fast as they can take notes with a pen. They take the notes first, then transfer the information into their computers after the call is completed. Do whichever works best for you.

I cannot tell you the amount of money that is wasted by brokers who run good ads that generate good calls but whose agents don't even meet the callers. You have an obligation as a salesperson to your broker and to your owner. You're also obligated to yourself and to your family to meet that potential buyer. It's amazing how we don't think about money spent unless it's our own.

Finally, you must be mentally prepared to win. When the phone rings, say to yourself, "I'm going to meet these people." Burn with that desire. When you meet them, you can determine whether or not they're qualified as buyers. I have had people call about a $30,000 fixer-upper, and I have ended up getting them into a $200,000 home. They called on the fixer-upper as an investment property. You never know.

Who is more motivated to own a home—the husband or the wife? Usually the wife is more motivated. The husband in many instances puts off the decision and lets her go look at homes first.

Who usually calls, though? The husband usually makes the call because he wants to eliminate you so he doesn't have to look at homes seriously. He'd rather stay home and watch the big game or go fishing. That's why you must learn to close the husband on the first appointment.

Envision the following: Steve and Jenny are reading the Sunday morning paper. Steve is reading the sports page. Jenny is reading the ads. She finds one that looks pretty good. This ad has attracted her attention. It's built her interest, created a desire, and caused her to act. Her action, though, is to get Steve to call on it. He reads the ad. The formula works on him, too. So, he calls.

Now, I want you to hear this call the right way and the wrong way. So, first, Steve is going to call Pathetic Realty and talk with Joe Schmoe. Old Schmoe has just arrived at the office—fifteen minutes late. He read about all the disasters in the morning paper. He is depressed and doesn't know why he even came into work. The phone rings:

Schmoe: "Pathetic Realty."

Steve: "I'm calling on this ad in the paper called a Touch of Heaven."

Schmoe: "Oh, yeah. That's one of my favorite homes. What can I tell you?"

Steve: "Well, does it have a large lot?"

Schmoe: "Sir, the lot on this home is one of the largest in the area."

Steve: "We didn't want to have a lot of yard work. Tell me this, how much is the down payment?"

Schmoe: "They're asking $10,000."

Steve (to Jenny): "Honey, they're asking for $10,000. That's all of our savings. You don't want to spend it all, do you?" Of course she doesn't, but she wants to see the home. So, he asks, "Well, I don't know if we're interested or not. Could you give us the address in case we decide to drive by and check it out?"

Schmoe: "Sir, we're not supposed to give out the addresses."

Steve: "If we can't drive by, I guess we're not interested."

Schmoe: "Well, if you promise you'll call me back . . ." He then gives out the address. Steve now has everything and Schmoe has nothing.

How to Do the Call Right

Let's see how the professional would handle the same ad call. The phone rings. The pro answers on the third ring. By answering sooner, you might scare them. If you answer too late, they may think you're not there. The moment you answer the phone, your voice creates an image in their minds. If you sound like you're suffering from a terminal disease, they won't want to meet you. Pick up that phone with a degree of enthusiasm. If you have a problem sounding happy, smile when you pick up the phone. It's difficult to sound down when you're smiling.

Let's go over three ways to answer the phone. Now, you must use the one that your broker approves, and say it exactly the same way each time. These are just some suggestions.

"Good morning. Champions Unlimited. How may I help you?"

"Good morning. Thank you for calling Champions Unlimited."

"Champions Unlimited, this is Tom Hopkins. How may I help you?"

Prospect: "I noticed this ad in the paper a Touch of Heaven."

When they tell you which ad, acknowledge the caller's interest and place them on hold.

Pro: "Yes, sir, that's one of the finest homes in our inventory. May I please place you on hold while I see if it's still available?"

Prospect: "Yes."

Pro: "Thank you."

If you ask the question just like that, they'll always say yes and allow you to put them on hold. Now why did you want to do that? If they're on hold, you can take a moment to gain composure, to get control, get the information on the home in front of you, and come back ready to close them for the appointment.

Never leave them on hold for more than seventeen seconds. They change. The warm, nice man who just called four minutes ago has turned into a raging wild man. You won't even know it's the same person. Take them off hold after seventeen seconds and close for their name.

Pro: "Thank you for waiting. My name is Tom Hopkins. May I ask who's calling, please?"

Prospect: "Joe Johnson."

Pro: "Yes, Mr. Johnson, may I ask what appealed to you in the ad?"

Prospect: "Well, it sounds pretty good. Let me ask you some questions."

Pro: "Yes, Mr. Johnson."

Prospect: "Let me ask you this. Does it have a large lot?"

Pro: "Mr. Johnson, were you and the family looking for a large lot?"

Prospect: "No, not too large."

Pro: "I see. Based on the size of the lots in the area, it's an average size. To see the home, would you like me to pick you up, or would you rather come by my office?"

Prospect: "How much is the down payment?"

Pro: "Down payments are flexible, Mr. Johnson, depending upon financing. How much of your savings would you like to invest in your new home?"

Note: If they say down payment, you should use it to answer their question. If you switch to initial investment just now, you might confuse them. After you've referred to the home as an investment, then make the change to initial or monthly investment.

Prospect: "Probably around $7,000." If the amount of money they tell you is more than you're used to getting, don't lose your composure. Whatever they say, act like it's perfectly normal. The same goes if it's less than you're used to getting.

Pro: "Fine. That should be feasible, depending upon the financing arrangements that best suit you. Again, I'm free now, Mr. Johnson, or would you rather see the home at 3:00 this afternoon?"

Prospect: "If you just give me the address, we'll drive by and if we like it, we'll call you."

Some of you have been giving out addresses because you feel if you don't, they'll call and get the address from someone else. If you learn the techniques I'm giving you, closing them for their name, phone number, and appointment, they aren't likely to call someone else. If there's one thing I can't stand, it's being used. And if you give out an address, you're being used. They will not call you back because you're clerking, not selling. Instead, they'll call a friend in the business or someone who's told them, "If you call me, I'll give you a little something."

To become a professional you need to stop giving out addresses. Use the following words instead:

Pro: "I would be happy to give you the address, Mr. Johnson. However, normally one of the conditions of our agreement with the seller is that we accompany each prospect to the property. Would it be convenient for you now or would you rather make it this afternoon?"

Prospect: "Listen, just give me the address."

Pro: "Mr. Johnson, I think I know a way to avoid invalidating our agreement with the seller. Let me call and see if they will give me permission to give out the address. If they don't mind, I sure don't. At what number can I call you right back?"

Prospect: "Look, I just want to drive by the property."

Pro: "I see. It's always a good idea to inspect the exterior of a home as well as the neighborhood. When do you plan to drive by?"

Prospect: "I guess it would be around 5:00 P.M."

Pro: "Fine. In order to save you time, I will be available at 5:00 P.M. to answer any questions you may have regarding the property. I can meet you at (neutral location). I'll be driving (color and make of your car). What kind of car will you be driving?"

Do you see what I'm trying to teach you? They may not want to come to your office. They may want to just drive by. You can meet them at a neutral location, near the property; I don't care where, just meet the caller! That should be your burning desire when you pick up that telephone.

If they really fight you, and some of them will, that should tell you something. They probably have the money. They're probably qualified. They've controlled every other salesperson they've met. In essence, they're real turkeys. But they're probably qualified turkeys. It could be that they've had a bad experience with another real estate salesperson.

One thing I've learned over the years is that the more upset people get, the warmer and nicer you need to become. If you lose your temper, they win. Also, it's hard to be angry with someone who's nice. That's why the professional says this: "Mr. Johnson, it sounds like you've had a bad experience with a salesperson. Am I right in assuming that?"

Prospect: "Yes."

Pro: "Would you mind telling me about it?"

If you let them tell you, they'll really tell you. It will give you insight as to what you should avoid doing with with this client at all costs. It also gives you an opportunity to understand where he's coming from.

Pro: "I can certainly understand how you feel. The longer I'm in real estate, the more I find that selling is an unnecessary act. The true skill is in finding a customer's likes and dislikes and then locating the home that best suits his or her needs. I've had great results in serving my clients, and I'd like to make a suggestion. Maybe this home is not right for you . . . then again, maybe it is. I would appreciate you giving me the opportunity to stop by your home this evening to meet you. Then we can discover what type of home would best suit your family's needs. That would be agreeable to you, wouldn't it?"

Prospect: "Well, I don't know . . ."

Pro: "I can bring information files on some of our finer properties, and in the privacy of your own home, we can go over what's available. Would 7:00 P.M. be convenient or shall I make it 8:00 P.M.?"

Prospect: "8:00 P.M. is okay."

The next step is critical. You must reconfirm everything. The average person won't remember what was said ten minutes ago. That's why the pros reconfirm everything!

Pro: "Thank you, Mr. Johnson. Do you have a pen for some pertinent information? Again, my name is Tom Hopkins with Champions Unlimited. I'll look forward to meeting you at your home this evening at 8:00 P.M. Your address is . . . ? Fine. In case something unforeseen should arise, may I please have your phone number so I can contact you? Thank you again."

Common Telephone Questions

Let me give you some of the most common telephone questions you'll hear and how you should handle them.

"Where's the property located?"

What are they really asking for? The address. That's why you must switch their base from the address to the general vicinity.

"The property is located in the (general area), are you familiar with that area?" Or, "Is this an area you would consider?"

"I'd like the exact address."

"I'd be happy to give you the address, Mr. _____. However, normally, one of the conditions of our agreement with the seller is that we accompany each prospect to the property. I'm free now, or would 3:00 P.M. be better?" Be sure to include the word *normally*. It's not always the case, and you don't want to tell an untruth.

"I'll meet you at the property."

Now, here's what a lot of them do. They tell you they'll meet you and get the address. Then, they'll either get there before you and take off or wait until the next day. Some of them will even have the audacity to set a time knowing that they won't be there. That's why you warmly say, "Fine. However, our office is not far from the property. To avoid the possibility of missing one another, can you come in at 1:00 P.M. or would 3:00 P.M. be better?" Unless they're really turkeys, they'll begin to see how professional you are—how you are trying to serve them—and give in. If they are turkeys and continue to fight you, you probably wouldn't want to work with them anyway.

If they call on a sign they've seen, they'll already have the address and try to get other information from you. In that case, you would say, "I'll be happy to meet you at the property in fifteen minutes with all of the information. I'll be driving (color and make of your car). What kind of car will you be driving?"

If they call on an ad, they might say, "We would just like to drive by the property."

Agree with them. "It's always a good idea to see the exterior of a home as well as the neighborhood. What time do you plan to drive by?" When they give you the time then you can say, "Fine. I'll be available at that time to answer any questions you may have about the property. Shall I pick you up at your home, or would you prefer coming to my office?"

Or, you could do it this way, "Fine. I'll be happy to drive you by the property, Mr. _____. However, it would be a shame to miss the home's beautiful rear yard (only say this if it has one). To save time, I can show it to you now, or would 3:00 P.M. be better?"

"What's the down payment?"

"They're asking 10 percent, but how much of an initial investment would you be willing to make to become the owner of the right home?"

This will give you the opportunity to find out approximately how much money they have to work with. Or you could say, "Down payments are flexible depending upon the type of financing arrangements that are made. What did you have in mind for an initial investment?"

"Why are they selling?"

Never, never answer that the home is too large or too small. If your caller hears that, they may feel the same way about the property before they even see it. Instead try something like, "I don't have the file on my desk, Mr. _____. How long have you been looking for a home?" Or "I'll be happy to obtain that information for you. At what number may I call you back?" You see, you're still closing for that appointment.

"What is the price of the home?"

"They're asking $295,000. Is this about the investment amount you had in mind? Better yet, today, most people are more concerned with the monthly investment. About how much did you wish to invest monthly in your new home?" If you learn what they can afford each month, any professional can compute what they can afford as the total investment and lead them to the right property for them.

"Will the owner take less?"

Isn't this a silly question? Why consider offering less until they see it? Some of them will, though. I always said, "I've learned never to make a decision for a client. However, would you be interested in buying the home if they would?" Here most people will say, "Not without seeing it," and give you another opportunity to close for the appointment.

"I want to bring my brother-in-law. He knows all about real estate."

Have you ever heard that? They just say that to protect themselves. If their brother-in-law really knew all about real estate, he'd have a license to sell it and they wouldn't be calling you in the first place. They just want that third party to be a buffer between you and them.

There will be times when there is a legitimate third party though. And some of you make a mistake here. You try to close the sale when the people you're talking to don't have the capacity to go ahead. It's just like when you take a woman looking for homes without her husband. Don't overclose her on the home. She isn't likely to make the final decision without her husband. Nor, will a man be likely to choose a home without his wife's consent.

You may take a couple out looking at homes who says they're getting the money from their parents. A professional never closes until they're in front of the person who has the authority to make the decision. So when they tell you about their third party, say, "You're fortunate to have someone to advise you. Most friends and relatives are reluctant to aid in a major decision and can only recommend against the purchase. May I ask if he will be living with you?" If they are living with them, you must consider how much say that person has in the final decision. If they won't be living with them, you can bypass this objection.

"The last guy we worked with showed us some really tacky homes. Are you going to waste our time?"

There are buyers out there with champagne tastes and beer budgets. You'll come across them now and then. Some salespeople lack what I call polish and tact. When the callers tell you that all they've seen were dumps, it's possible that's all they can afford.

But the person showing them homes did not have the ability to communicate that effectively. They could have helped these people realize that they have an opportunity to get involved in a stepping-stone home, one that would allow them to "express their creativity and personality." Based on that expression, they would increase the value to the point where they can reap a tremendous profit, which will help them afford the home they now can't afford but want. It's not so much what you say, but how you say it. Use these words:

"Ideally, sir, I strive to show only two homes to each prospect. One to determine the prospect's likes and dislikes and the second only when I have selected the right property for them. When can you see number one? Now or would 4:00 P.M. be better?"

Or: "No, sir, but to assure you that your time is not wasted, I'll prepare information on several fine homes and mail the information to you for your consideration before you visit the homes. That sounds fair, doesn't it? If you'll just give me your address, and what's your phone number?" If the prospect has accessibility to the Internet, you could offer to e-mail them links to some properties your company is showing online.

"I prefer not to give my name (or number). I don't want to be bothered."

"I understand how you feel. No one likes a pushy salesperson trying to force something unwanted on them. However, the longer I'm in the business, the more I realize that selling is an unnecessary act. The important skill is to find a home that really suits a family, then to show them how they can own it, don't you agree? If an exceptional property becomes available, how may I reach you?"

"I talked to another salesperson, and he said he'd call me back but didn't."

"Sir, I hope you won't judge me or my company by the performance of another company or agent. Please give me your number so I may recontact you and provide you with my finest service."

Now that you have the material, I challenge you to learn it. Use it on your very next call. Sure, it'll sound rough at first, but once you've internalized it and it comes out naturally, you'll do great. Read and role play the answers to the questions above with a loved one or a fellow associate.

One top producer told me that she took all the telephone responses, enlarged them on cue cards, and just read them over the phone to the caller. Soon the words became hers, and she started getting eight out of ten appointments to show properties from the calls she received.

Remember, you're first and foremost in the people business, and you move people to making decisions by using the right words.

CHAPTER 21

Open House Opportunities

Before we go into how to professionally demonstrate properties, let's cover another powerful method of meeting buyers. It's called the open house. Many salespeople will tell you an open house is a waste of time, and it is—unless it's conducted properly. A well-planned open house can put you face to face with a large number of buyers.

Before you commit a whole day of your time to an open house, you must plan well. Review your listings carefully before choosing the home. Don't choose a property because the seller wants you to hold an open house there. A good open house must have five qualities.

1. THE HOME MUST BE PRICED RIGHT.

Whatever you do, don't hold an open house in a home that's overpriced for the current market. It will not only have a negative effect on your reputation with buyers, it'll make the sellers angry when no one buys the home. Most people who stop at open houses already have some knowledge about the neighborhood. If they know most of the homes run about $200,000 and you've got this one listed for $225,000 they're not going to want to do business with you on this home or any other in the area.

Another thing to be concerned about in holding an open house in an overpriced home is that the neighbors who stop by will all be watching to see how long it's on the market and if you really sell it for that amount. If by some odd chance, you do sell it that high, you'll be getting calls for more overpriced listings. If you don't, they'll remember you and never use you or your company when they're ready to sell.

2. THERE MUST BE PLENTY OF TRAFFIC.

The first concern of any business in looking for a retail location is traffic flow. They can be sure that a certain percentage of the people who drive by will stop in. The same goes for your open house. It must be in an area where a large number of people will be driving by and seeing your signs. In many areas, you can create a certain amount of traffic flow with good directional signs or other attention getters, but it doesn't make sense to hold an open house that's hard to find.

3. YOU MUST KNOW THE AREA WELL.

Always hold your open house at a home in your normal service area. The people who stop in are going to do so because they think they want to live in that area. If this isn't the right home for them, you'll need to know of other homes in the same area that may fill their needs.

4. MAKE CERTAIN YOUR SELLERS ARE GONE FOR THE DAY.

You must explain to your sellers that no buyer will relax in their home if they are there. Discuss this with them when you set up the open house. If they won't leave, choose another home. It would be a waste of your time to be there when the sellers' presence will be frightening potential buyers away.

This may take some time, but you'll need to make the sellers feel secure in leaving you alone in their home. Tell them exactly what you'll be doing to preplan the day and build traffic. Be honest with them about your expectations for this open house and make them happy to leave it all up to you. You may have to assure them that no one will destroy their home and that you won't leave the premises unattended. The extent to which you'll have to carry this conversation will depend on the sellers' emotional situation regarding the sale of the home.

5. THE SELLERS MUST BE PREPARED TO WORK AS HARD ON MAKING THE HOME LOOK GOOD AS YOU DO ON GETTING PEOPLE TO COME TO IT.

Most sellers know enough to have the home looking neat both inside and out. Sometimes they need to be made aware of how much a little paint and some extra elbow grease can enhance the value of their home, making both of you a lot of money. If the sellers have a lot of plants in their home, be sure they're trimmed up nicely for the open house. The condition of the plants tells a lot about how the sellers have kept up their home.

Invite the Neighbors

Now that you've gone through the criteria we listed and made your arrangements with the seller, it's time to get to work on that traffic flow. Advertising and promotional flyers can accomplish much; however, I recommend that you first consider the neighbors. Hand deliver twenty invitations to the open house to neighbors. Don't mail them, put them in the hands of those neighbors yourself. It's a good opportunity for you to meet them and demonstrate your professionalism.

I recommend you deliver these invitations the day before your open house. You might wonder why you would ask the neighbors. They just might have some friends or relatives wanting to move to the area. Or, they might know what a good investment the area is and want to purchase another property themselves. Or, it's even happened that neighbors like the area, but wish they had bought a home facing another direction or even envied the landscaping, design, and upgrades of a home they look at every day. People do move across the street or down the street in a neighborhood. It happens. That's one of the reasons you want the neighbors to know about your open house.

In hand delivering these invitations, here's the phraseology to use: "Hello. My name is Tom Hopkins, representing Champions Unlimited. As you know, we have a home across the street that we're helping the owners to market. Tomorrow, between noon and five, we're going to have an open house. Now, the Smiths will be gone for the day, and I'll have refreshments. If you'd like to stop by, it's an exciting value. You may have a friend or relative who's looking for a great investment so I wanted to be sure to invite you and your spouse to see it."

The key phrases here are, "The Smiths will be gone for the day," and "I'll have refreshments." Then, you want to put the idea into their minds that they ". . . may have a friend or relative who's looking for a great investment."

One of two things will happen here. They may come to look it over and find out what it's listed for to get an idea of the value of their home without directly calling someone in real estate. That's okay because it'll give you an opportunity to list their home at a later date. Or, they may bring friends with them who want to move into the area. If they don't choose that home, you will most likely get an opportunity to show them other homes in the area.

Now, many of your sellers might not want their neighbors in their homes. By making them understand that a great percentage of people who buy in a given area already have friends or relatives living there, they'll very often change their feelings. If your sellers absolutely insist on no neighbors, honor their wishes and don't directly invite the neighbors.

Signs

Next, you need to drive the neighborhood and decide on the best locations for your signs on the day of the open house. Do this several days beforehand—not the morning of the open house. Always take the time to get permission to put a sign on someone's private property. It's a simple thing, but means so much to the home owner. Some people who live on busy corners find directional arrows on their property nearly every weekend. By taking the time to ask permission and guarantee to repair any damage from the sign, you'll make yet another contact who will eventually want to move, giving you the opportunity to sell their home and/or help them relocate to another area.

I recommend the following phraseology for meeting these people: "Good morning. My name is Tom Hopkins with Champions Unlimited. A family in the neighborhood is employing us to professionally market their home. I'll be having an open house on Saturday from noon until five and I'd like to ask you a favor. Could I use a small portion of your lot for one of my directional signs? When I'm finished, I'll replace the sod and you'll never know it was there. Would you mind?"

In most cases, they won't mind at all. You're one of the few who had the courtesy to at least ask their permission. So, always ask. If you don't ask, they may turn the sign around or lay it down. As soon as you have their approval, ask for their name and send them a thank-you note.

"Dear Mr. & Mrs. James, I want to thank you for letting me put my sign in your yard. We are expecting a tremendous amount of activity at this open house. If I can ever serve the real estate needs of you or any of your friends, please feel free to call."

They'll not only appreciate your asking, they'll remember you because you're different from all the other agents who didn't ask.

A Little Help

Another thing you must take into consideration during your preparation for the open house is what you do if a qualified buyer comes in wanting a home in that area, but not this particular home. You can't just leave the open house to show them other homes. If they're really interested enough to look today, you need to show them other homes today. They may buy from someone else by next week. That's why I suggest you have another agent at your open house. Preferably, they will be with you at the open house the whole time. In some cases, however, you may have to rely on someone being on call within a few minutes drive to cover for you while you show other properties. However, you won't be able to get anyone to work with you at all if you don't handle the details required to get a lot of activity at this home. Another agent won't want to tie up a potentially productive day at your low-traffic open house.

Black or with Cream and Sugar?

Plan the refreshments you'll serve at your open house carefully. Most people who come to open houses don't really want to take the time to meet you or risk getting involved with a real estate agent. They just want to breeze through to get a feel for the home and get out. They don't want to give you their name for fear you'll try to sell them something. So you have to plan refreshments that will slow them down and, you hope, get them talking.

The best thing to slow them down is coffee that's fresh and hot. Be careful not to have it hot enough to burn anyone. You don't want to create a lawsuit. Now, you don't ask them if they'd like a cup. Assume they'd like one and simply ask them how they take it. Serve the coffee in a real cup—not a plastic disposable cup. You can either use your own or the seller's, if they give you permission. Then, your prospects will feel obligated to stay long enough to at least have a few sips of coffee and move slowly through the home so as not to spill it or break the cup.

A nice technique one of my champions has used during the hot summer months is to give qualified buyers one or two quarts of ice cream on their way out if he isn't going to be showing them other properties that day. Where are they going with two quarts of ice cream? Most likely, they'll return home. They won't drive around looking at other homes and leave the ice cream melting in their car.

Information to Give and to Get

Prepare a one-page information sheet about the home. List the overall square footage, carpet color, various room dimensions, and other amenities that someone planning to live in the home would be interested in knowing. Include in this list all of the things the seller is leaving in the home such as refrigerator, doghouse or pet door, swing set or fireplace screens, and utensils. I have sold many pet doors that happened to come with the homes I had listed.

Be sure you also bring some sort of guest book for your open house guests to sign. Besides giving you a list of prospective buyers, it shows the seller the type of activity you had that day.

Keeping Busy

Be sure to bring work materials with you. Even the most successful open houses will have some slow periods. You can accomplish a lot of work in a brief, quiet period, if you are prepared. You can write your thank-you notes, catch up on some reading material, write ads for the next week's campaign, and complete many other highly productive tasks.

Be careful not to spread your work materials out over an entire counter or table. You'll have to rush to gather them up when someone comes into the home, and you could risk misplacing valuable information. Only work on one item at a time and quickly place it in your briefcase if someone enters the home.

Opening the House

Always plan plenty of time in your schedule to prepare the morning of your open house. Allow yourself time to get all of your signs placed. Then, arrive at the home at least an hour before the open house is to begin. The sellers probably won't leave until you get there and will want to see what you are doing to show their home effectively.

I recommend that you open all the drapes in the home and turn on all the lights. If your open house is during the warm months and the home has air conditioning, turn it on. Keep the temperature just cool enough that people will notice the air conditioning immediately upon entering. If you have it too cold, they'll want to hurry through the home.

Light a fire in the fireplace if there is one. Even in the summer, this is a good idea. It lends a certain emotional appeal. A small fire is all that's necessary. If people ask you about it, and most of them will, you can explain that you wanted them to get a feel for the home setting in a different season.

If you're holding your open house during the colder months, keep the home comfortably warm so there are no doubts about the effectiveness of the furnace. A small fire is still a good idea. If you have a roaring blaze, that one room may become uncomfortably warm. If this same home has air conditioning, be sure to note it on the information sheet you have prepared. Or, to be different, you might even want to hang an attractive sign on the thermostat that there is also central air conditioning in the home.

To involve even more senses in the home, many real estate salespeople I know bake a tin of cinnamon rolls or cookies during the open house. The wonderful aroma of home-baked goodies does a lot for emotional involvement in a home. For those of you who have a fear of baking or might become too distracted to keep track of something like that, don't risk burning the rolls. Instead, put a few drops of vanilla extract in a pie plate and place the oven on warm.

If the sellers don't have much in the way of decorations in the home, to brighten up the rooms, bring in some vases of fresh flowers or blooming plants.

They're Here!

Okay, you're ready. It's noon on the day of your open house. You've done everything to make it successful. The home looks great, your signs are well placed, your refreshments are ready, and the neighbors have been invited. Before you meet any prospective buyers, you should have internalized the techniques covered in the previous chapters. If you haven't, you risk losing every prospect. It would be a terrible waste after you've put so much time and effort into this open house. I'll run through a few of the techniques here so you'll see how they should work.

There is a couple coming up the walk of the home. Don't let them see you peeking out the window or door. Stay busy. When they knock or come in the door, don't jump at them. Go to the door, open it, and say, "Hello. Won't you please step in and make yourselves at home?" As you say this, back up. Prepare yourself beforehand to know in which direction to step. It's not as effective if you back into a wall or piece of furniture. This body language invites them to step farther into the home.

Step back until they are well inside the door. Then stop. Look them in the eyes, smile warmly and say, "My name is Tom Hopkins with Champions Unlimited." Don't offer your hand for a shake unless they do. Only shake hands if they offer first. Stand there until they offer their names. It'll force their names out of them. Don't be afraid of silence, and don't move any farther into the home. Just keep smiling. They'll give you their names.

After you get their names, tell them it's nice to see them and step aside. It's critical that you get out of their way now. If you ask them more questions at this point, they'll feel pressured and withdraw. To avoid that, simply say, "Why don't you folks just walk through the home by yourselves. If you have any questions about the home, the area, or the real estate market in general, please feel free to ask."

Now, you might be thinking, "What? Let them loose in the home by themselves? What if they miss the great closet organization system the sellers have installed?" The average agent will go out of their way to show the prospects every nook and cranny of the home—boasting of the wonderful job the sellers have done. Most prospective buyers either won't care about those items or will disagree with your term *wonderful job*. It's more important to let them tour the home alone and get the feel of the house before they begin looking for details. Let's face it, if they don't like the overall feeling they get in the home, they aren't going to care about the amenities.

When they get to the kitchen, be ready with your hot coffee and a few nonthreatening questions. See my Buyer's Analysis for Better Service form in the next chapter for an idea of the information you need to know to decide how to proceed with them. Don't hover over them or write down the answers to these questions, just use them to strike up a conversation.

1 . Do you folks live in the area? If they're neighbors, you'll handle them differently than if they're from out of town.

2. How long have you been looking for a home? You need to know if these people are professional open house visitors. If they've been looking for months, they're probably not too motivated. If they say, "Only a couple of days," they may be highly motivated, and you'll have to act fast or they'll go through someone else.

3. How many are in your family? The answer to this will give you an idea of whether or not the size of this home is feasible for them.

4. Have you seen any homes you like yet? Some open house visitors already have purchased in the area and are just out to compare to see if

they got a good buy. If it's a case where they have found one but haven't purchased, you need to know why. Ask what prevented them from owning that home. You want to discover if they made too low an offer or if they couldn't qualify.

5. Are you looking for a good investment as well as a good location to live in? Most people will answer yes to this one. Some, however, will give you even more of a response. For example, they may say, "We're really concerned with the investment opportunity. We like where we live now, but we have a large equity in the home and are thinking of moving up."

At this point, you'll know if they're serious about buying a home. To gather more information on their specific needs, ask them to comment on the home. Tell them it's information you want to give the seller to help them sell the home. In telling you their likes and dislikes, they'll be telling you if this is really the home for them. If it is, ask them to re-tour the home with you so you can be sure they've seen all the amenities. This is when you point out the space-saving closet, the low-maintenance landscaping, and the refrigerator that matches the built-ins. I cover specific demonstration techniques in the next chapter.

The Perfect Home

If this is obviously not the home for them, match their needs in your head to a home in your inventory. Try to find a perfect house for them. Then tell them, "Mr. and Mrs. Brown, based on what you've told me, I can't help but see in my mind's eye a home that might have everything you're looking for. The amenities are beautiful. The location is excellent. There are quality carpets and draperies. Now, it does have four bedrooms. You mentioned you wanted a fourth bedroom. It's one of the most exciting homes I know of that will fill your specific needs."

You must sound excited to build their desire in wanting to see this home as soon as possible. Enthusiasm and excitement are contagious. They'll start thinking you've really got something to see.

You would then continue with, "It's nearby, and we have a key. You might want to follow me by it this afternoon." That sentence has a very strong effect on buyers. They're thinking, "Okay, it's not too far so it won't take long. The key is available so maybe the sellers will be gone from there, too. We can follow the agent and not get committed to driving together and seeing a dozen homes today." It's a nonthreatening situation with a lot of potential for success if you build it right.

Keep in mind that you must truly have this home in your inventory. It must be close by. By that, I mean within five miles. And you must have access to the key. Otherwise, you'll lose them right from the start by not being able to fulfill your promises.

If you don't have another agent to cover your open house for you so you can leave right now, use this technique to set an appointment to show the home as soon as possible.

Getting to Know You

In a case where you've determined this isn't the home for them, and you can't think of a home in your current inventory that meets their needs, you have to get their address and phone number. As they're preparing to leave, ask them to sign the guest register as a courtesy to the sellers. Explain that you want to show them the amount of activity the open house has generated. It's really an evaluation of how well you did your preparation.

At this point, the buyers like you and trust your knowledge of real estate in the area. Have your business cards handy and use this method for getting their permission to recontact them. "Mr. and Mrs. Johnson, some of the finest values come on the market and are sold before the signs are even put on them. If a fantastic value comes to my attention (pause), here, let me give you my card. Here's my office phone number, and let me circle my home phone. You can reach me twenty-four hours a day for service. How can I reach you?"

By using these words, you're unthreateningly offering your service, then asking for a means of contacting them. The psychology behind this close is powerful. The average salesperson would ask for their number first, then when they didn't get it, offer their card and probably not see or hear from them again. Once you have their permission to service them, you can set appointments for demonstrating properties.

CHAPTER 22

Qualifying the Buyer

You have an appointment with a couple that responded to one of your ads. You've cleaned off your desk and are waiting for them to arrive. What are you going to do when they come in?

First, you want them to let you help them. And they won't let you help them unless they like you, right? Therefore, you need to establish a positive rapport. Let's go over some ideas to help you do just that.

Have a neat, clean desk. When people walk into your office, they look at everything and judge you. Always keep one drawer in your desk empty. Then, when you are busy, have a lot of paperwork to handle, and have a new prospect coming in, you can put everything from the top of your desk into it. It can't get lost, and you can take it all back out when they've gone. If you have a family, place a picture of them on your desk. People want to know if you're like them.

Relax your prospects by being relaxed. Even if you have never done this successfully before, you must act relaxed. Would you like and trust a nervous salesperson? If you act nervous, they'll get nervous. If you have no self-confidence, they won't have any confidence in you either.

The first impression is so critical. I can't impress this on you enough. The moment people see you, they start evaluating you. Your appearance must be neat and clean. Take a moment before their arrival to check your clothing, your shoes, your nails, hair, and breath. If you need some spiffing up, do it!

You must be careful about your handshake. What does it trigger when you meet someone for the first time, and they reach out for you? Some people expect it. Others back off. And you won't immediately know what kind of people your prospects are. So, to avoid putting them off, don't reach for them, unless they reach out first. Now, this can't look like a fumbled football play. Simply keep your right arm angled so your hand is about at your waist. Then, you'll be ready to shake their hand if they reach out for you.

Qualify them where you intend to close. If your office has a conference room that is used for this purpose, use it. If you do this type of work at your desk, then get them there for the qualification sequence.

If you change rooms between qualification and closing, your prospects will fight you because they'll feel they're going to be sold. When you use the same area, they'll feel comfortable the second time they're in it, which, hopefully, is when you close them on owning the property.

Determine the best area for you to close and use it all the time. Once you've earned professional status, you will instinctively know where the best place is for you to close the sale. In some cases, it might be in the home they've just fallen in love with, providing the sellers will be gone for a while. It could be in your office, in their home or apartment, even on the hood of your car, or in a local coffee shop. A lot will depend on how excited they are and what you know about their ability to qualify.

Wherever you choose to qualify and close your buyer, be aware of the potential for interruptions and do what you can to limit them. The two areas of qualifying and closing are so delicate that even a minor interruption can cancel out all the hours you've put into the process thus far. You must concentrate only on the needs of the people in front of you when you're with them. By this, I mean both their emotional needs and financial needs.

The first thing you want to say when potential buyers first come into your office is this: "Mr. and Mrs. Jones, why don't we step into the other room so we can have a little privacy, while we discuss some of the things I need to know to help you possibly find the right home today."

Once you've settled them in, you're ready to qualify. Why do you think I have you qualify them immediately? Have you ever shown a buyer several properties, wasted a lot of time, a lot of gas, and a lot of effort and then found out that they couldn't qualify to own a home even if you found them one? Qualifying them before showing homes helps you determine the right course of action.

Buyer's Analysis for Better Service

Qualifying the buyer is one of the most critical aspects of any selling career, but especially real estate. Before you begin asking your potential clients questions, ask their permission like this, "May I, in order to serve you better, ask you a few questions on my Buyer's Analysis for Better Service form?"

The Buyer's Analysis for Better Service form is nothing more than the questions we're about to cover typed on a piece of paper. You can re-create them on your computer with your company logo on them. It's up to you. The important thing is that you ask clients these questions and write down their answers.

If they are reluctant and say something like, "We just want to go see the home we called on," you would say, "We could do that, but I've found that eight out of ten people who call on an ad invest in another home. It would be a shame if on the way to this home there's another excellent value and we miss the opportunity to stop by, wouldn't it? So may I ask you a few questions?"

The questions you should have on your form are these:

1. Is this your first visit to our community? You might already know this from your earlier conversation. In that case, don't ask. The whole purpose of this questioning device is to give you the information you need to discover what they're really looking for.

If they live in the area, they may own a home they need to sell before getting involved with a new home. They may be slightly familiar with the area. This is when you would use the piggyback technique we discussed in Chapter 9.

2. How long have you been looking for a home? The answer to this question will save you a lot of time. If they say they've been looking for three or four years, you may decide that today you have more important things to do and after qualifying them you may make an appointment to show them homes at a better time for you.

BUYER'S ANALYSIS FOR BETTER SERVICE FORM

[**Note:** Precede each question with the name(s)]
1. Is this your first visit to the community?   Yes   No
    A.   If yes, where are you from? _____
2. How long have you been looking for a home? _____
3. How many people are in your family?_____
    A.   Number of children _____
    B.   Names _____
    C.   Ages _____
4. Where do you live now (address)? _____
5. How long have you lived there? _____
6. Are you investing in your home or do you rent? _____
7. (If they own) How is the resale market in your area? _____
8. May I ask Mr. _____ where are you employed? _____
9. How long have you been there? _____
    *Piggyback: Ask a question about the answer to the last question to keep rapport building.
10. Have you seen any homes you really liked?_____
    A.   What prevented you from owning that home? _____

URGENCY QUESTIONS
1. How soon had you thought of making a move? _____
2. How much time will you have to see homes today? _____
3. How many bedrooms would best suit your needs? _____

IF THEY OWN A HOME
1. How much do you feel you will realize from the sale of the home? _____
2. Will it be necessary to sell your present home to purchase the new one? _____
3. Will you be converting any of your other investments to complete the purchase? _____

CALL FOR DECISION
1. If we are fortunate enough to find the right home today,
    will you be in a position to make a decision to proceed?   Yes   No

FINANCIAL QUALIFYING QUESTIONS
(Preface with, "Not to be personal, but to do a better job for you, may I ask,")
1. How much of your savings did you wish to invest in your new home? _____
2. What price range have you been considering? (Pause)
    Better yet, since most people today are more concerned
    with the monthly investment, how much do you feel you could
    comfortably invest each month in your new home, including everything? _____
3. A rule of thumb most lenders use is the monthly investment
    should be approximately one-fourth of a person's gross
    monthly income, after long-term bills. Are we in line here?
    (Note: Use on low- to medium-price range properties.) _____
4. **(To wife)** Would you take a moment to describe
    your present home to me, telling me your likes
    and dislikes?_____
5. Do you have any special requirements
    that you are looking for in your new home? _____

If the buyers are sincerely motivated and qualified, they will buy within seven days. Here's one of the biggest problems most of us have: When buyers are sincerely motivated, when they have the capacity, when they have the need, we can't risk losing them because they will buy a home from someone within seven days. That's why when you have a qualified buyer, you have to stay with them.

3. How many are in your family? Have you ever asked prospects how many children they have? There's a potential in that question for embarrassment. Perhaps they've had the unfortunate instance of losing a child or they haven't been blessed with any and do want them. Either way, you're stepping into potentially dangerous territory. That's why I prefer that you word the question as I've given it. Then, if they say there are five in the family you can say, "Oh, then, you have three children?" If there is instead a situation where a grandparent or other adult relative is living with them, they will then tell you.

4. Where do you live now? If they answer by telling you that they're renting, you've gotten what you need to know. If they give you a general answer such as the name of a city, ask for their address.

5. How long have you lived there? If they've been there a long time and they own a home, you can get excited because they probably have a rather large equity in that home to work with. If they've only been there six months and they own the home, you may have a challenge getting them successfully moved.

You may encounter people with this type of situation. They've invested in a home in another area, perhaps even in another state and within six months they feel they've made a bad decision and want to start relocating. It can be difficult to work with these people because they don't have any equity built up. In other words, they don't have the financial capacity to make a move at this time. They may have to consider renting the other property for a year or so, depending on their financial situation. There could be a hefty prepayment penalty on the loan for that home if they resell within three years. These are all factors that could negatively impact your ability to serve them today.

6. Are you investing in your home or do you rent? You would only ask this if it hasn't already come up through the other questions.

7. (If they own their home) How is the resale market in your area? This question may prompt them to tell you that they found the resale

market very good because their home has already sold. Then, you know they have capital to work with on the new home.

If they tell you that they don't know about the resale market, they may be telling you that they haven't seriously considered the move. They could be ignorant as to what their equity position is, which is what you need to know. Or, their home could become a potential listing for you. If they've had their home on the market for a long time and it hasn't sold, it could be that it's overpriced. You have to consider all of these possibilities.

8. May I ask, Mr. _____, where are you employed? It's a given that you must ask both the husband and wife this question.

9. How long have you been there? This would be a piggyback question based on their answers to the last question. The type of business they're in and the length of time employed will tell you whether or not they'll be able to qualify for a new loan. If they have had eight jobs in the past two years, they may not be able to get a new loan. Typically, the borrower has to demonstrate two years of income stability. If they're self-employed, they'll have to show proof of verifiable income. And, unfortunately, too many self-employed people do not have that information readily available.

10. Have you found any homes you really like yet? If they are already involved in a new purchase, you're wasting your time with them. Perhaps they've made an offer on a property and just thought they'd look around a little more while it was pending. They aren't going to buy from you. If they have already found one they like, ask, "What prevented you from owning that home?" You need to know. It could have cost too much. The initial investment could have been too high. All of this information will lead you closer to the property that will be right for them.

Urgency Questions

1. How soon had you thought of making a move? If they have children of school age, they may plan to wait until after the school year is over. They may be ready to move today.

2. How much time will you have to see homes today? When they an-

swer that, you will know at what pace you need to proceed today. If they have plenty of time, you can take a slower pace than if they have only today to look, perhaps in the case of a transfer.

If your buyers are being transferred into the area and have only the weekend to look at homes, it may be necessary for you to spend the entire weekend with them. You may have to totally educate them about the real estate market as well as the amenities of the various sections of town. It's possible that they will need to see as many as twenty homes in different areas before they feel they can make a decision. If this is the case, always plan to take a break after showing them four properties. At that time, ask what their likes and dislikes were and move on to the next group of homes. Ask them to forget what they've seen so far, as you are zeroing in on the right property for them because you don't want them to get confused.

3. How many bedrooms would best suit your needs? Don't ask them how many they would like. They might like twenty. If they say they'd like four, then you know they can handle three. If they say they need four, then you know they probably have a three-bedroom home now and need something larger.

If they own their home, ask the following questions also.

1. How much do you feel you will realize from the sale of the home? Whatever they tell you, prepare to discount it by 25 percent because most sellers have expectations higher than what they actually receive. I often find them a home with a lower initial investment than what they told me. Don't try to find them something that has an initial investment of exactly what they told you, and never show them one that's more. In most cases, they'd have to struggle to make it on what they told you. If you try to get them to stretch too far, you'll lose them.

2. Will it be necessary to sell your present home to purchase the new one? They may want to use it as a rental property.

3. Will you be converting any of your other investments to complete the purchase? If they are, it would be good for you to know. If they don't have any, they'll be flattered that you asked.

The next question will ultimately weed out the *lookers* from the *buyers*. It must be used word for word as it is written here. Memorize it.

"If we are fortunate enough to find the right home today, will you be in a position to make a decision to proceed?" This is a tactful way of asking, "If we find a home today, are you going to buy it or not?" This question should trigger any objection they might have in the back of their minds. It should bring forth any third parties involved such as the lawyer who has to approve anything they "sign." There could be a relative who is lending them the initial investment.

There are some money questions you should also ask at this time. Providing this information to you can cause them some discomfort. After all, it's personal information. Whenever you must ask a personal question, you need to couch it or warn them it's coming rather than jump right into it. You may want to say, "Not to be personal, but to do a better job for you, may I ask . . ." Now, they want you to do a better job for them, don't they? Of course they do. They won't hold back any information if it's for their own good. Here are the questions:

1. How much of your savings did you wish to invest in your new home?

This is much better than asking them, "How much money do you have?" If they tell you that, you might want all of it. If they have a limited amount of funds, they can act like the amount they tell you is only part of what they've got, thus saving face and feeling good. Remember, one of the keys to selling is to make them feel good with you. You want them to feel good about every step in the buying process. You can't turn them off here.

2. What price range have you been considering? (Pause) Better yet, since most people today are more concerned with the monthly investment, how much do you feel you could comfortably invest each month in your new home, including everything?

This question is very important. In some cases they won't know what to tell you about the price range because some other salesperson has shown them everything from $50,000 to $300,000 homes. The figure they give you will be close to or higher than what they're paying now.

3. A rule of thumb most lenders use is the monthly investment should be approximately one-fourth of a person's combined gross monthly income after long-term bills. Are we in line here?

(Please note that lender's qualifications regarding income to monthly investment ratios may vary. Know the figures for your area.) This question will make them stop and think. If they question you as to what is considered long-term bills, it's anything that would show up on a credit report. For most areas, that would include car payments, other major purchases, and credit cards if their current balances would take longer than six months to pay off.

To compute an approximate figure, take the amount they tell you they gross in a week, multiply it by 4.3 weeks. Then divide by four. If they give you what they make hourly, multiply it by 40 hours, then by 4.3 weeks again. Sometimes they'll tell you how much their long-term debts amount to. That's great. If they don't tell you or seem hesitant here, go with the ballpark figure you get without knowing their debts. You will know then to stay under that amount for a monthly investment.

Beware here that if they want to look at $400,000 homes this question may insult them. If they earn $150,000 per year, in most cases, they should be pretty financially sound—but not always. You have to be the judge as to whether or not this question is appropriate.

4. Would you take a moment to describe your present home to me, telling me your likes and dislikes?

The wife is more likely to begin answering this question. If either of them shows any hesitation say, "You see, I would like to be sure that you retain the things you like most in looking for your new home." For some people there are features they just love about their home, and those features, if found in another home, can become one of your major closing points.

If they fail to give you any negative comments, you must ask for them. They're just as important to you as the things they love about their home. You would ask, "Not to be negative, but if you were to change anything in your existing home, what would that be?" I cannot repeat often enough how important it is that you write these things down. If you forget one little negative and it's in the first home you show them, they'll begin to doubt your competence. Don't let that happen.

5. Do you have any special requirements that you are looking for in your new home?

Anything they say here is important. To demonstrate, let me tell you about one couple I got happily involved in a home. When I asked this question, the wife said that they had a small dog and every home they've lived in with that dog had a doggie door in the kitchen. Now, I made a note of that, but didn't tell them the home I was going to show them had one. It wasn't a major selling point. However, when they saw the home I had chosen for them, they were delighted when they discovered it had one. Something that small may help you overcome other challenges.

What you really need to learn here is whether or not they have any health-related needs. If they're allergic to orange blossoms, for example, you know not to show them any homes near orange groves. They may need a basement. They may need a one-story home if one of them has a hard time getting around. They may need air conditioning. Now, in the case of air conditioning, in some areas of the country your listing sheet may say yes to air conditioning when the home has an evaporative cooler. You must know for sure what type of air conditioning the home has before you show it to them or you could lose your credibility completely. They'll blame you for not knowing. You can't try to blame the listing sheet. That's weak.

If there's absolutely no way you can get your prospects into your conference room or to your desk to ask them these questions, be prepared to ask them in the car. Now, you won't be able to write down their answers in the car. What you would do here is to hand one of them the Buyer's Analysis for Better Service form and have them go over it in the car. Sometimes this will work so well that they'll actually qualify themselves.

Deciding What Property to Show

Now that you have a good idea of what they're looking for and what they can afford, you need to choose four properties to show them. Never show them more than four properties at a time. If you show more than four, they'll get confused and you'll lose them. Besides, you're a professional real estate salesperson, not a professional tour guide. We'll go over how to find them the right home after showing only two or three. In instances where you do have to show more than four homes, ask them to wipe their minds clean before going into that fifth home. Help them to look at each home individually, not compared to the others.

I suggest you ask their permission to show them homes that are less expensive than they can afford. You might phrase it like this, "Mr. and Mrs. Jones (use first names if applicable at this point), may I have your permission to show you a couple of homes that are less than you can afford? You see, if I can find you a suitable home for less money, you'll be under less financial pressure and have more money to enjoy your new home. May I?" They'll not only say "Yes," but they'll be amazed to meet the first salesperson who is trying to save them money. Another reason for doing this is that too many salespeople begin by showing homes that are at the top of what the buyer can afford. Then, if they are not satisfied with those properties, the salesperson starts moving them out of their financial range and ends up showing them properties they can't afford anyway.

You should begin by choosing four homes. The third home you'll show them will be the one you feel best suits their needs. The fourth home will be an alternate in case number three is wrong for them. Now, you may have been told, "Show them two dumps first, then close them on the nice one." That's not the idea. You show them two homes prior to the one you've chosen as their home to get feedback to confirm that you've made the right choice for them. If, after the first home, you realize the third one won't do, you will be able to make a change. That is why you always have a fourth home in reserve.

You might excuse yourself from the room for a moment to call the sellers of the three homes you plan to show this couple and make appointments. Once you are prepared, you are ready to get them in your car and begin demonstrating properties.

CHAPTER 23

Demonstrating the Property

Demonstrating the property involves strategy, just like qualifying and closing. It isn't something you just do without proper preparation and a certain amount of technique.

The most critical point of preparation for demonstration is never to show a home you haven't seen. You'll absolutely destroy yourself. You'll do nothing but create unnecessary challenges if you rely just on reading the listing sheets and deciding what sounds good. This is where knowledge of inventory will make or break your career.

Setting Up a Showing Sequence

There is a truth about showing homes. Most people don't know what they want. However, they do know what they don't want when they see it. Many times a buyer must see one or two properties they don't like so they can give you the feedback you need to pinpoint the type of home they will enjoy. In other words, pick out two or three homes for comparison to the one you think they will buy. This will also give you a better idea as to whether or not the home they called about, or the one you feel is right, really is.

If at all possible, don't try to set the appointment with the seller while sitting in front of your prospects. These are complete strangers you are trying to impress. Perhaps they just walked in off the street or you talked them in on an ad call. When you call the seller, you say, "Mr. and Mrs. Johnson, I have some nice people here with me that I would like to show your home today." The seller is glad you called but not because you have a potential buyer. They're glad because they have some problems they want to talk over with you. They tell you that the last person who showed their home left the door unlocked. Your side of the conversation would go something like this, "No, I didn't show your home the other day. We would never have left your door open. I'm sorry for any challenges that might have caused you." Now, what are your prospects thinking about you? They're doubting your competence. They're beginning to wonder why they're talking with you. You can't afford to let that happen.

Another reason you leave the prospects to make the appointment is that you could be calling at an inopportune time for the sellers. Granted, they should be prepared to have their home shown at any time; however, there may be something going on that you aren't aware of and the atmosphere isn't quite right. You wouldn't want your prospects to hear any of that. You can't allow any negativity to enter their minds prior to seeing the home. Also, if for some reason you can't get the appointment, the prospect may want to postpone seeing other properties until they can see that home. They may feel it's the right one and feel slighted if they can't see it.

Here's what I say before leaving the prospects to make the calls: "Based on the information we've got here, I have some excellent properties to show you. Let me go and call to arrange for us to pop by. Why don't you just chat for a moment and enjoy your coffee. Then, we'll go see the homes."

Note: Based on your office configuration, you may have to qualify, set appointments for showings, and close your prospects at your desk. If this is the case, you must develop strategies for your particular situation. For example, you might want to make arrangements with another agent whose desk is at the far end of the office from yours to make your calls to sellers from his or her desk.

Getting Them into Your Car

This next point is so critical. They must ride with you to the homes. One of the reasons for this is that most people will not fight in front of you. I had it happen, when I was new and they didn't ride with me that when we left the first home everything was okay. But, when we got to the second home, they had changed. They'd just had a knock down, drag out fight on the way to this home. Now, I was lost. Anything I said or did could have been the wrong thing and I'd lose them. To prevent that from happening, always have them ride with you. How do we get them to do that?

First, always try to park your car closest to the office door through which you plan to exit. That way it'll be easily accessible. You simply walk toward your car and open the door for them to get in. If they say what they usually say, "Why don't we just follow you" or "We'd like to take our car," you would say, "Oh, you'd rather drive? Fine." Close your car door and say, "I can ride with you."

If they try to get away from you say, "I understand. Would you let me do one thing, though? Would you let me do my best today to serve you?" Of course they'll say yes. Then, you follow with, "You see, by showing you the schools, the shopping, the amenities, and the overall area, everything that makes the decision of investing in a new home possible, you'll be more apt to make the right decision and that is what we want, isn't it? So, why don't we ride together? Shall we?" It'll be hard for them to say no when you're so nice. You're only trying to help them.

What do you do if they've brought four or five children with them? It's impossible for you to fit in their car. It's also impossible for all of them to fit in your car. What you do in this case is to suggest to the parents that a couple of the older children ride with you. Some parents simply won't go for that. They don't know you all that well and they don't know if they can entrust the safety of their children with you. Asking this question, though, may make one of the adults offer to ride with you so the kids can stay with Dad or Mom. They may even bring along one of the children. If the group is too large to manage well, suggest to the parents that they make an appointment to see the homes when the children can be watched by someone else. It will make the process go much more smoothly. Once they've selected a home or, at least narrowed the choices, they can then include the children in seeing a home or two to get their feedback.

Now, there will be times when you will encounter children who are less than well behaved. It should go without saying: Never strike another person's child! Also, be careful what you say when you speak to the children. Some parents take offense to anyone else correcting their children. Oh, you may want to torture them for what they're doing to your car, but don't do or say anything that could cause their parents to turn against you.

If the children are truly misbehaving or being annoying, explain to the parents your concern for their safety and that you want them to be happy during your time together. Choosing a home for the family is a major decision, and the parents shouldn't be distracted from seeing the amenities each home has to offer. Some parents will have the children wait in the car until they see if a property is even feasible.

I've had instances where teenagers would find everything wrong with the homes I showed. They didn't want to move, period. That's why you need to try especially hard to get them to like you. If they like you, they may even help you. Some teens helped turn the tide when it came to deciding between two houses when they found out there was something in it for them—a swimming pool, a friend who lived close by, a major mall in the area, etc.

For little ones, I suggest keeping coloring books, colored pencils, small puzzles and games in your car. If the parents like the home and want to make an offer while still there, sit the kids down to play quietly while you discuss the offer.

Driving to the Homes

It's important that you select the best route for getting to the homes, especially to number three—the one you think is best for them. You want them to see the nicest benefits of the area. If they've told you it's important for them to be near schools and shopping, take them by the shopping center and school when going into the neighborhood. If you know there's a house at one end of the street that hasn't been kept up well, don't take them by it. It'll give them a negative opinion of the neighborhood even before they've seen the home you've chosen.

Before you even think about getting a prospect into your car, you must be prepared with what you'll talk to them about on your way. I like to suggest that you go to your local chamber of commerce and learn everything you can about your area. Do you realize how impressive it is when you can tell your prospects the population, the anticipated growth, community events, average temperatures (if they're moving from an area unlike yours), and information about major employers in the area? Remember: Always sell with the facts. Learn them and use them.

Another thing to be concerned with once you get them into your car is how you drive. If you've always wanted to be a race driver, now is not the time to show them. It could be that they've been in an accident before and are nervous about being in a car with a strange driver anyway. Don't do anything that might make them more nervous. If they're taking the time to worry about whether or not they'll see their loved ones again, they won't be thinking about owning a home.

If you have someone sitting in the back seat of your car, adjust your rear view mirror when you get in so you can glance into their eyes in that mirror as well as see out the rear window. Tell them why you're doing this so they don't think you're some kind of weirdo. Say something like this, "Mary, I'm going to tilt my mirror to see you so we can communicate during our discussion on the way to the property." The person in the back seat will appreciate it. You're keeping them involved. If you'll be driving in heavy traffic, tilt the mirror back to where it's most beneficial to you as the driver—not the real estate agent.

Keep your conversation moving while in the car. Also, make it fun. Ask them questions about their hobbies, sports interests, and employment. Tell them a couple of jokes (only cute, clean ones). Never tell an ethnic, religious, political, or off-color joke. Even if they tell you one, don't you ever tell them one. It'll alter their image of you.

Always have respect for both parties. If you're a man, don't get so involved in a discussion with the husband about football that you alienate the wife. If you're a woman, don't get off on tangents with the wife that aren't of interest to the husband.

Also, be extremely polite at all times. If you're in doubt about your manners, go to your library and get a book on them. Don't find out the hard way that you have offended someone.

Ask if there are any special requirements in the home they're looking for. I know you've already covered this on your Buyer's Analysis for Better Service form, but something else may have come into their minds. By asking this question again, you may find that they need something they hadn't thought of telling you before, something that could help you close the sale. Perhaps in your discussion of hobbies they say they enjoy something that requires a lot of space or a certain type of lighting. Ask where they currently display their collectibles or work on their hobbies. Remember those answers when you're showing them the right home.

Arriving at the Homes

As you drive up to the first home, look on the opposite side of the street. Get them looking at the other homes in the neighborhood to get a feeling for the area. Park across the street from the home you're showing. If they begin to fight you here, if they say, "I don't think this is what we're looking for," it's okay.

Remember, we're showing them this home, which is less than they can afford, in order to get feedback. To get them out of your car, if they balk at this home, simply say, "It is less money. But as long as we're here, why don't we just take a quick look. I did call the people and make an appointment. I would hate to hurt their feelings." If they see this home and hate it, it's more likely they'll go for home number three, which is what you want, isn't it?

Before you cross the street to the home, use this phraseology: "Mr. and Mrs. Johnson, would you please take a moment to appreciate the exterior of this home? This is what friends and relatives of the owner of this home will see when they visit. (Pause) Would you mind commenting on it?"

You're trying to get them mentally living in the home and in a situation where friends or relatives are coming over for dinner. What will that trigger for them? Lots of things. They'll give you the feedback you need. You want them to tell you exactly what they love and hate so you can use that information to sell home number three.

Before you enter the home say, "John, Mary, before we go in, I'd like to ask you a favor. When you look at the home, try to pretend it's vacant so you can picture how your furnishings would fit if this is the right home." You do this in case the present owner's furnishings detract from a very nice floor plan. You see, when your prospects first look at the homes, they're decorated in a way the prospect probably wouldn't have done it. That's why you must try to get them to picture the home empty. Then, they can mentally move their own furniture in and not be influenced by someone else's taste.

At the door, have your buyers behind you. When the seller comes to the door, use these words: "Good afternoon, Mrs. Reed. I'm Tom Hopkins with Champions Unlimited. This is Mr. and Mrs. Johnson. We'd like to take a look at your home and should any questions arise, we'll come and get you. May we step in? Thank you."

What have you just done? You've very nicely told the seller to get lost. If the seller hangs around, you'll have problems. Don't take the time to introduce the sellers to your prospects. The sellers can say one thing and destroy you. For example, they say, "Oh, yes, you'll love this neighborhood. There are 348 children in just one block." The prospects don't have children and are looking for a quiet neighborhood. Can you see what the sellers have just done? Don't give them the opportunity to trigger anything negative with your prospect. You must stay in control.

Also, the buyer will want to meet all of the other sellers. That will only create room for challenges for you. Now, you can't tell your prospects that you don't want them to meet the sellers. They'll wonder why and start doubting everything you tell them. You're actually doing this to protect the sellers from themselves.

As you step into the home, warmly suggest that the buyers make themselves comfortable. Give them the opportunity to ask a lot of questions. You want them to feel relaxed in the home and with you. Here's where you really have to watch them without letting them know they're being watched. Because this is the first home, and very possibly not the right home, you must remain rather subdued. Watch and listen carefully for positive or negative responses from your prospects. Make mental notes of any comments made about things this home lacks that they'll find in the home you've chosen for them. It's important that you keep your emotional level the same as theirs. It'll give them the feeling that you're with them—that you understand.

After they've seen the home and you return to your car ask, "Mr. and Mrs. Johnson, in order for me to do a better job in the selection-of-inventory process, would you please share your feelings regarding your likes and dislikes of this home? And, please, be very candid." Or, you might ask, "John and Mary, how are you feeling about that home?"

They've got to tell you to help you select inventory. Obviously, you've just shown them a home they don't like so they're going to want to help you. By asking them to be candid, you're telling them it's okay to lay it on you. If they hate it, you want to know. We were trying to save money by looking at this home, but maybe we can't do that and make them happy.

The key here is that the more upset and negative they get, the warmer you get. If they feel the home is a disaster area and are surprised that you would even show it to them, here's what you say: "Mr. Johnson, I'm happy to hear your comments. They are very close to what I expected, but I had to be sure. By getting a better feeling for your tastes, I can much more easily find the right home. That's what we really want, isn't it?"

Now you're going to the second home. You'll need to remind them of the same things we did at the first home. Get them to notice the exterior, picture the home vacant, relax, make themselves at home, and be candid with their likes and dislikes.

After they've given you the feedback on the first two homes, you have a decision to make. Is the third home, the one you've chosen for them, the right home? Did they tell you something in one of the other homes that disqualified it? If so, go to your alternative home. Perhaps that home also is not right for them. If that's the case, I suggest you stop for some coffee or a bite to eat and excuse yourself. Get away from them and either call your office or refer to your notes on other homes in inventory to choose the right home for them.

You see, a real estate professional doesn't always work with what the buyers want in a home. Too often they don't know what they want. The professional works by eliminating those things they know they don't want in a home. And when you eliminate what they don't want, you end up with what they do want.

Sometimes you may have to requalify them at this point. You may have a home you know will satisfy their needs, but it costs more than they originally said they could afford. Rather than just taking them to that home, you have to ask their permission. You would say something like this, "John, Mary, based on the monthly investment we agreed you could afford, we shouldn't look at homes over $200,000. I think I have a home that will suit your needs, but there's a challenge. It's a little more than you wanted to invest at this time. May we go a little bit higher if I find the home that will satisfy your needs?" If they can go higher, great! If there's no way they can, it's time to choose another number three.

If you don't know of another home you can call for an appointment, call your office. Get your broker, manager, or a veteran salesperson to help you choose another home. Call the sellers for permission to pop by and get back to your prospects. If you leave them alone for too long, they'll begin to doubt your competence, especially if they really hated the first two homes.

When you get near the third home, they should begin giving you some positive stimulus, if you've chosen the right one for them. This is when you begin using the questioning techniques we covered in Chapter 9. Let's say, for example, the wife comments on the nicer neighborhood. You would then say, "This neighborhood shows real pride of ownership, doesn't it?"

Once you feel you're in the right home, you must be careful about your emotional level. Don't get too excited, too fast. Stay with them on their emotional level. If they start to get excited, build that excitement. This is where you begin using your minor closes. You want to help them get emotionally involved in this property. In many cases, if it's the right home, they'll begin closing each other and you won't have to do anything but watch until it's time to handle the paperwork.

You may not always have to use the closes. Only use them when you need them. If you've done everything right to this point, the closing sequence will just flow. In fact, closing is nothing more than the end result of an eloquent presentation.

Now, you must be careful not to try to close too soon. Also, don't use any of the closes too often. They'll know what you're doing and you could lose everything you've built to this point.

Demonstrating the Property

Let me give you some ideas on demonstrating while you are in the home. First, keep people together. By all means, do not let children get separated from you during the demonstration. As we already covered, not all children are well behaved. Should an accident occur where one of them breaks something or gets hurt, you'll have a whole new set of issues to worry about.

Let the buyer discover things. Don't show everything. Try to save something for a surprise. I can't tell you how many homes I marketed simply because they *discovered* an intercom system, a rose garden, an extra large master bedroom, or even a pool, when they thought they couldn't find a home they could afford with those amenities. When they get into exploring, they're having fun, and if they're having fun, they're relaxed and being honest about their reactions to the home.

If you have a home with an extra room, help them find a use for it before you show it to them, like this, "If you had one more room, a room you didn't even know about, what would you use it for?" In many cases, the couple will say they'd use it as a study, a sewing room, or a craft room. Maybe they'd use it as a playroom for the children or a workshop or just an extra place for storage. It could be a dream come true for them to have such a luxury.

Here's another very important caution for you. Don't walk into the bedrooms with them, especially the master bedroom. There's a very simple reason I'm telling you this. You take up space. Anything that detracts from the size of the room could negatively influence the sale. Escort them down the hall. Allow them to enter the room but stay in the doorway. If you must enter the room to talk with them or to watch their reactions, stay close to the wall so they can feel the size of the room. If the seller hasn't already done so, turn on the lights in the home as you go so the home has the appearance of being bright and cheery.

If you receive positive stimulus from them about this home, brag about any challenges you are aware of with the home. Let's say it needs painting or some other cosmetic repairs. Don't avoid mentioning it because they'll see it. They may bring it up as an objection later. Anticipate it and brag about it so it's overcome before you begin closing. You could say, "One thing that's exciting about this home, John and Mary, is that someone is going to have an opportunity to express their creativity, thus increasing the value of the property because of a little elbow grease and some paint. It's almost like you get paid for all the work you do. That's exciting, isn't it? Also, you get to choose the colors. If the home is newly painted and it's a color you don't like, that would be a waste, don't you agree?"

Learning to turn challenges into opportunities is critical in this field. Let me tell you a little story. My salespeople and I marketed eighteen homes in thirty days that a builder said he couldn't sell. He was going to let them go into foreclosure.

Here was the challenge. The builder built these homes very close to a railroad track, and the track was used daily. The builder kept lowering the prices and couldn't give the homes away. Over the years, he had developed a real dislike of real estate salespeople as many builders do.

I contacted him and told him I could sell the homes for him. We met and he asked, "What do you want me to do, reduce the price further?" I said, "No, let's increase the price of these homes back to where they were in the first place." He thought I was nuts! I also told him he needed to purchase eighteen color television sets, one to be included with each home. He agreed to give me and my salespeople a chance to sell the homes.

First, we put out a sign stating that the homes had a unique quality, so unique that the homes will only be shown in group showings at 11:00, 2:00, and 4:00. That's when the trains went by. When people saw the signs, it got them curious. On good days, we'd have seven or eight people all show up at the same time, which would create a little excitement.

In the hallways of the homes, my people would stop the group and say, "As we've stated, these homes all have a unique quality. Would you all please just be quiet and listen right now?" They would do so. What they heard was the air conditioning running. Then we'd say, "You know, you all heard that air conditioner because we wanted you to. Normally, you would tune it out. Let's step into the living room."

We would then walk into the living room and turn on the color television. "This color TV is included in the home because the builder of this home is concerned that you may suffer an inconvenience by living here. I now want to turn the television up to the normal volume it will be at and we'll show you what will happen. Please listen now and check your watches because the noise you are about to hear will last about seventy seconds."

Luckily for us, the trains ran pretty much on time. And because of all the preliminary work we did prior to the trains passing, most of the people agreed that they would be able to tune out the noise for seventy seconds three times a day. That's how we marketed those eighteen homes in thirty days. We bragged about the objection.

Common Objections

Let's go over some of the most common objections you'll hear and how to overcome them.

"We really wanted another bedroom."

When they say this, what does it really tell you? They don't need it. They were really hoping for it, but the odds are good they can't afford a home with that fourth or fifth bedroom. What you need to do here is to change their base. "John, Mary, I know when we first talked you were hoping to find a home where you could possibly have a fourth bedroom. Knowing inventory the way I do, I've done everything in my power to find a property with that fourth bedroom. But I have to weigh something like that with what is most important to you—having that fourth bedroom, or having a home with the three bedrooms that you need and can afford. I don't want to put you under any financial pressure. If I do that, I'm not doing you justice, don't you agree?"

"I don't feel we've seen enough homes yet."

You will hear this objection when you find the right home. When you're good and you find that right home so quickly for them, it might scare them to death. "John, Mary, I feel that you're rather apprehensive because I've found a home that's suitable so fast. I don't blame you for that. I hope you realize, though, in essence I am your eyes. There are over three thousand homes for sale in this community. Rather than show you all of them, which is ridiculous, I decided to show you only those homes that meet your needs not only financially, but physically. I think I've done that and I can assure you that this home, in my opinion, is most feasible for your family's needs. That's why I'd like you to consider getting you and your family happily involved in this particular property rather than wasting your time seeing for yourself that this is truly the best home for your needs."

"The third bedroom is too small."

They would never say this unless they were considering the rest of the home. You would begin handling this objection by using the porcupine. When they elaborate, try to change their base. Perhaps the children have a lot of things, and they don't think they'll fit.

In some cases here, if the husband objects and the wife loves the rest of the home, she'll overcome the objection for you. If you must go into it yourself, here's what to say, "John, seriously, on what do you think we'll base our decision today, on the livability of the home and everything you like about it or a few inches of space in the third bedroom?" In other words, you are asking which is more important to him. If they absolutely must have a larger third bedroom, then you need to find them one. However, the majority of the times you hear this objection, those words will help you overcome it.

"The home is too far from schools."

A lot of people use this as a way out of committing to the home. Try saying this: "I can understand your concern about your children as far as the distance from the schools. Please consider, though, that in our world today it's necessary for children to grow up much faster than they used to. This is because they must deal with a society that's maturing more rapidly than ever before. Because of that, it can be an advantage having the school farther away. They may have to take a little longer bus ride, but at least they'll have the opportunity to learn responsibility and punctuality. Besides, the bus stops for them right here on the corner and we know with the amount of public concern for our children today that we can trust the bus drivers, can't we?" What I've done here is to try to change their base again. The distance from school really isn't the problem; it's whether or not their children can get there and back safely.

"The home across the street is in terrible condition."

I love it when they say this. Here's how to handle it: "You saw it, too." When they ask what you're talking about continue with, "You saw one of the advantages I saw when I first looked at this home. You see, the average American moves every three to five years. I don't know the people in that home, but there's a good chance that they'll be moving a lot sooner than you will. I'm sure the condition of the home across the street has reflected on the value of this home today. When the new home owners move in, they'll probably fix it up, just like you would. That will in turn enhance your property, giving you the profit to overcome the challenge that we have right now. That makes sense, doesn't it?" Almost anything that is a concern has a good side to it.

"We think our parents should see the home first."

If you try to talk them out of letting their parents or whomever they mention see the home first and don't do it right, you'll lose them. Approach the matter the same way we did with the telephone caller who has a friend or relative in the business. "You're fortunate to have someone to advise you. Most friends and relatives are reluctant to aid in a major decision and can only advise against it. I would like to ask, and I'm not being disrespectful, but will they be living with you?"

In most cases they'll say no. They may say they've promised their parents. If so, you would say, "Then I think we should help them. We should help them by letting them know you've made the decision subject only to their disapproval. If it's critical that you get your parents' consent, I'd like to make our transaction contingent upon their disapproval of the property. By this, I mean that if I meet your parents and let them know everything I've done to help you in this decision, and they still feel that it's not right for you, then you've lost nothing but time." By making it subject to their disapproval, that means the parents have to disapprove something that their children have already okayed, which means they'll be taking something away from them. I'm sure we can agree that's a very difficult thing for a parent to do, especially when their children are grown and striking out on their own.

"The home doesn't have a dining room."

Many homes today do not have formal dining rooms, but it seems everyone today is determined to buy a formal dining room set. You will encounter other people like this who will buy a piece of furniture they love and then try to find a home to fit it. What you have to do in a case like this is to take a room that's not used very much and create a dining room plus a combination living room. In many homes today the living room is unused. It's a showplace, isn't it? Therefore, it can be made into a lovely dining room with a simple partition. Some people use draperies, others use the traditional wood partitions.

Another suggestion would be to use the living room as the family room—with the television and other equipment. Most family rooms are adjacent to kitchens and convert nicely to formal dining areas.

Too many of the homes that do have formal dining rooms will cost $10,000 to $20,000 more than those without. It's so much more practical and more fun to create a dining room from a room that's otherwise not used very much.

"We did want a fireplace."

If this is the only objection, mentally put a fireplace in for them. Help them visualize one there. Suggest that there is room for them to design and build one. A home with a fireplace may cost $3,000 more to purchase. And with that additional amount financed over a period of twenty to thirty years, they'll be paying so much more than if they added a fireplace on their own. It will also increase the value of the property for resale.

Fixer-Uppers

If you are in an area with quite a few of what we call the fixer-upper homes, you can sell them all by bragging about what's wrong with them and telling the buyers how awful they are because that's what they're looking for. Listen to how it's done. "Mike, Joan, before we go to see any properties, I must ask you, are you looking for a good value?" What are they going to say? Of course they're looking for a good value.

"Would you like to be able to be repaid for all the work you do to a home, in fact, also make a nice, sizable profit? I know a home that really fits into this category. I personally like this type of home because I can visualize what people can do with it. When you get a good value, with a little paint, some elbow grease, and a little creativity, you can also get a tremendous appreciation in value." On the way over to the house, tell them how awful it is. When they walk in, it's never as bad as they thought it would be.

If you try to hide the objections and they find them, those challenges seem worse than if you bragged about them. That's why a professional is prepared to brag about or overcome objections that are most commonly encountered in demonstrating a property.

CHAPTER 24

How, When, and Where to Close the Sale and Get the Commitment

The key to getting a commitment accepted is knowing how to obtain a good one. How to obtain the commitment is a strategy with several steps.

1. Show the homes with a definite pattern.

2. Keep your emotional level the same as theirs. You can't get ahead of them because you risk losing them. If you get behind them, you might never catch up.

3. Keep building rapport throughout the entire presentation. Some of you may use this material to build rapport during the first hour or so, but then you think you've got it made and stop. You've got to keep building all the way through to the close and after the sale to get referrals. The best way to keep building rapport is not by telling them things, but by asking them questions.

4. Always keep a certain degree of calm. Some salespeople get so excited that they make the buyer nervous. If a buyer tells you that you're moving too fast, it's because you're too emotionally excited and they can't stand it. They become afraid that if they become too caught up, all of a sudden they'll own the property without really making a decision to own.

5. Involvement is of the utmost importance. They must be participants, not spectators. You must do everything possible to get them to participate in the experience mentally, physically, and emotionally. Give

them a map of where you're going. During the showing, ask them to make notes on the properties, especially of anything they'd like to ask you later.

One professional I know gives a small pad of paper and pen with his name, address, and phone number on them to each of them so they have something to take notes on.

When to Close the Sale

When you begin receiving positive feedback, use your test closes. A test close is a minor close that, if they agree with it, shows they may be ready to go ahead. It might be something like, "John and Mary, do you see why I was so excited to show you this home?"

A professional real estate person is test closing all the time. Again let me stress that you don't need to use every close, every technique, on all sales. I've seen salespeople talk themselves right out of a sale by going too far. By talking and talking and talking, they've given the buyers the opportunity to cool down or change their minds.

So when you receive positive feedback from your buyers, use the test closes to build their enthusiasm for the property to the point where they're ready to close. You're the only one who will know when they're ready. The way to learn this is by closing too soon and too often, thus developing a closing instinct. Great closers operate on reflex, but to develop that reflex, they must have learned by closing too soon and too often. The average real estate salesperson is afraid to make a mistake and gain from that error. You can't develop a closing instinct without practice.

What types of positive feedback or clues are you looking for?

If they start asking about personal property, they're very likely to be seriously considering this home.

They might ask to go through the home one more time.

They may make more eye contact with each other.

They may begin asking more questions about the area or the home itself. If they want to know the average utility bills, they're picturing themselves already living there. When you see or hear this type of thing happening, you're ready to start test closing. But, you do that by using the questioning techniques you learned in Chapter 9.

You can't be too abrupt. A pro never asks them if they want to buy the property. The test closes they use answer that. Never move on to the close until you've received positive stimulus from a test close.

Another good test closing question is this: "John, Mary, how are you feeling about this home so far?" They'll either be positive or negative. If they're anything in between, help them review some of the positive things they liked about the home that might get them off the fence.

You can use the alternate of choice. Ask, "John, Mary, would a 30- or 60-day possession date best suit your needs?" If they answer that question, they're ready to move into the closing sequence. If they won't commit to either answer, you know they're not ready yet, and you should continue showing the benefits of the property.

With the next positive stimulus you get, try another test close. It could be regarding painting the home or even just one room. "Would you do the painting yourself or have it done?"

Or, perhaps they'll give you positive stimulus regarding the landscaping. "You've mentioned that you enjoy working in the yard. Do you feel you would need a gardener or would you do it yourself?" If they tell you they'd enjoy doing it themselves, they're mentally moving into the home. That's what your test close tells you. If they're mentally moving, the next step is to get them physically moved in by going for the close.

The problem with too many salespeople is that they try to close before they've test closed. When they do that, in most cases, they've gone too far and begun to alienate their potential buyers. That's why I'm teaching you to test close. It's so powerful.

I have had people tell me after they've gotten involved in a home that they would send others to me because I was so patient and low pressure. It's true. Great real estate salespeople don't apply pressure. They persuade or guide people to wise decisions just by asking the right questions. It's the right question if the answers confirm they should have the property. Real estate professionals don't push. They just ask the right questions in a warm, nonthreatening way. It's done with a concern that they make the right decision. There's nothing more powerful than asking the right questions.

That's what you do when you start closing, too. I used to say, "The sellers are interested in giving possession of the home in 30 days, how does that fit into your plans?" I've had them say that the possession date was fine, but they really weren't ready to make a decision. That's when I would come back with, "I know that, but you can't make a decision until you've reviewed the facts, isn't that right? Why don't we sit down and I'll outline all the details for you. Then you'll have something to consider." We all sit down and I get them happily involved in the opportunity after about forty-five minutes of helping see all the benefits of this home.

Your goal at this point is to help them rationalize the decision. As we've already discussed, people make their decisions emotionally, then defend or rationalize the decisions with logic. Your job is to keep the emotional involvement strong while you help them rationalize the decision.

You must be careful not to impose your prejudices or biases on them. You may love something about a home, but they don't. Don't mention anything you like about the property unless you know it's one of their requirements. Otherwise, you might as well be the one buying the home since you'll sell it to yourself, not to them. Always remain a sounding board. Use their comments to emphasize the benefits of a particular property. Keep your own comments to yourself.

Don't get too excited too fast. Don't begin test closing until your potential buyers have seen the entire home. They may get very excited about the entry, living room, and kitchen, but their enthusiasm falters when they see how the bedrooms are laid out or when they see the size of the yard.

You need enthusiasm to do well in this business. In fact, enthusiasm built on your clients' enthusiasm is your strongest closing tool. When they begin to show excitement about the home, start asking the questions that will help generate even more enthusiasm throughout the rest of the showing.

Where to Obtain the Commitment

Once you've received positive answers to your test closes, you must select a location for the closing sequence. This can be done anywhere. That's why a professional is always prepared. I like to compare this situation to hunting. If you were to go hunting, when would you load your gun, when you see the rabbit or before you start walking? If you wait until you see the rabbit, by the time you get your gun loaded, it's almost certain to have vanished. You must be prepared to close at any time, anywhere.

You should be carrying a legal pad binder or something similar for taking notes. Under the fourth sheet in your note pad, staple a purchase agreement. Also staple one under the eighth, twelfth, and sixteenth sheets. Then, you will always have four purchase agreements readily available. In other words, your gun is loaded.

Too many salespeople wait to get the purchase agreement out of their briefcases until they think the buyers are ready. Believe me, when you open that briefcase, they know what's happening and they'll change emotionally. It's physically impossible to write through the top of your briefcase, so keep your purchase agreements in your note pad. They've seen you writing on that pad all day. They won't even think twice when they see you lift a few pages and make more notes—on the purchase agreement.

The best place to close is in the home, if they're ready and the seller is gone. You just sit down at the kitchen table and close. Sitting there in the home will make it easier to highlight the major selling points and dwarf any minor objections they may have.

Don't be afraid to start closing. If you just get started, you're halfway home. When you've done everything correctly up to this point, don't be surprised if you fill out the paperwork, review it with them, ask for their approval, and get it!

If you feel this is the right home for your buyers, ask the seller to be gone for two hours. If they think you'll be able to sell the home while they're gone, they'll be happy to stay away.

If your buyers aren't ready to close on the home, when you get back to your car you can say, "You know, John and Mary, fate is a funny thing. I know you're not really that concerned if this home were to be sold, but at this point you don't know if this is the right home or not because you don't have all the details. I'd like to take a moment while we're here and it's fresh in our minds. Could I just outline the details on the property for you so you have something to consider?" Do it right there in the car. This is especially effective if the home is being shown by several salespeople in the same day. If you're lucky, another salesperson will drive up to show the home while you're leaving, thus emphasizing the fact that they may lose the opportunity to own this home.

You don't have to wait and drive back to your office before you close. They could cool off by the time you get there. They could talk themselves out of it. They may get buyer's remorse before they even make a decision to own it. In cases like that, head for a restaurant. Suggest that you stop for a bite to eat or a cup of coffee to go over the details of the last home while it's still fresh in their minds.

The office is the best place for new people to close because you can get help there if you need it. If you started them in the conference room when you first met, take them back there. If you were at your desk, that's where you want to go. If they try to leave you at the door, encourage them to come inside in order for you to outline the details for them so they will have something to consider. Once you get them settled inside, go into the closing sequence.

Steps to Filling Out the Purchase Agreement

You may not believe this now, but you will, at sometime in your career, encounter people who don't have to be closed. They will see a home they like and make the decision to go ahead. When this happens, go with them. Don't try to close them. They've already closed themselves. Simply pull out your purchase agreement and fill it out. Here are the steps you will need to follow when this happens:

1. Begin by choosing the location for filling out the form. It could be the countertop in the home if it's available, or the dining room table, if the seller is gone. It could be in your car or you may have to go back to your office.

2. Stay composed. When this buyer lets you know they want the home, remain subdued. Don't get overly excited. Express the need to just put everything down on paper to see if it makes sense for them.

3. Cover the financial details. Always cover all the financial details before moving onto the form. Once they have an understanding of the total investment, monthly investment, interest rate, loan charges, and closing costs, then just say, "Why don't we just draft up our thoughts on the paperwork, then we can see how it looks."

4. Begin with a nonthreatening question. Ask the wife's middle initial or another reflex question such as the correct spelling of their last name (don't ask this if their last name is something very simple), today's date, and so on.

5. Move through the form quickly and smoothly. As we covered earlier, you must be able to fill out your form rapidly while simultaneously relieving pressure with intermittent conversation or chitchat.

6. Turn the form around for their approval. When you have completed the form, turn it facing them, lay your pen down by the signature line and ask them for their approval. Then, shut up and wait for them. They will either pick up the pen and approve the paperwork, or give you a stall of some sort.

This is when you should be ready to start using the major closing techniques in the next chapter, if necessary.

CHAPTER 25

Getting a Commitment on a Property

The average real estate person knows two closes and uses one. Maybe you've heard them. They go like this, "Well, what do you think?" And the real powerhouse is this, "Shall we go ahead?" That is not closing. It's clerking, and that's why those people earn a clerk's income. In analyzing the people we have trained, the top closing specialists accomplish the final closing of the sale after the fifth major closing attempt. If you only know two closes, maybe that's why you don't make much money.

The Definition of Closing

What is the definition of closing? It's a well-filled ink pen in the hand of a sane, mature individual who affixes a signature to a predetermined dotted line with no physical help from the salesperson. That's one definition. The one I prefer is this: professionally using a person's desire to own the benefits of the property, then blending in your sincere desire to serve them and help them make a decision that's truly good for them.

As I've taught you in the previous chapters, you have no right to help people make decisions unless you have knowledge of inventory, knowledge of financing, and have perfected your performance. Then you not only have the right to help them make the decision but you also have an obligation to help them.

The day you turn pro is the day you choose to use your techniques to help them make a decision that is good for them. If it's not good for them and you influence them to do it, you're not a professional. You're a con.

There's a very fine line between a professional salesperson and a con artist. The con artist is prepared to sell anything to anybody anytime, whether it's good for them or not. They use techniques. They know their "product." They know ways of getting a person's money. But they don't care if what they're doing is good for the buyer. And the buyer will never see them again once they hand over their money. Those people need to be locked up. We need to protect the general public from salespeople who would help customers and clients make decisions that are not good for them.

The Importance of Closing

You might not be in real estate a year from now. The reason for this is simple. You won't learn how to lead people to make good decisions. If you don't learn how and make yourself do it well, your success is subject to the marketplace. Without the ability to call for the decision, everyone loses. The sellers lose the opportunity to complete the transaction, thus not selling their home. The buyers lose because they need to keep looking at homes, wasting their time, money, and gas. You lose a fee for service, and, finally, your family loses because you weren't doing your best and earning a good income. That's why it's so important for you to learn the closes and use them. You must take this business seriously if you're going to provide for your family. Don't cheat them by not learning how to close.

You must learn to balance two basic drives in order to close—your empathy and your desire to help them make a decision. If you decide to remain that warm, easygoing, overly empathetic person, you're going to stay average. They'll love you all right, but will they buy from you? Not very often. If what you want is to stay average, that's okay. As long as it makes you happy.

If you decide to become a professional, you must learn to use the techniques. And you should be proud of what you do. Professional salespeople are a rare breed today. And you deserve to make a lot of money. You deserve to become rich because of the commitment and effort you have made to become a true professional in this industry.

However, you must understand a basic truth before you can become prepared to sell. The average American cannot make rapid buying decisions. Do you know that indecision and procrastination have become acceptable today? Procrastination is living yesterday, avoiding today, thus ruining tomorrow, which is what average human beings do. They want to go home and think about everything. And that's just what they'll do if you don't close them. The reason they can't make a decision is the fear they have of making a bad decision. They're so afraid of making a bad decision, they won't make any decision at all.

Insecurity breeds procrastination. That's why they want to go home and think it over. They're insecure. The key to getting people to invest their security—their money—is to make them feel secure before they invest. If they become insecure, they begin thinking about giving up $10,000 of their savings, which took them years to accumulate. Are people willing to do that if they're insecure? Of course not. They'll keep looking for someone who makes them feel secure about the decision to own.

People love to buy after they own. That's a very simple statement, but think about it. I've had people who looked at homes for six weeks and finally I made the decision that they were going to own. I helped them see that it was a wise decision for them and six months later they were thanking me for doing so. They were so happy in their home, and yet, they probably would have still been looking six months later had I not gone ahead and helped them arrive at a good decision.

People need someone to help them rationalize the decision they really want to make. They don't really enjoy driving around every weekend looking at home after home. The fact that they're even taking the time to look tells you that they want to own a home. Don't believe them if they tell you they're just looking. It's only a stall. No one is just looking. They're looking for the right property to own.

At What Point Do You Close?

When you demonstrate property as I've taught you, the third home is the one that you've chosen for them. However, if they walk into the first home and they want it, let them have it. Don't keep showing them homes or ask them to wait until they've seen the other homes you have for them.

The more you say, the better chance you have of losing. The more you ask, the better your chances of winning.

If they begin to slow the pace down that's a sign they're ready. If they were approaching the whole matter with a passive attitude and they begin to get excited or speed up the pace, that's a sign. When they require more information that's a sign. This means especially technical information about the property—lot size, square footage, or the average cost of utilities, taxes. They wouldn't care about that information if they weren't seriously considering the home.

Another sign is if they start to linger or ask to see the home again. If this happens, 70 percent of the time you can close them on that property.

The Anatomy of a Close

There are certain ingredients that are a part of every close. If even one of them is missing, you won't be able to close them. We'll cover them in four steps.

Step 1. You must understand the buyers' needs. If you don't understand their needs, you can't close. It doesn't matter what your needs are. We all know what you need. You need that brokerage. However, if they see the dollar signs in your eyes, they won't let you close them. You can't look at them as if they're your mortgage payment or car payment. To understand their needs you must qualify them. By using the Buyer's Analysis for Better Service form you'll know what they need. Then, by using their buying motives and asking the right questions, you'll be able to get them happily involved in a home.

Step 2. Recognize buying signs. The average buyer will let you know that they want the home not by what they say, but by what they do. Learn to recognize the buying signs we covered in Chapter 24.

Step 3. Based on their positive stimulus, make the decision that they will invest. If you aren't sure they're going to own, how can you close them?

Step 4. Close the sale. You would do this by leading them to the same decision you've just made by asking the right questions.

Concerns

I've stressed to you the importance of learning the techniques to the extent that they become reflexive. But buyers have reflexes, too. They have built-in reflexes for stalling the decision, which are called objections or concerns. We've already covered some of them. They sound like this:

"We're not going ahead until we talk to our parents."

"We don't jump into things."

"We have a friend in the business who's going to give us some advice."

"My attorney said he'll handle the paperwork for us."

"We really don't need a broker."

"We're not paying a brokerage."

"We're just the type of people who think things over."

"I feel it costs too much."

"Will they come down?"

"Can we just make them an offer?"

The difference between you and the great ones at this point is that as soon as their clients start coming up with these objections, the professional already knows how he's going to close them. And you probably don't. Never fear, I wouldn't present a challenge to you without including the solution.

On occasion, you will encounter a buyer with a condition. A condition is a valid reason for not going ahead. There are only two conditions you should accept—no money or no credit. There are no other conditions. And if there is no condition and they don't own, it's your fault. You, as a professional, should be able to overcome anything other than their not having the money or credit to get them into a home.

Let me give you the definition of an objection. An objection is merely a request for more information. Also, please understand that objections are to be expected. If they don't object to something, they aren't going to own. I've developed a step-by-step method for handling a buyer's stalls (or requests for more information) so you do it smoothly—without causing them to come up with more concerns.

Steps to Handling Concerns

Step 1. Hear them out. Don't try to anticipate their objection before they finish their sentence. If you answer the wrong objection, you've given them a new one to stall with. Listen to them. Let them explain the entire objection to you before you utter a sound.

Step 2. Feed it back. When you do this, you're asking them to elaborate on the objection. You want to know as much as possible about this objection.

Step 3. Question it. After they elaborate, question their explanation to be certain you understand every detail of the objection before you handle it.

Step 4. Answer the objection.

Step 5. Confirm the answer. You must confirm that they understand your answer and that the objection has been handled once and for all. Otherwise, they could keep coming up with that same objection later in your closing sequence.

Step 6. By the way. Use those three words to take you from handling the objection into the closing sequence.

Let me demonstrate the steps for you. We're going to use the objection that the bedroom is too small.

Buyer: "This bedroom is too small."

Salesperson: "John, this bedroom is too small? Could you elaborate on that a little for me?"

Buyer: "I don't feel all of the children's things will fit in here."

Salesperson: "So, John, really the thing that's keeping you from owning this home, which you both seem to enjoy, is the fact that this one bedroom is too small. Is that right?"

Buyer: "That's right."

Salesperson: "Tell me, John, what will we base our decision on in finding a home, the livability of the entire home or a bit of space in the children's bedroom?"

At this point, if the wife wants the home, she'll jump in and close him for you. However, you must still confirm the answer.

Salesperson: "So, I guess that settles that, doesn't it?"

Buyer: "I guess it does."

Salesperson: "By the way, I'd like to show you something else."

Your objection is handled, your concern addressed and you now dismiss it with the words, "by the way" and move on to another topic—always moving closer to the final decision about ownership.

Reduction to the Ridiculous Close

The major concern you'll encounter in most sales is money. Most people will have a challenge with the money because they want to find a way to offer less for the property. Or it could be that they are increasing their monthly investment but would rather it not be too great of an increase because they're afraid. That's why you want to try to lead them gently to the money decisions. Let's see what you should do if they say, "It costs too much."

Buyer: "It costs too much."

Salesperson: "John, you feel it costs too much? Well, I'm happy about one thing. You wouldn't even be negotiating as to the value unless you were seriously considering the home, am I right?"

Buyer: "Yes."

Salesperson: "So, may I ask how much too much you think it is?"

Buyer: "$10,000."

Salesperson: "So, in other words, it's just about $10,000 more than you feel you should commit to and that's what's bothering you, is that right?"

Buyer: "Yes."

Salesperson: "Then, right now, the only thing standing between you and the home is the $10,000, isn't it?"

Buyer: "Yes."

Salesperson: "If it weren't for the money, you might go ahead?"

Buyer: "Yes."

Now you know exactly the amount of money it will take to get them into this home and that the money is their final objection. There's no other reason for them not to go ahead with this home. This is when you would use the reduction to the ridiculous close.

Your ability to use this close successfully depends on knowing your math. This is a critical area, and if you make a math error, you'll be defeated. You want to reduce the total amount they're objecting to down to a monthly, weekly, and daily amount to show them how minimal the amount really is, thus overcoming the money objection. Let's continue with our example.

Salesperson: "John, sometimes we don't put things in the proper perspective and I think we should. First, before we go any further, of the homes we've seen today, you did like this one the best, didn't you?"

Buyer: "Yes."

Salesperson: "John, let's look at it from the money standpoint. Please take my calculator and enter the $10,000 that's standing between you and the home. If you were to own the home, would you say you might live here 10 years?"

Buyer: "Probably about that long."

Salesperson: "Would you divide that $10,000 by 10 years? That's $1,000 per year, isn't it?"

Buyer: "Yes."

Salesperson: "If you were living here, enjoying the beautiful kitchen and spacious family room and took a two-week vacation away from the home each year, you'd be spending 50 weeks each year in the home, right?"

Buyer: "Yes."

Salesperson: "John, would you divide that $1,000 by 50 weeks? What does that give you?"

Buyer: "$20 per week."

Salesperson: "If you and the family were living here, delighting in all of the amenities that attracted your attention seven days a week and we divided that $20 by seven days, what would we have?"

Buyer: "About $2.86."

Salesperson: "Honestly, do you feel we should avoid having the home that you both obviously love for $2.86 per day?"

Another way to look at this is to do the mortgage calculations on the listed amount and an offer made at $10,000 less. Over the span of a 30-year mortgage at 6 percent interest (just for figuring sake), the difference is roughly $60 per month more on the monthly investment. That's two dollars a day if you then reduce it to the ridiculous. Get creative with their money and show them the math. If they stall on the home for $60 a month, they didn't really want it in the first place.

I've had instances where the wife spoke up and suggested that if they gave up smoking or cut back on soda or some other habit, which they've wanted to do anyway, they could afford the home. Most often, they'll agree with you once you demonstrate to them that the sum is a minor amount of money when they look at it on a daily basis. Only use this close if you know they can afford it. It won't do you any good if you show them it's only $2.86 more, but they already can't afford the daily amount. You may get them to agree with you on this point, but they'll still want to offer less. Should they ask if the seller will take less, use this phraseology: "I have learned never to make a decision for a client. Please realize that I'm only authorized to quote the listed value; any less would have to be negotiated."

You'll always have people who want to offer less. Your job then becomes adding value to the property to help them rationalize offering the full listed amount. That's only fair to the seller and we must always remember that we represent the seller. Put your buyer in the seller's place by saying this: "John, I have a feeling you and your family will be happy in this home for many years. When you see the service I'll give you, I know you'll call me when you're ready to sell it. Would you like me to get you what you want for the home when you're ready to move?" Of course they'll agree with you. If they still insist on offering less, take it. After all, you have an obligation to the seller to take a deposit. Then, prepare the buyer for a possible counterproposal.

As I stated, it's critical that you know the math to use this close. Do yourself a favor and figure out the yearly, weekly, and daily amounts for $5,000, $6,000, $7,000, $8,000, and $10,000 so you'll be prepared when you hear this objection.

Order Blank Close

You won't always find out about the money concern before you ask for their approval on the paperwork. In fact, most closing sequences will begin with the order blank close. The order blank close is nothing more than asking questions and writing the answers on the form. You have your order blank, deposit receipt, and purchase agreement under a few pages of your legal pad binder. The way to start this is to ask a reflex question. The best one I know is to ask for the favorable spouse's middle initial. They'll answer this without thinking.

If they stop you, and you've already used the "I organize my thoughts and keep everything in the proper perspective" phraseology, you would instead say, "Let me just outline the details for you so you'll have something to consider." The exciting thing about this is that many times they won't stop you. If they don't stop you, they've bought the home. It's just a matter of filling in the paperwork and getting their approval.

Ben Franklin Balance Sheet Close

You would use this close when they are honestly having difficulty in coming to a decision on the property. The words I'm going to give you for this close are critical. You must learn them word for word. If you use these words properly and have a sincere desire to help them make the decision, it will work even though it'll probably be obvious to them that you're using a technique. Here are the words:

"History has proven that most great decision makers believed that a good decision was only as good as the facts. Now, the last thing I would want to do would be to influence you to make an unwise decision. However, if it proves to be a good decision, you would want to make it, wouldn't you? Fine. Do you mind if I help you? Let's draw a line down the middle of this legal pad and on this side list the facts favoring this home. Then, over here, we'll list the reasons against it. When we're through, we can simply add up the columns and at that point make the right decision. (Shoot for six reasons for the decision. Then, let them come up with reasons against it.) Okay, let's add up the columns and see what we've got. By the way, this technique was used by one of our most famous men, Benjamin Franklin. We've all considered him one of our wisest men, haven't we?"

The Similar Situation Close

In using this close, you're going to be telling your prospects about someone else who was in the same situation they find themselves in now, what they decided to do about it, and benefits they gained from that decision.

Every time you make a sale, start writing down what happened.

If you start doing this, you'll have new similar situations to use all the time. For those of you who haven't yet made a sale, you can quote me. You can say, "I was reading about a situation someone else had like this recently" and go into the appropriate story below. These situations should always be based on the *feel-felt-found* formula. It's like this, "I understand how you feel. Others have felt that way. Here's what they found." Here are a few stories to get you started:

If they're in no hurry to make a decision use this:

"I was reading recently about a case in which the people wanted to wait to make their decision. The buyers loved the home but just weren't ready to make a decision. The Realtor let them go home, and he was very sad because when they called him later that night to tell him they wanted the home, he had to tell them that it was sold. I wouldn't be so persistent about your making the decision today, right now, unless I truly felt this is a home you and your family will enjoy for many years to come."

If they want a home that has a larger investment than they can afford:

"A few years ago, a young family, just like you, was in a similar position. They had only a limited amount of money to invest in a home, and they couldn't own as nice a home as they wanted with that investment. They couldn't decide whether it would be wise to wait a few years until they could save a larger initial investment or to go ahead and invest right then in a home they could afford. Fortunately, they decided to go ahead and buy what we call the stepping-stone home. Just recently they sold that home and made a sizable profit, which allowed them to invest in the type of home they originally wanted sooner than if they had waited and saved for it. They were very happy that they quit paying rent and started building equity when they did. I'm sure you can agree with me that they did the right thing, can't you?"

The "I Want to Think It Over" Close

This is not a final objection. It's only a way for them to put off making the decision. When you hear them say this, agree with them that it's a good thing to do. Don't fight them. You just want to get them to tell you what it is they want to think over (their objection), so you can handle it. The key to having this technique work is to act as though you've been defeated. In other words, you haven't done your job properly or they would already have made the decision. Here's the phraseology:

"That's fine, John. Obviously you wouldn't take the time to think it over unless you were seriously interested, would you? Since you're that interested, may I assume that you'll give the home very careful consideration? (They'll usually assure you they'll give it careful consideration.) John, you're not telling me this just to get rid of me, are you? (They'll say no to this not to hurt your feelings.) Just to clarify my thinking, what is it that you want to think over (don't pause); is it the location of the home? Is it the landscaping? Is it the layout? Is it the carpets or draperies? Could it possibly be the money?"

If they say it is the money, ask if there's anything else they're unsure about besides the money. Once you've confirmed that the money is the final barrier, determine the exact amount that's the problem, and you use the reduction to the ridiculous close.

The Best Things in Life Close

Some people just need to be reminded about other big decisions they've made and been happy about in order to feel confident about making this decision. These words have been extremely effective. Learn them and use them.

"Isn't it true, John and Mary, that the only time you have ever really benefited from anything in your life has been when you said yes instead of no? You said yes to your marriage (optional: and I can see how happy you are). You said yes to your job, your previous home, your car—all the things that I'm sure you enjoy. You see, when you say yes to me, it's not really me you're saying yes to, but all the things you enjoy about this home. Based on this truth, it just makes sense to say yes, doesn't it?"

The Secondary Question Close

With this close, you pose the major decision with a question, and without pausing, ask a secondary minor question. When they answer the minor question, the major decision is carried.

"As I see it, John and Mary the only real decision you have to make today is how soon you'll start enjoying life in this wonderful home and great neighborhood. By the way, would you prefer to take possession of the home in 30 days or would 60 days suit your needs better?"

The Wish I'da Close

We all have things in our past that we wished we'd have handled differently. Remind your buyers of those situations and move them away from having another regret.

"John, we are all members of the 'wish-I'da' club. Wish I'da bought real estate in Arizona fifteen years ago. Wish I'da invested in some stock twenty years ago so I'd be rich today. Wish I'da grabbed a chance to gain an exclusive advantage and so on. Wouldn't it be great to get rid of at least one wish I'da by saying yes to a home that you really want?"

Two-Party Indecision Close

In most cases, you will be working with more than one decision maker. They each have their own ideas about what is right for them even though they may both agree on the basics of what size home, what neighborhood, etc. If you reach a point where they are not in agreement and you do firmly believe this is the best home for them, use this close.

"John and Mary, when two people are required to make one decision, it's often impossible to find one solution that satisfies both of them. So, life becomes a matter of compromise. Now the measurement of each decision is through the use of this question: 'Does the home satisfy most of the wants of each of the parties?' So, do you feel this home does?"

In most cases, they'll realize the point of disagreement is minor compared to all the benefits the home does have for them—if you've done your job.

Multiple Closing

As I stated earlier, the great ones accomplish the final close after the fifth closing attempt. After your fifth attempt at closing, you will get to your last close by apologizing for being so zealous. The last thing you want to do is to make them feel that you're pushing them. This will let them feel you're backing off and they'll relax. Go back to the beginning by covering all of the benefits of the property that they have agreed upon and slowly take them through everything you've covered so far.

You may feel uncomfortable repeating yourself, but please understand that your presentation and closing are very similar to a speech. There are three phases to a professional speech, which must be a part of each of your presentations. They are

1. Tell them what you're going to tell them.
2. Tell them.
3. Tell them what you've told them.

In other words, repetition is vital to any selling situation.

Silence Is Golden

Once you've overcome all their objections, agreed on their offer, and there's no reason for them not to go ahead with the home, simply turn the paperwork around to them for their approval. Here you must develop your own final closing question or statement. Try using these words: "John and Mary, I'm excited for you and with your approval right here (point to signature line). I'll do my best to get you your home tonight."

Now, let me give you the most critically important instruction about closing. Whenever you ask your final closing question, SHUT UP. Never forget this: SHUT UP! The first one who talks will normally own the home. If you talk, it relieves all the pressure for them to go ahead, and you'll be left sitting there with an unsold home.

If they talk, they'll normally go ahead.

This is so important! If you remain silent when you ask for their okay, approval, endorsement, or authorization, they can only do one of two things: go ahead or give you the final objection. Either way, you are prepared to handle the situation because you've been practicing, drilling, and rehearsing, haven't you?

If you feel you must break the silence use these words, "My mother once told me that silence means consent. Was she right?" What you're saying to them is that by not giving you any objections, they must be agreeing to make the offer on the property. You'll be amazed how well this will work for you.

Mentally Preparing Your Buyer

Once they've approved the paperwork, don't yell Yippee and dash out to the seller. Take the time to reinforce your commitment to do your best to get them the home.

Thank them for their confidence and trust in you.

Suggest the possibility of the seller making a counterproposal if they are proposing less than the listed price.

Ask them to wait up that evening until they hear from you. Explain that you may have to wait to see the seller, and it could take a while to go over all the details with them. In most cases, they'll be so anxious to know the outcome they won't mind staying up very late, if necessary.

Also, it's important that you set them up for buyers' remorse. This is what happens once a major decision is made. People tend to start second guessing themselves and doubting whether or not they made the right decision.

What I did was to take one of those apothecary-type vitamin bottles and put a label on it that said, BUYERS' REMORSE PILLS. I then filled the bottle with M & Ms. The phraseology for this technique goes like this: "One thing might happen tonight. If you're normal, you may go home and start to worry a bit. If that happens, I've got a little something here I'd like you to take. These are candy, but I call them buyers' remorse pills. If you get nervous, would you take two of these? And, please don't worry, I'm committed to do my best for you."

In most cases, they'll laugh, but believe me, it works! You've prepared them to expect buyers' remorse and told them that it's normal, which should ease the amount of stress or anxiety they feel. This may just eliminate the possibility of a cancellation of the offer.

If you don't feel comfortable with this technique, at the very least be certain to let them know it's normal to be worried while waiting for the sellers to accept the proposal. It just shows how excited they are about their decision to own this particular property. Again, reassure them that you're doing your best to get them the home they have chosen so they can get happily moved and start building memories.

CHAPTER 26

Presenting the Proposal

The first thing you must be aware of in presenting a proposal is that the seller is emotionally unstable. Anyone involved in selling a piece of real estate is going to be emotionally unstable. For most people, it's the single most valuable thing they own, and they want the most for it. They're already mentally spending the money they think they'll get. Therefore, you must proceed with caution. You can expect to become the brunt of all the anxiety they've built up during the selling process.

If it's one of your listings, you should have less to worry about because you will know the sellers have been treated properly throughout the selling process. If it's another person's listing, be prepared for anything.

Setting the Appointment

Do yourself a favor and have a third party arrange the appointment. If you do it, the seller will try to find out all about the proposal on the phone and when you tell them you prefer to wait until you see them in person, they're going to be in a bad state emotionally. They'll wonder what you're trying to hide from them, and they'll think the worst. They'll think it's not a good proposal, that there's something wrong with the buyers, or that they might not qualify.

Save yourself and them needless worry by having a neutral third party set the appointment. I used to have the office secretary do it for me. Give her the information regarding what time you'll be by to see the sellers and something positive, but noncommittal to say—perhaps just that you're very excited about the deposit you've taken. Then, step out of the office so she can honestly tell them you are out of the office and asked that she set the appointment for you.

Preparation Prior to the Appointment

Compute the seller's net proceeds.

You must have this figured before you arrive at their home. You can't afford to wait until you're with them to do it. You could make a math error there and put a dent in your credibility. If you're presenting the proposal with another salesperson, double-check their figures on the net proceeds. You should have a good feeling for whether or not the net amount will be acceptable to the sellers if it's your listing.

If the property has an existing loan, there may be a reconveyance fee. That is to return the title to the property to its original owner.

A home warranty is offered by a division of the National Association of Home Builders through certain builders. The program sets standards for construction and requires warranties ranging from one to ten years in duration on everything from minor defects in workmanship to major structural problems on new home sales. Warranties may also be obtained on resale properties to cover major problems that occur during the first year of ownership, such as a major roof leak, heating or air-conditioning failure, or the like.

Discover what the property's activity has been. You need to know how much this home has been shown. If it's only been shown three times in four months, that information will help you close them. If it's been shown forty times in two months and it's only had one proposal, you need to know that, too. This information will help you in closing the transaction.

Also, how eager are they to move? What is their situation—a job transfer, divorce, moving up to a nicer home, or needing more room

ESTIMATED SELLER'S PROCEEDS

Seller's name_____ Date_____

Property address_____

Broker _____

Sales representative_____ Selling price $_____

ENCUMBRANCES

First Mortgage	Source: Seller ❑ Lender ❑ Document ❑	$
Second Mortgage	Source: Seller ❑ Lender ❑ Document ❑	
Other		
Encumbrances	Source: Seller ❑ Lender ❑ Document ❑	
TOTAL ENCUMBRANCES	....$	

GROSS EQUITY $

ESTIMATED SELLING COSTS

Policy of Title Insurance $

Estimated Escrow Fees

Termite Inspection and Report
   (Possible repairs not included)

Prepayment privilege (if any)
   None

Conventional   Varies, but safe to figure 6 months interest
             on unpaid balance

Reconveyance fee (only if existing loan is being paid off)

Lender's Demand or Beneficiary Statement

Proration of interest on existing loan
   (Interest is always 1 month in arrears.
   Allow 1 month's interest maximum.)

FHA or VA loan discount fee of new loan

Brokerage

Home Warranty

Appraisal

       APPROXIMATE TOTAL COSTS $

       APPROXIMATE SELLER'S PROCEEDS $
       (GROSS EQUITY LESS TOTAL COSTS)

POSSIBLE CREDITS OR DEBITS $

Proration of property tax

Return of balance in Impound Account

This estimate has been prepared to assist the seller in computing his/her costs. Whenever possible, we have used the MAXIMUM charges that can be expected. Lenders and escrow companies will vary in their charges; therefore, these figures cannot be guaranteed by the broker or his/her representatives.

I have read the above figures and acknowledge receipt of a copy of this form.

Seller _____ Address_____

Seller _____ _____

Presented by _____ Telephone number__(_____)_____

because the family is growing? You need to know as much as possible about the situation you're going to be walking into tonight.

Find out about any past offers and why they weren't accepted. What is the emotional state of the seller? If the property has been listed a long time, you may have to go in there and remotivate them to sell before you can attempt to close them on this proposal. Are there any other offers to be presented? Some pieces of real estate are such a good value that there may be two or three offers to be presented. In that case, you have to be prepared to have a better performance than the other salespeople in order to get your proposal accepted.

Things the Seller Will Want to Know

List all the benefits of the proposal. Tell them about the qualifications of the buyers. The seller will want to know about the people who have made this proposal. This would include type and length of employment, credit rating, and approximate income level. Write down the deposit amount. You need to let them know how many there are in the family and a little about them as people so the seller will relate to their personal situation. Tell them about their hobbies, community activities, and what they liked about the home, particularly if it's something you know the seller is proud of.

Make a note of the closing date. If you know from the listing sheet that they want a 30-day closing and the buyers have agreed to that, you've got something you know they'll agree to. Be sure to cover this early in your presentation.

Make notes on the benefits of the type of financing the buyers will be using. On the subject of financing, please realize that terminology differs throughout the United States and foreign countries. However, there are some basics that you should learn and adapt to your presentation of a proposal.

For example, when a buyer pays all cash or cash to the existing loan, there are definite savings and advantages to your seller. If a buyer offers a low down payment and the seller must carry back a secondary position in financing, this could have disadvantages. However, you will find some sellers don't need the cash and will enjoy the higher interest rate usually afforded from a second mortgage or trust deed.

Also, keep in mind that if government financing is used (FHA or VA), you must consider the time necessary for appraisals, possible repairs required, and a longer closing period. In other words, always analyze the financing that the buyer is proposing. You must be able to find the benefits of any type of financing and explain them to the seller.

Steps to the Signature

1. Sit at a table with them across from you. Try never to let the sellers sit across from each other where they can nonverbally communicate without you seeing them. They'll work against you. All couples have specific meanings to looks and gestures that only they understand. If they can use them without you being aware of them, you won't be able to control the situation.

2. Compliment them on the condition of the home, if applicable. Thank them for having the home in such good condition that it showed beautifully, resulting in you getting this proposal.

If you're warm and nice with them before you go into your presentation, they'll feel more comfortable with you. You can't go in there and just get down to business. This is because you are dealing with people's emotions.

3. Be assumptive and begin with bottom-line articles. The bottom-line articles are minor things they'll agree with that will carry the major decision. These would be things such as possession date and personal property. Here also cover any personal items the buyer would like included that may not have been on the listing sheet, such as the refrigerator, a metal storage shed, fireplace equipment, throw rugs, or a swing set. Cover them this way, "First of all, Mr. and Mrs. Jones, I want you to know that I have a very nice family that wants your home. They are agreeable with the 30-day possession date. If everything else is agreeable, is that still acceptable?" They'll say yes because it's one of their qualifications on the listing sheet. When they say yes to this point, they'll mentally start moving out of the home.

4. Cover the buyers' qualifications. Spend a lot of time telling them

about the buyers. People buy people. Go over their length of employment, approximate income, credit rating, and so on. Assure them the people can qualify for the necessary financing.

5. Hand them the purchase agreement and watch their expressions. What they do now is so important. They'll either be with you or against you. Don't lose your composure if they get upset. And, whatever you do, don't fight with them. Let them vent their anger and get it all out before you continue.

6. Don't purposely upset the seller. By this I mean, don't knock the home. If the buyer offered less than the listed amount because they didn't feel the home was worth that much, don't tell the seller that. Instead use these words, "Our buyers, based on their financial position at this time, sincerely felt they could not go any higher." Everyone has at some time or another been in a financial position where he or she couldn't spend more than a certain amount on something.

7. Keep reminding the seller that you are working for them—that you only want what's best for them. Use the words fiduciary responsibility. That's what you have toward the seller—a position of trust. Let them know that you wouldn't jeopardize that trust by taking a deposit that is outrageously lower than the amount for which they were asking.

8. Keep reselling the benefits of your proposal. Don't be afraid to be repetitious. You have to repeat yourself. The entire basis of selling is repetition. They may not hear you the first time or even the third time if they're thinking about the money. You have to repeat the benefits until they have an effect on the sellers.

If they ask whether you think the buyer will increase their offer, use this phraseology: "I don't know. All I do know is that I have an executory document, which is not binding at this point." If they need further explanation, tell them, "If I go back to the buyer and they've cooled off about wanting this home, we could lose the entire transaction."

9. If pressure builds, ask for a glass of water. In other words, if they start getting a little too tense, change the subject for a little relief, then begin again. Break the pressure. Then go back into your presentation again.

10. If interrupted, don't start where you left off. Instead, sit patiently and do a benefit summary before continuing. Go over everything that they've agreed upon so far to get them back emotionally to where they were.

11. Use minor closes. The one I've found to be most successful is the "Two buyers for your property today" minor close. You would only use this when you have a good proposal for the home and they're fighting you. Here's how it goes: "John, Mary, we've been discussing this for some time, and I've been unable to get you as excited about this transaction as I am. I'm sad about that. You see, at this point, we really have two buyers for your home. I was hoping my buyer, the Joneses, would own your home today. They're wonderful people and really love your home. I knew when I came in that one of our buyers would own this home tonight. I wish it were the Joneses. You see, if you can't accept their proposal, then you've suddenly become the buyer of your home. Do you really feel that you'd pay what they're offering for the home today?" I've had them agree that they wouldn't pay that amount for their home and go ahead and accept the proposal. You have to be warm and sincere when you use this close. If you come off smart-alecky, they'll destroy you.

Another minor close you can use is to have them approve their rejection in writing. If they won't accept the proposal or even make a counteroffer, have them put their rejection in writing. This would be used when they're really being stubborn about not accepting or giving a little on this proposal. Make them sign away the transaction. If you have to use this technique, it'll often make them think more seriously about what they're giving up and reconsider the counteroffer.

Normal Seller Objections

Please realize that it's perfectly normal for the seller to object to the proposal at first. There are many objections they'll give you that you can expect to hear hundreds of times in your selling career. Let's cover them and how to handle them.

"Your offer is less than I paid for the property."

In a case such as this, it's probably because the sellers have been in the home a very short time, perhaps less than a year. In that case, it's not really wise for them to want to sell and expect to make a profit on the home. You will have to explain this to them. Use your comparable market analysis to show them that the proposal is compatible with the current market. If applicable, remind them of how long they've had the home on the market and the few showings or offers they've had.

"I won't pay loan points."

Remind them of adjustments made when they listed their home. "Loan points may seem a bit too much at this moment, but let me explain the parallel between loan points and the second trust deed you plan to discount and how the listing broker made adjustments for you in price at the time you listed your home. Do you recall . . ." Go into detail.

"Do we have to have a termite report?"

"I understand your reluctance to have this done, however, it is required by the lender. In fact, it was done for you when you purchased the home. Besides, it's really the businesslike thing to do in selling a home. You can understand that, can't you?"

"The Martins, down the street, sold their home for more than we're getting."

You have to know this before they mention it and why that other home sold for more. Use your comparable market analysis for their neighborhood.

"The house has only been on the market for a week. I don't want to take a quick offer."

In a case like this, they're afraid it's been too easy and that they might get a better proposal. Say this, "No one wants to make a wrong decision when selling a property, but I'm sure you will agree there's no reason why the first proposal can't be the best one." Go into further explanation of possibly not getting another proposal for some time. Refer to their reasons for moving. It'll make them want to go on to their next home and get settled more quickly.

"I'm in no hurry to sell. I'll wait until I get my price."

This is only a stall. Use this phraseology: "I envy the position you're in. You are quite fortunate, but let me show you how this proposal equals your price." You must be prepared to talk about their net, interest rates, the second trust deed, and the cost of waiting.

"I want my attorney to look at the offer."

This is another stall. They are merely afraid of making the decision. Say this: "I don't blame you. I think it's wise and good business that any time we are unsure of something that we don't approve or sign anything until it's clear to us. Now, let me ask you this, what area of this agreement can I help you understand? Is it the possession period? Is it the initial investment? Is it . . ." Keep asking about every detail until they tell you what they don't understand so you can help them.

The Counterproposal

If the seller agrees to everything but the money and gives you a counterproposal, go immediately to present it to the buyers. Their emotional level will change overnight. Even if it's late at night, try to get the buyers' permission to come over right then. Tell them you want to stop by on your way home to go over a few details. Don't let them know over the phone whether it was accepted or not.

Try to get the sellers to go more than halfway on the counterproposal. Don't split the difference. They always want to split the difference. Say this, "Please give me something to go back to my buyer with to show your sincerity and willingness to work with them." Even if they only go $100 past the halfway point, that $100 has made the difference in getting the transaction approved for me many times.

Go over everything with your buyer that was accepted first. Then, hand them the counterproposal. Watch their expressions. If they've cooled off, you have to resell the home. Keep reminding them of the reasons why they wanted the home. You may have to get their emotions to the level of excitement they were at when they made the original commitment.

If they're still hesitant, take the home away from them warmly. If they say they won't accept the counterproposal say, "Please don't do that. Do you understand what you've done? You've gotten the seller to reduce the property down to an excellent value for someone else. Whoever sees this home next will be the one who benefits from this and not you if you let this opportunity slip away now."

If there's no way they will accept the counterproposal, you may have to go for a counter-counteroffer. In that case, make them go more than halfway. There may be days when you go back and forth between the buyer and seller several times until they agree on an amount. You can't let it get you down. Just keep using the techniques.

CHAPTER 27

Building a 100 Percent Referral Business

I was on a 747 one day waiting for it to take off, and I thought of how much the plane was like someone in real estate. You may think I'm crazy, but I live and breathe real estate and the profession of selling. I'm always looking for new ideas, strategies, or interesting ways to present existing ideas. This day an analogy struck me. A 747 must be at full throttle to take off. However, once it reaches its cruising altitude it backs off almost half of its power to maintain that altitude. That's what it's like to build a 100 percent referral business.

If you operate at full thrust for one solid year, giving it your all, you'll take off to an altitude you can stay at while reducing your thrust to half. If you want to increase your altitude, you merely have to increase your thrust.

Don't be like the average salesperson. He or she is constantly taxiing and never takes off. They work half-heartedly or don't work the business to its fullest for that first year. They're just *trying* real estate. They haven't made the commitment necessary to succeed. That's why a year from now, they'll be working for someone else, probably in an entirely different field, and telling people how hard it is to succeed in real estate.

Do you realize that the easiest sale to make is to a referral? It's almost as easy as falling off a log. The trick is to serve your first few clients so well that they are eager to refer their friends, relatives and associates to you. When the referred folks have already accepted you, based on their friend's or relative's recommendation, the rest is easy.

But you have to really work hard to get to that level. It won't be easy that first year, but it truly will pay off if you're willing to work hard. Understand that the pain of working so hard will be forgotten once you reach the level you choose. You'll be so busy enjoying your active business life and satisfying personal life that you'll forget about the long hours of work and intense training you put yourself through to get there.

You see, my definition of work is anything you're doing when you'd rather be doing something else. You will have to *work* for awhile, but soon you'll find yourself in my shoes. I haven't worked for years because I thoroughly enjoy what I'm doing. I don't see it as work at all. It's fun! And real estate can become fun for you, too, if you're willing to pay the price.

The whole thing begins by doing everything in your power to build a referral business. I'm going to explain to you how I did it. The first thing I suggest is to live by these words:

I Must Do the Most Productive Thing Possible at Every Given Moment.

You must have priorities. Set up priorities for yourself so you always know what the most productive thing is at every given moment. Some people take time off for nonbusiness activities when they shouldn't or do something that's relatively unimportant and feel guilty when they do. Then, they can't really enjoy themselves. That's why you do the most productive thing. Why make yourself feel guilty?

The next thing is to treat every prospect with the attitude that your relationship will continue for the next ten years. If you do your job well, it will. Don't be one of those people who isn't sure if they'll be in the business in three to five years and neglects to send thank-you notes or holiday cards. Do you know you can spend your next twenty years working with those people again and again just by keeping in touch and giving good service? People today are clamoring for it. If you will just take the time to give people good service, you'll build a magnificent referral business.

You also must keep your files up to date. How can you help someone if you don't know where to find them? I've seen people in this business who literally keep all their client information tied up in rubber bands. Their contact information is on 3-by-5 index cards and held together with rubber bands. How can you do business if you never take the rubber bands off? They'll forget you if you forget them and look to someone else the next time they need service. Besides that, few prospects will feel comfortable working with an agent who does not demonstrate proficiency with the latest technology. It will reassure them of your overall competence when they see you using the latest tools of the trade.

True professionals in this business pay fast attention to details. You won't be able to do that unless you have your details somewhere you can find them easily. File all the details you have about each and every client. It doesn't matter if you use file folders, a Rolodex or the latest high-tech software system. Just use something that works for you. Keep information on everyone you work with—buyers, sellers, other real estate agents, title company representatives, mortgage brokers, landscapers, painters, and so on. Keep in touch with your buyers and sellers, even if they move out of state, because you know what will happen? They'll meet someone who is moving to your state and give you that referral.

I once sold the home of a family that moved from California to Utah. Even though they moved out of state, I still sent them a card every ninety days. After a while the people who bought the house decided to make another move. I immediately contacted the original owners and let them know that there was a possibility their house would be on the market again soon. It turned out that they had been thinking of moving back into the area. I got them their old home back, and they were so happy. It all came from my keeping in touch.

Here's the information you need to keep on the people you do business with:

Names—first and last
Addresses and phone numbers
Date of purchase or sale
Names and ages of their children
Employment—what fields they are in
Any special attributes or hobbies
Birthdays and wedding anniversary date

By keeping in touch with your buyers, sellers, and friends, you'll be able to take advantage of their *itch cycles*. The itch cycle for the average family today is to move every three to five years. If you keep in touch with them, they'll be doing business with you. You'll be there when they need to scratch that itch.

With reference to sending anniversary cards, let me state that it is wise to send the card to arrive about three days before the anniversary. I've had husbands call me to thank me for reminding them. It's saved them a lot of grief. It's one of the little things that makes a difference.

Thank-you Notes

Send your people thank-you notes as often as possible. In fact, you should send them to everyone, not just those you've done business with. By sending them to others, too, you'll expand the realm of people you could do business with in the future. Here are some that I suggest you send regularly:

THANK YOU TO BUYER AFTER SHOWING

It was my pleasure, Mr. and Mrs. Johnson, meeting you and having the opportunity to show you homes. You can rest assured that I will do my best to help you find the perfect home and get you happily settled.

THANK YOU AFTER PURCHASE

Nothing excites me more, John and Mary, than helping someone find their new home. I am very happy for you and feel confident we will have no problem getting you happily settled. Please call me if any questions arise.

THANK YOU TO BUYER AFTER CLOSE OF ESCROW

It's been my pleasure, John and Mary, helping you get settled in your new home. I am sure you will enjoy many happy years in our community, and hope you will call me if I can be of service to you or any of your friends.

ANNIVERSARY THANK YOU

It's with great pleasure that we wish you a happy anniversary. It was just one year ago that you let us serve you in finding your new home. We are proud to have you as one of our satisfied clients and hope you will enjoy many more happy years in your home.

REFERRAL THANK YOU

Thank you for referring the Smiths to me. You can rest assured that I will do my best to help them and to justify your confidence in me.

THANK YOU AFTER TELEPHONE CONTACT

Thank you for talking with me on the telephone. In today's business world, time is precious. You can rest assured that I will always be respectful of the time you invest as we discuss the real estate opportunities available to you.

THANK YOU TO ANYONE WHO GIVES YOU SERVICE

Thank you. It is gratifying to meet someone dedicated to doing a good job. Your efforts are sincerely appreciated. If my company or I can serve you in any way, please don't hesitate to call.

THANK YOU TO PEOPLE WHO DON'T BUY FROM YOU

Thank you for giving me the opportunity to show you some homes. I enjoyed meeting you and appreciate the time we shared. We couldn't get together on your needs at this time, but I hope that in the future when you think of real estate, you'll remember me. Please let me know if there is any way I can be of service.

That last card will net you some surprises. In many cases, the next time someone mentions real estate around them, they'll think of you.

Remembrances

Get in the habit of giving a gift to each family who buys from you when they move in. The average salesperson doesn't want to do it. The professional knows how important it is. It can be anything. I suggest plants, personalized door knockers, doormats, or a night out to dinner. Don't send them cut flowers unless you know they particularly enjoy them. Give them something they'll be seeing for a long time to come. Every time they look at it, they'll think of you.

I used to show up late in the afternoon on the day I knew my buyers were moving into their new home with dinner for them—pizza or Chinese take-out. On moving day, people tend to lose track of time and rarely plan dinner.

Send a letter, card, or small gift for special occasions. This would include Christmas, Hanukkah, Thanksgiving, Easter, Halloween, Valentine's Day, anniversaries, and birthdays. Just as we covered in the listing portion of this book, the idea is to use these events as an excuse to get your name in front of them.

How to Ask for a Referral After the Sale

When you stop by with their gift after they've moved in, ask if they have a moment to sit down to talk and use these words:

Salesperson: "My goal is to help as many people as I can. I'd like to ask you, John, you do participate in activities outside the home, don't you?"

Owner: "Yes, I'm in a golf league."

Salesperson: "Is there anyone you play golf with who has mentioned the possibility of having an interest in owning real estate lately?"

Owner: "Well, Bill James has mentioned it. He and his wife have been living in there home for four years. I know his wife would like something bigger. He could probably use some help."

Salesperson: "Mary, are you in any type of group activity?"

Owner: "I'm in an exercise class."

Salesperson: "Is there anyone in your class who might have a real estate need?"

Owner: "Well, Nancy Green is living in an apartment now but she's expecting and they'll need more room."

Salesperson: (Write down names) "Let me ask you about Bill. It sounds like he truly has a need. Do you know what street he lives on?"

Owner: "He lives on Forty-third Street."

Salesperson: "And how about Nancy, do you know where she lives?"

Owner: "She lives down the street from our old place."

Salesperson: "That was on Second Street, right?"

Owner: "Yes."

Salesperson: "Mary, would you do me a favor and get your phone book, please?"

Owner: "Sure. What are you going to do?"

Salesperson: "Would you help me and just look up the addresses of those two people?"

Owner: "Okay."

Salesperson: "You found them, good. John, would you mind calling Bill and telling him about your new home and how happy you are? I'd appreciate it if you'd encourage Bill to let me help him like I've helped you."

Owner: "No, I don't mind. In fact, I've been telling him for some time now that he should look into getting a bigger home."

Salesperson: "Fine. And, Mary, would you mind calling Nancy for me?"

Owner: "No, I wanted to talk with her today anyway and invite her over to see our new house."

If they won't call, get them to just let you use their names. If they'll let you do that when you contact the people, it's a referred lead, which is much easier to close than an unknown voice over the telephone any day. You can open your conversation with the referred person by saying, "John and Mary Smith asked me to contact you."

The main element of this technique is to isolate faces for your buyers to see. Get them thinking about family members or groups of people they know. They're bound to come up with someone who they've talked with about their new home who may have a similar need.

The problem most salespeople have when they ask for referrals is that they give the buyer the whole world to look at. The average salesperson will say something like this, "Can you think of anyone else you know who is looking for a home?" Few people will come up with names when asked that way. When you begin instead by isolating a group of people they know by asking about a hobby, sport, or social group, they see specific faces—the faces of people they would have been talking to about their new home.

CHAPTER 28

Implementation

Now that you've read the techniques covered in this book, it's your responsibility to decide if, when, and how you are going to start internalizing and benefiting from this material. Let me remind you that all of the information in this book has been proven to work by thousands of real estate professionals around the world. It can work for you, too, if you make the commitment to use it properly.

Only 10 percent of the people who read this book will actually do what has been taught here. Most will give one or two things a try, but they won't internalize the material—make it theirs—and truly succeed. If you have already decided to become a member of that 10 percent group, I congratulate you. If you're still uncertain how to begin, this chapter will help you.

The first step in implementing this material is to decide exactly what you want to achieve. In other words, you must define what success means to you.

If I ask a hundred people to define specifically what success means to them, I will probably get a hundred different answers. To some people it's earning twice what they made last year. Others may have to earn five times last year's income to deem themselves successful. Many people define success in terms of lifestyle rather than dollars. It doesn't matter what your definition is. However, it must be specific and be something that makes you happy.

My definition of success is this:

Success is the continuous journey toward the achievement of predetermined, worthwhile goals.

The journey of life is what's fun. Predetermined means you've thought long and hard about where you're going. Worthwhile means that you can feel good about what you're after.

Once you determine what success means to you, you need to establish a plan for achieving it. I like to compare life planning to planning new construction. No competent person would attempt to build a structure without a set of blueprints. I strongly advise you to invest some time in drawing up a set of blueprints for your life.

As an example, let's look twenty years into the future. How old will you be? How do you expect to be living at that time? How much money would you need to do so? What physical condition are you in? Who are the most important people in your life? Think seriously about your answers to these questions. You may have trouble picturing your lifestyle twenty years from now. If you do, I recommend you think of someone you admire now who is twenty years older than you are. What do you admire about them? How do they live? Is that what you want to be like?

Once you determine what your life will be like twenty years from now, write it down. Include all the details you can visualize. Once you've done that, you've set a goal. Wasn't that easy? Too many people think goal setting is so involved they never do it. There is also a fear of not getting what you write down and being a failure. Or, in some cases, changing your mind about what you want and having this goal carved in stone.

I cannot stress enough the fact that goals are not carved in stone. They must be flexible and you must reevaluate your goals regularly. The important thing is that you put your goals in writing. If they're not in writing, they're just dreams and wishes. Therefore, one of your first steps toward achieving the success you want is to put in writing what you want and when you expect to achieve it.

By vividly imagining your goals, you will find yourself becoming very detailed in your description of them. For example, if your goal is to have a new car by the end of the year, go out and look at the models available before writing down the goal. Once you've chosen what you want, picture yourself driving it, smell it, feel it, and enjoy the pride you will have in showing it to others. In your description of the car include model, year, color, options, even the license plate if you plan to personalize it. Get a picture of the car to put up where you'll see it several times each day perhaps on the sun visor of your current vehicle.

Once you've made your twenty-year goals, consider what you would have when you're halfway there—your ten-year goals. What do you have to achieve in the next ten years in order to be where you plan to be in twenty years? Write it down. I recommend breaking those ten-year goals even further into five-year, one-year, monthly, and weekly goals. Since life can only be taken one step at a time, you must begin to do whatever is possible now to stay on the right path to those twenty-year goals.

The only caution I must give in setting goals is that they must be believable. Don't set a goal to run a four-minute mile by the end of the month if you aren't already in top physical condition and running regularly. You have to take into consideration where you are starting from.

An area where most people have the least amount of information is their net worth. Do you know what your net worth is today? Do you understand exactly what time and effort commitments you need to make to achieve whatever your goals are?

Net Worth Statement

You can't set a goal for the future until you know where you stand today. Now, let's assume all of your productivity goals are going to be aimed at an ultimate personal goal of achieving a certain net worth. What is your current net worth, and what are you aiming at? Take some time to gather the data required by this statement. Don't be surprised if your net worth is less than you thought it might be. Most people don't ever take the time to make that determination and guess that it must be a certain amount because they're living a certain lifestyle. Lifestyle is a reflection of net worth to an extent; however, it is not a determining factor. As we are well aware, a good many people live beyond their means. If this is you, I strongly recommend a book by Dave Ramsey titled *The Total Money Makeover.*

Another point I need to make here is that you don't need to have fig-

NET WORTH FORM

Net Worth of (name) _____ As of (date) _____

Financial score card for 3-month period of _____

ASSETS

Cash	Checking	$_____	
	Savings	$_____	
Residence	(fair market value based on CMA*)	$_____	
Furnishings and effects		$_____	
Automobiles		$_____	
Investments	Stocks and bonds	$_____	
	Real estate (fair market value based on CMA*)	$_____	
	Other	$_____	
Other Assets		$_____	
	TOTAL ASSETS	$_____	(1)

LIABILITIES

Mortgage on residence	$_____	
Other mortgages and bank loans	$_____	
Contracts on autos and furnishings	$_____	
Amount due on credit cards	$_____	
Other Liabilities	$_____	
TOTAL LIABILITIES	$_____	(2)

TOTAL ASSETS	$_____	
− TOTAL LIABILITIES	$_____	
= **NET WORTH†**	$_____	(3)

Fill in Net Worth from line 3	$_____	(4)
Net Worth, prior, as of last quarter	$_____	(5)

NET WORTH GAIN OR LOSS FOR THIS QUARTER‡ .... $_____

Net Worth goal for next quarter _____

* Comparable Market Analysis

† To get Net Worth: Subtract your total liabilities (2) from your total assets (1). What remains is your Net Worth.

‡ The difference between (4) and (5) lets you know your financial score. Have you gained or lost this quarter?

ures for every category. These categories are just the most common ones. Don't rush out and invest in stocks just to put something on this statement.

Once you've determined your current net worth, decide what you want it to be. Set your twenty-year net worth goal. Then break it down until you have a goal for the next quarter. Use this goal to help you set goals for all the other areas of you life. What do you need to do to achieve the next quarter's goal? We'll cover productivity information next. I recommend that you refigure your net worth at the end of each quarter and make the necessary adjustments in your activity goals.

Setting up a reward system for your goals is a very good idea. As we've already discussed, once you get the new car that you set a goal for, you have the car. However, for goals you set concerning intangible things such as weight loss, quitting your smoking habit, doing more prospecting, or learning new skills, set up a reward for yourself upon their achievement. If you lose ten pounds by November 30, reward yourself with a really spectacular outfit to wear during the holiday season.

By doing more prospecting, you'll receive a reward of more activity, thus more sales; however, give yourself a gift or remembrance of the achievement as well. These things will keep you motivated when you have a weak period of not wanting to do what you have to do to achieve another goal in the future.

What should you set goals for? Well, set them for what you really want, but consider all areas of your life.

As I mentioned in Chapter 1, there are four aspects that must be kept in balance if you want to achieve true happiness. They are financial, physical, spiritual, and emotional. After all, what good is financial success if you're a physical wreck? And what do you think it would be like to be healthy and financially well off, but have an emotional or spiritual void in your life? That's why balance is important.

It's also important to include your loved ones in your goals, especially the goals that will affect their lives. If you set a goal to spend more time prospecting for clients, talk it over with your spouse and children if it takes you away from them. By helping them understand the benefits you'll gain by being away prospecting, they'll be more supportive when you need it. It's so easier to achieve your goals if you're not fighting to get them.

I also recommend you set goals as a family. When everyone works together for something, it makes the achievement that much more enjoyable. It's also a good way to help your children learn the benefits of goal setting. Help them set goals for themselves. You'll be surprised how quickly they adapt goal setting to all aspects of their lives.

Start right now setting both long-term and short-term goals. Long-term goals will take you anywhere from ninety days to the rest of your lifetime to achieve. The specific date of accomplishment is up to you. A short-term goal is something you can achieve in less than ninety days. Set a goal right now for what you'll accomplish in the next week. Maybe it could be to reread and begin internalizing the techniques in this book and then to begin applying them to situations with your clients on your next appointment.

Getting a Firm Grip on the Slippery Minutes

It's easy to procrastinate in real estate, easy to spend the whole day actively doing nothing. That is, it's easy until a month is gone, and you have nothing to show for it except bills.

Do you have organizing and time-planning challenges? If you do, you're fortunate. Great salespeople aren't naturally organized. They're not detail lovers. What they want is to get out there, meet the people, and sell or list the house. Curses on the paperwork.

But you're paid for doing what you don't want to do whether it's paperwork or prospecting. Both those things can overwhelm you unless you've learned how to pull effective action out of the raw material of life. And what is that raw material? Nothing but a lot of slippery minutes strung together. That's all any of us have to work with—bunches of fast-fading and easily misplaced minutes. So, to be successful, we have to find ways to gain firm traction on life's slippery highway. If I can get you to plan your time and organize your action, you'll get so much time traction that the results—in terms of more money in your pocket—will amaze you.

Being organized allows you to cope with problems efficiently. I often say that the real estate business—when worked professionally—is a gold mine. It's also a mine with challenges. If you ignore the challenges in real estate, will they go away? Or will they grow from little creatures into huge monsters? Untended problems in real estate don't fade, they flourish. When we try to hide from them, they grow so big they eat us alive when they catch us, which usually happens about fourteen hours before the transaction is scheduled to close—but won't unless the challenge is resolved.

The Three Basics of Time Saving for Success

Is there a professional way to handle challenges in real estate? There certainly is. A four-letter word, *fast,* sums it up. When challenges arise, and in real estate they will as surely as corn grows in Iowa, your clients must be made aware that you have done everything a skilled and professional agent has the power to do toward solving the difficulty. They also must be made aware that you acted promptly. But solutions won't always be within your power, will they? As long as you do your job quickly and keep them informed—demonstrating once again that you're operating with their best interests in mind—that's all right. The first basic of time saving is: Do it now if it can be done now—especially if it's unpleasant.

Otherwise, all the fear, guilt, and evasion that'll fester in the shade of the challenge you're trying to avoid will make you waste far more time and money later than it would take to cope with it now.

Hand a loser several phone messages and what'll he do? First, he'll groan and suffer about the ones he was afraid he'd get. Then he'll call the easiest one in the pile. And the problem calls? He'll leave them until tomorrow, next week—or never.

Hand a champion the same phone messages and she'll call the toughest one first—and if there's a challenge, she'll get it on the road to a solution before she'll make her easy calls. As usual, the champion arranges things so that she can finish on an up note and walk away feeling like the winner she is.

Doing it now if it can be done now, especially if it's unpleasant, doesn't just apply to problem solving. This concept should be your guide to everything you know you should do in business—and maybe in your private life as well. But we're constantly faced with situations where more than one thing must be done right now. Which of them gets our attention first?

The average salesperson says to himself, "Okay, I can't do everything at once, so I'll set priorities. First, I'll work on the item that'll make me the most money because that's my reason for being in business. Then, when that's out of the way, I'll go out prospecting."

Champions have a completely different priority: They get the difficult things and their activity goals achieved first. Then they jump on the things they're looking forward to doing. Why? Because champions know that what's hard and what makes the most money are usually the same things in the long run. They know that every time they handle a hard task today instead of avoiding it, they raise their prestige, increase their self-respect, and make their tomorrows easier, happier, and more profitable.

The second principle of time saving and success is to take time every day to think. People don't realize they are deliberately shutting their brains off by keeping them filled with trivia all through their waking hours. By the way, it's not thinking when all you do is review your prejudices, reinforce your fears, and excuse your evasions. Take time every day to look clearly and openly at who you are, where you're going, and how you're going to get there.

The third principle of time saving for success is short and sweet: Be organized.

Think of all the things you can't do if you ignore this principle.

1. You can't make much money unless you're organized. In real estate, it takes a large volume to create a large income—and details left unattended can break more transactions than the fastest tongue can open.

2. You can't make efficient use of your time unless you're organized. A large volume of real estate transactions comes only from a large volume of meaningful contacts with people—and this is something that only a time-efficient agent can achieve.

3. You can't build a referral business unless you're organized. Maybe you think they'll only remember that you finally sold their turkey. No such luck. If you failed to give them service, they won't remember anything except the calls you didn't return, the promises you didn't keep, and the frustrations they felt. Sure they'll give you a referral—when fish start singing.

4. You can't enjoy any time off unless you're organized. As any veteran of the business can tell you, it takes effort and organization before a real estate person who is successful can take time off. Some people do well in this business for a short time and then burn out because they never figure out how to take time off.

Preparation is half the battle for time off in real estate; the other half is being determined to let nothing, and I mean nothing, stand in the way of your time off.

The key is preparing the people you're working for. I told all of my clients, "Here are three phone numbers: my office, my home, and the phone in my car. Except on Wednesdays, you can reach me twenty-four hours a day at one of these numbers. Wednesday is my day off, and I'm not available then, but at any other time, you can always get me on the phone right away. If something that can't wait overnight comes up, John Smart at my office will take good care of you but every day of the week except Wednesday, I'm just a quick call away."

The test of whether you can stay away from Burnout Island comes when an agent catches you right before your day off and says he has a hot offer on one of your listings. The only moneymaking answer a champion can give is; "That's wonderful. I'm delighted to hear that. Call John Smart at my office and he'll take care of everything. I'm off until Thursday morning."

"But . . ."

"John will take good care of you. And thanks for calling. Goodnight." But this is only for champions. When you're new in the business, you can't do that; you have to kiss your day off good-bye and go fee hunting instead.

If you're a budding champion, here's a valuable tip: When you're able to give top priority to the taking of one day off a week, don't stay home the night before. If you're going to be late, head out of town directly from your last appointment and meet your family a few miles down the road.

Otherwise, somebody will catch you before you can get away the next morning and dump a little something on you. That little something will probably be a challenge, but it might be a possible opportunity. Either way, when you have that item taken care of, all chance of getting a quality day off will be lost. It's so easy to let this happen over and over—and it doesn't take long to destroy your family's faith in the whole idea. When that happens, so much anxiety will hang over your days off that most of the benefit will be cut out of them.

After your first six successful months in this business, nothing will do more to ensure that your success will continue than locking into one day off a week. After being on this schedule of having assured time off for a month, very few calls will come in for you on your days away because everyone knows you're not there. That's how it worked for me.

Select your day off with care; then stick to it. Switching around kills the system. I recommend having your day off printed on your business cards: "Available 24 hours every day except Wednesdays, call _____."

Flick Through the Files Day

Start a habit of going through all of the names in your contact list every other day. Ask yourself these questions:

What are they thinking about real estate today?
Are these people about to change from warm to hot?
What can I ask them or tell them to justify my dialing their number right now?

Since an essential part of the follow-up that creates your income is done with these calls, take long enough with each card to bring the person to mind. Think about their situation for an instant. Then, act on your hunch. Keep on doing that for three weeks and you'll discover that you're developing a sixth sense for the hottest opportunities in your file. Every time you call any of your prospects, note the date you spoke to them, the next time you look at their information, you'll know how long it's been since you've worked with that person on the phone.

The Action-Oriented Desk

If you plan to rise above the average level of success of real estate salespeople, you need to have a certain attitude about your place of business.

I'm not referring to the company you work for here. I'm referring to your desk. When it all boils down, the specific place you conduct business is at your desk. Think of any other business and what their front office looks like. They're usually neat and clean with a few decorations. It's a pleasant and welcoming atmosphere.

Take a look at your desk and see if its appearance is welcoming to clients. Is it a warm and pleasant place to conduct business? Will your clients feel like they're invading your private place because it's cluttered with tons of private papers? You see, people consider the paperwork involved in the sale or purchase of a home a private matter. It's their personal knowledge what they paid for a home and what they're willing to sell it for. If they see this type of information handled less than personally in your place of business, they'll feel you will do the same with them.

If you don't bring clients to your desk, think about your associates. If your desk looks like you live there—too cluttered—they'll think there's an open invitation to drop by and chat. If you have a clean, neat desk, they'll think you won't be in too long and keep their business short and to the point.

I recommend that you only have the things at your desk that you need to make money. You need the basic business tools such as a phone, phone books, computer, calendars, calculator, pens, pencils, and so on.

You need pictures of your family to draw strength from and to help develop rapport with close-mouthed clients. Pictures of your goals are also helpful. However, if your goal is to have a car that's above what your clients would drive, put it away when they come in. There's no need to make them feel uncomfortable. They need to think you're like them.

In your file drawer you should have:

1. EXPIRED LISTINGS

Label a folder EXPIRED LISTINGS to hold copies of your expired listings and all important documents relating to those expirations. You must have this information handy in your desk so you can react quickly when these former clients call you about becoming active again.

Maybe you're thinking right now, "I'm not going to have any expired listings." Good luck. I believe that the greatest lister in the world will, after a few years in this business, have had many listings that expired. Most people can accept that their home didn't sell and not blame you if you kept them informed, showed them that you cared, and exposed their property well. What they hate is when you don't give them service and they never hear from you. That's why you call your sellers and follow up with them regularly.

The market changes constantly. You can write a listing tomorrow that, three weeks ago, would have been gone in seventy-two hours—but there's been a ripple in the market and that beast just sits there. The veterans of this business all have war stories about listings they've had that should've sold and didn't. If you've done your job, the clients can't get mad at you when the listing expires, but they feel bad. The world doesn't like their home. That heavy rejection makes a lot of people say, "We'll just wait then." What they're really saying is, "You don't like our home, world? Then we aren't going to let you see it anymore."

But they're still itching to move. In 60 to 90 days, that house will be back on the market; if you haven't kept in touch, it'll show up on someone else's inventory, and you lose. So let them see your smiling face and hear your sweet voice scratch, scratch, scratch on that constant itch of theirs.

2. CLOSED SALES

Please keep a folder in your desk that has information on all your closed sales. If your broker wants the original documents to stay in the office's main file, run copies of the important ones for your desk. With this data at your fingertips, you can immediately start talking knowledgeably when any of the people who've bought a house from you call, wanting to sell. You'll probably have more information about their property within reach than they can locate without a lot of effort, which is the position a professional likes to be in. But don't roll all your facts out over the phone. Get over there and talk face-to-face to them before another agent moves in on you.

3. INCOME TAX AND BUSINESS RECEIPTS

This is another vital file that should be kept handy in your desk and added to regularly. Almost everything you spend money for in the business end of real estate is deductible—if you can prove that you spent the money. The best way to keep good tax records—that is, the method that takes the least time and has the least risk of missing deductions—is to make a permanent record of your expenses the same day you spend the money. Get in this habit. It'll save you a lot of time and money every April.

Keeping a little box or envelope in your car to pop receipts in is handy, but don't overlook having some form of diary. The IRS requires this for any entertainment expenses you're planning to deduct. Your appointment book or planning software can serve this purpose.

Planning/Appointment System

Most champions keep an appointment book or time management software within reach throughout their business hours; they simply have too much going on to function efficiently without a convenient, take-along record of their appointments and of the details they must follow up on each day.

You can find a variety of daily diary/appointment books in stationery stores; other good ones are advertised in business magazines. Try to find one that you are comfortable with. A good diary/appointment book will have the following standard features: lines for appointments broken down at least in half hour increments, space for listing your priorities or goals for the day, as well as room for a things-to-do type of list. Your diary/appointment book should also have calendars showing the full month as well as a breakdown for each week of the month. Many of them will also have sections for names, addresses and phone numbers, mileage, and other business expenses.

The most important aspect of the diary/appointment book is that you must rely on it every day. It should always be with you. Find one that doesn't tell you to give up and go home at five or six o'clock. By not having space organized for evening appointments, that's what most of them do. Since the best listing appointments usually take place at night, why set yourself up to feel bad every time you write one in your book? Get one with spaces you'll feel good about filling.

If you choose to work with time-planning software, you'll need to be able to include the same information. Be certain your software doesn't have limits as to how many characters are allowed for any entry. You need room for a lot of details. Do yourself a favor and print out the information for each day after you complete your entries. File that paper away in a safe place just in case your computer has challenges when you fire it up tomorrow. Also, learn how to back up all of your computer files and do it religiously.

The Strength of the Standard Week

In most jobs, we have to be in a certain place doing certain things for certain hours of the week. The boss does the time planning for us. All we have to do is punch in, keep breathing as we do the job, and then go home.

People who come to this business from a job that involves a company-imposed workweek are often bewildered by the average real estate office's free atmosphere. Without someone telling them what to do, they're lost. They just don't get anything done that'll make money.

The champion is the same. He'd be lost without someone telling him what to do. But there is one important difference: The champion fills that vacuum by being effective at telling himself what to do—and generally he demands more of himself than he'd give any boss.

He or she sets life goals as we discussed earlier, and then breaks those goals down to ten-year goals; and finally to yearly, monthly, and daily goals. Then the champion translates those money and accomplishment goals into the action that will achieve them.

This is done very simply: by scheduling enough daily activity to reach the desired result in the desired time. In other words, you schedule a successful life the same way a factory schedules its production.

Companies would get into trouble fast if they tried to operate without schedules. So will you. If you force yourself to operate without a working routine, every day, perhaps every hour, you'll find yourself debating what the best course of action is right now.

One of the solid pillars I built my real estate career on was the standard week. Hot buyers pulled me off it. Ready-to-list sellers pulled me off it but little else could. And, when an interruption was over, I picked up my standard week again. In the beginning, it was two early hours in the office, then out meeting people by 9:30 every morning; lunch, then return calls, research houses, and make afternoon calls; dinner, then evening appointments. Every night, I ended my regular workday plus work evening with a short planning session for the next day.

As my skills and knowledge grew, my standard week evolved steadily toward higher and higher production. Everything learned about the area and its inventory of houses helped me reduce the amount of time that adequate research took. And, as my referral business grew, I had less time or need for prospecting.

In my fourth year, I hired a full-time secretary and encouraged her to get a real estate license so she could work with my clients on anything I wanted her to handle. She was a tremendous help and only cost me a listing a month. After hiring and training her, I was able to spend most of my time working with clients. When not showing properties and closing buyers, I'd be running through my techniques with sellers and listing them. What happened to my income then? It really took off.

First, get efficient; then go for the big volume. After you've done the first, the second is easy. That's right. Real estate is an easy business to make big money in—after you've worked hard for two or three years at developing your professional expertise and building your clientele.

Keeping to a standard workweek is one of the basic methods that helped me achieve what I achieved as a real estate salesperson. After taking some training, I worked out a pattern for my weeks. Sure, it was a demanding pattern. I wouldn't ask anyone to work as hard now as I did then, but a large part of my results came from always knowing what I wanted to do at any given moment, and then just doing that thing. I had goals for every day: Every weekday morning I did certain things; every Sunday afternoon I did certain other things.

For all the basic activities that spell success in real estate, there are some hours of the week that are best to do them. For every hour of the day from seven in the morning until nine at night, there are some best things that you can do to make more money. The limits on how much you'll do and on how high you'll fly are set by you and nobody else. Most people do that by never thinking about it. You're different. You're going to set goals, plan your days around a standard workweek, and achieve great things, aren't you?

Keep at each new standard workweek until you grow enough in professional stature to move up to a higher level. If you make yourself decide everything every day, you'll make a lot of bad decisions about how to spend your time. Instead of wondering what to do next, it is a great relief to operate smoothly and confidently along previously decided lines, knowing all the time that you're on target for achieving the success you want. Commit yourself to a standard workweek that's a high-production schedule; then stick to that plan until you're ready for a better schedule that will create even greater production. You'll be astonished at the heights you'll reach when you work systematically.

Do your scheduling in writing. Unless you commit it to black and white reality, your plans won't have enough impact to make an impression on your present habits. Review your progress daily. This is crucial, especially in the beginning. Keep working at it. You'll find that developing and getting in the habit of following a powerhouse schedule takes time and effort. What you're looking for is a standard workweek that pushes you without beating you and makes the most effective use of your time that's possible with the degree of expertise you've attained so far.

Finding More Hours Through Time Planning

If you think about how much a few individuals get done and then compare their output to how little so many people accomplish, it seems like the effective few must have ways of manufacturing minutes.

In a sense, we do. What's amazing is how simple these minute-manufacturing methods are. Let me tell you how to use the plan-your-work, work-your-plan method:

1. Tonight, list all the things you have to do tomorrow.

Set priorities on those things by red-flagging or numbering the most important items. Now you're ready for the most crucial thing in this step, which is to commit yourself to completing your top-priority items at the earliest possible hour tomorrow.

2. Tonight, review your daily activity goals.

These are all the things that your plan calls for you to do each day—prospect with fifteen people, for example—in order to make your money and other goals come about. Compare your list of things to do with your daily activity goals; then work up an hour-by-hour plan for tomorrow that'll make the best possible use of your time.

3. Tomorrow, follow the plans you develop tonight.

It's really that simple, but let me warn you: In the beginning you'll often be shocked at how firmly you can commit to the next day's plans, only to have the things you didn't do last week, or last month—even last year—come crashing down and blow your plans sky high. Or your old work habits, your old personal commitments, your lack of familiarity with all these new techniques prevent you from carrying out your plan as well as you want to.

Don't worry about it. Just keep planning your tomorrows and working your plans to the best of your ability until these new habits become you. Then you'll find that it's happening with much less stress and effort on your part. Remember, a new habit only takes root in your personality when you follow it for twenty-one days. This means doing it, not just wanting to, not just trying to. And you can't mark those three weeks off in bits and pieces to make your new standard of work stick; you've got to put together a string of twenty-one days in which you plan your work and work your plan every day.

It will take some practice and some learning by trial and error. You may have to become more assertive with a few people who have been wasting your time. You may have to get very tough with the worst offender in this regard. That person might possibly be you.

Build plenty of flexibility into your plans. Avoid locking onto a rigid schedule so tightly that if anything prevents you from carrying it out in every detail, you'll lose your friendly attitude. One of the main purposes of time planning is to reduce frustration, not expand it.

Follow the plan-your-work, work-your-plan concept, and you'll find a lot more productive minutes in every day than you ever knew were there. These manufactured minutes add up quickly into extra productive hours that will add important money to your income. Foresight cuts wasted motion and lost time to the absolute minimum.

Every highly productive person I've talked to about this subject has told me that they plan tomorrow tonight, and they consider this small, basic idea one of the most important elements in their success. What an upsurge of productivity there'd be if all the people who control their working time suddenly adopted this system. Slowly, very slowly, that's happening; but most people never plan their days; they simply crash into whatever comes their way. And, just to make sure the confusion is complete, they put off everything they can, which turns everything that happens into a crisis. The future is always filled with nasty surprises for those of us who never look at it a day early.

If you've been playing that tune all your life, please invest the time and effort it'll take to learn how to create an effective work plan each night, and then put it into effect the next day. Do this, make this habit your constant companion, and it will revolutionize your productivity. The time to start is this evening. That's right, tonight. No matter how busy, tired, or discouraged you are, you can make a start on this vital new habit tonight. You can list at least five things you need to do tomorrow.

In the beginning, you'll need about fifteen minutes a night to plan each tomorrow, but as you gain experience with this technique, the time required for it will drop drastically. What'll happen is that you'll be thinking and maybe making notes all through the day of what you'll need to do tomorrow. When you sit down in the evening for a few minutes to complete your plan, you'll be able to make all the necessary decisions, and then commit yourself to them, with quick confidence.

What a relief it is to have all your work decisions made, and simply go out and do the job. Believe me, all it takes is commitment to success, which means commitment to accepting the pain of change, commitment to accepting lots of trivial rejection, commitment to doing the most productive thing at every given moment.

Be sure to include your life's most important people and things in your time planning. Otherwise, you'll create forces that'll tear you down faster than your hard work can build you up. Schedule time for:

1. FAMILY

Please, treat your family better than you treat your clients. They're more important to you in the long run, aren't they? Yet so many of us forget that truism in the day-to-day hustle to make a buck—and this attitude is so counterproductive, so unnecessary, so harmful to your life. Schedule time for the family. Keep track of the days and things that have special significance to each person you love—anniversaries and birthdays, the school activities your children want you to attend, the events you've promised your spouse you'll attend together.

You can find a new client anytime by knocking on ten doors, but your family is unique and irreplaceable. So if you have to be late for a date with them, call. And, when something is especially important to your spouse or child, don't let the possibility of losing a fee override the certainty of disappointing them. A missed anniversary will be remembered in sorrow twenty years after. A fee you might possibly miss will be forgotten in as many days. One of the main reasons you plan your time and push yourself along all day every workday is to have time for your family.

2. APPOINTMENTS

If you have one appointment a week, you won't miss it but when you get busy, you'll miss scheduled listing and sales appointments unless you keep track of them. Maybe you don't think you're busy enough to need an appointment book. Don't worry. If you follow the suggestions in this book, you soon will be. When the surge of business that's coming at you hits, don't add to your burdens by having to learn how to schedule your time too.

3. RELIGION

If you have one, as I do, don't lose it getting rich. That's stupid. I mean it. If you're supposed to go to church, go to church. I know I was supposed to go, and I wanted to go, but sometimes my best buyer would call. Finally, I went to the pastor and said, "Father, make me an usher. That way I have to be here." It worked.

Other things are important besides making money. Commit yourself to doing those things outside of business that are of the greatest importance to you. They are the things that make life worth living; they give you the strength to keep on going instead of burning out about the time you start to make some real money.

4. RESEARCH

Our business is based on keeping up with the market and with the latest developments in financing and owning real property. All these things are constantly changing; the only way you can gain—and then keep—professional status is to be constantly updating your knowledge. Every day you're not fully occupied with clients, schedule time for viewing property. When should you do that? During the least productive hours for prospecting.

5. PLAY

If you work hard, you're entitled to play hard. If you'd rather not do that, go off for some high-quality loafing when you've earned it. I'm fortunate in knowing many of the top real estate people on this continent, and I can tell you that most of them play as hard as they work and they don't feel guilty about it either because they know they've earned it.

If you haven't done enough yet to feel good about taking time off, don't. Wait until you've convinced yourself that you've earned it. Otherwise, guilt feelings will wipe out the benefits you would have received had that vacation, in your own mind, been well-deserved. We can't fool ourselves as much as we think we can.

6. PROSPECTING

Until you've built up a referral business, the limit on your income is how much you prospect. Commit to prospecting, schedule it and don't fight a battle with yourself every day. Just get out there and do it. Now you know the phraseology; you know how to build the right attitude; you know how to make it all easier for yourself—so you know that you can do it all.

7. HEALTH

The tensions and pressures that are built into this business will get to you fast if you don't heal yourself every day with some physical exertion. Why? Because tensions and pressures throw more adrenaline into our blood than is good for us. The only way to get rid of that excess adrenaline is through physical exertion. This is very basic. Your body has only one way to react to pressure and tension, and that is the same way it reacts to fear—by running or fighting.

Any physical exercise can take the place of the fighting, but for most people, competitive sports create as much tension and pressure as their work does. Keep that in mind when you select your exercises for healing tension and pressure, and give yourself every possible break.

Your highest priorities for exercise and recreational activities, as you battle to establish your real estate practice, should be to heal yourself, to protect and improve your health, and to avoid creating new problems for yourself. Jogging may be a better choice than tennis, and walking may be better than jogging. For many people, doctors recommend a brisk half-hour walk instead of jogging. Whatever exercise you choose, commit yourself to it. You'll feel better, make more money, and enjoy life more and longer.

8. SPECIALTY

By now, you should have a good idea of what your first listing or selling specialty is going to be. Will you devote your primary efforts to your listing bank? Possibly you've decided to specialize on by-owners, or to work open houses most heavily. Or you might choose to work mainly with transferees to and from major corporations in your city. Whatever specialty you select, be careful to provide enough of the right hours for it in your daily time planner.

9. FRIENDS

Something has to give if you're on a strong drive for success, and what's likely to snap is your relationships with old friends. For many people, this is too rough—they cave in when the peer pressure to stay average hits them, and they remain as they are. But if you're strong enough to resist this pressure, and you'll have to be if you're going to succeed in becoming a new and remarkably more successful person, there'll come a time, perhaps much sooner than you expect, when it comes down to choosing between success and your old friends. Before long, you'll be growing emotionally, professionally, and financially in noticeable ways—but most of your present friends will be staying on the same levels they occupy now.

Before long, the old relaxed feelings and the community of interests that pulled you together in the first place will be gone, never to return. Very few friendships can survive a considerable change in the status of one friend that's not matched by a similar development in the other person. When you turn into an eagle, you can't eat sunflower seeds with a pigeon anymore.

Accept that life is set up this way. Don't worry about it because there's nothing you can do, short of giving up your drive for success, to hold onto the past. If that parting of ways is going to happen it will, naturally, and in due time. You're sitting there playing cards with old friends and suddenly your beeper goes off. You toss in the hand, stand up, and say, "I'm sorry but I have to go present an offer now."

If your friends don't understand, if they resent it, that's their privilege. If (I really should say *when*) you become uncomfortable with your old friends, find new friends among the many who, like you, are moving up. Or, find them among the people who already are at the level you want to reach.

Daily Activity Chart

During your working hours, there are certain things you should be doing—certain activities—that will generate the productivity you desire. I broke these activities down and charted them. That way, if I saw that my productivity was slumping, I could look at my chart and see where I was lacking.

Set a monthly goal for each category on the chart and enter them in the appropriate column. Then, record the points you earn each day. Do it at the end of each day, before reviewing your goals and to-do list for the next day. Determining how successful you were today will help you decide how active you must be tomorrow in order to achieve your monthly goals.

Let me define for you what counts toward points on this chart. In regard to the various contacts listed, you must actually talk with someone in authority. In most cases that's the owner of the property. Please, as a professional, don't count talking with children or babysitters. They won't remember who you are or care enough what you do to tell the owners. To determine whether or not this contact counts, consider the information you gain from it. You should at least get the owners' first and last names, a confirmation of the address, about how long they've owned the property, and when they might consider moving. You can't count points for knocking on doors that no one answers or dialing calls where no one is home. Remember, you must be honest with yourself on this chart if you are to benefit from the information.

DAILY ACTIVITY CHART

Days 1 – 31

Give yourself one point (1) for any of the following:	1	2	3	4	5	6	7	8	9	10	11	12	13
Phone canvasing contacts													
Phone canvasing appointments													
Door knocking contacts													
Requested mail-outs													
Appointments from mail-outs													
Other contacts													
Other appointments													
FSBOs contacted													
FSBO appointments													
Expireds contacted													
Expired appointments													
Ad call contacts													
Ad call appointments													
Open houses held													
Open house contacts													
Open house appointments													
Referrals received													
Listing presentations													
Listings taken													
Number of showings													
Other listings inspected													
Education													
Unsolicited mail-outs													
Thank-you notes sent													
Listings sold													
Closed sales													
DAILY TOTAL													

Post point total each day on your 90-day activity graph.

14	15	16	17	18	19	20	21	22	23	24	25	26	27	28	29	30	31	TOTAL

TOTAL POINTS FOR MONTH

In giving yourself points for appointments, I only want you to include appointments made and kept. Broken appointments don't count. Also, don't overlap your information. A listing presentation appointment only goes in the category Listing Presentations. I am assuming you use the two-step listing approach that I teach and your first appointment with any seller is just an information-gathering appointment. Your initial appointment with buyers, however, may include showings. In that case, you must list the number of homes showed. If you show a particular property six times in a month, that will count for six showings.

As an example of using the chart, let's say you have an appointment with Mr. and Mrs. Smith that you originally met at your open house. You would give yourself one point for holding the open house, one for making the open house contact, one point for the open house appointment, and one for each home you show them.

I have given you the Other categories for contacts you make that don't quite fit anywhere else. For example, you overhear an employee of your dry cleaner mention that they are looking at homes and start up a conversation. That would be an *other* contact. When you arrange to visit with them to assist them with their needs, that would go under "other appointments."

If you are lucky to have children like mine, you might have them tell you about their friend who has an aunt or uncle who wants to move into the area. I know this sounds quite removed; however, you'll often be happy to learn that they have just begun considering it and haven't really contacted anyone in the industry as yet. You can then nicely offer your services and perhaps send them market information to consider before they arrive in town. In this case, they probably won't see you as an eager salesperson. You're just being friendly in offering them the information they need to make a start.

In the Closed Sales category, only give yourself points for other agent's listings. If you sell your own listing, it would go into the Listings Sold category. Again, I'm trying to ensure you don't duplicate your information.

Give yourself one point for each property you inspect that's listed by another agent.

In regards to Education, give yourself one point for each hour spent in reading up on current market information, listening to audio training programs, or attending sales meetings or seminars.

Total up your daily points at the end of each day. This point total will show you how productive you've been. You'll then want to record that number on the 90-day activity graph we'll cover in a moment. I explained earlier that it's easy to be busy but not be productive. The Daily Activity Chart helps you keep busy with productive work. And once you determine your contact and sales ratios, it keeps you on a highly productive schedule. We'll get into the ratios in just a moment.

At the end of the month, total across each category and look at the results. By comparing monthly totals and ratios over a period of time, you'll see patterns emerging that will help you understand the areas in which you need improvement to increase your sales. You will find that you have more closed sales when you have a large number of referrals. That is the goal of every professional real estate agent. However, you need to learn what other areas you are good at that bring you those referrals and work on those areas.

Figuring Ratios

At the end of a month, you can determine what area has been most productive for you and plan your strategy for the next month to become even more productive by concentrating on the areas in which you have the best ratios. Or, if you know you can do better in a weak area, concentrate on improving your technique there to make yourself more well-rounded.

Let's say it takes you twenty-five phone canvasing contacts to make one appointment. That makes your ratio 25:1. Then, figure the ratio for contacts-to-appointments in each of the areas on the chart. As you go down the list, your ratios should be progressively better. It's only natural that you'll make more appointments with referred contacts than those reached by phone or even in person knocking on doors. These people are already somewhat qualified while the former group is not. The closer the two numbers in the ratio, the better the area is for you.

Let me offer a word of caution here. If you're new in the business, don't let one month's information determine what type of specialist you become. Keep your charts for at least six months before deciding. Next month could be a whole different story. If you haven't yet had time to concentrate in one of the contact areas, you might want to figure out an overall average for yourself by totaling the number for contacts and appointments. If you're not satisfied with this figure, spend more time internalizing the phraseology for getting an appointment in Chapter 20 and set a goal for higher activity next month.

Your ratios are also a good indicator as to whether or not a change you've made in your approach or technique is working. If your productivity seems to be dropping after a week of the change, don't stop using it. You just need to get more comfortable with it and try doing it better for at least another week. Your best determining factor will lie in a change that's made for at least a 30-day period. So don't give up if your average days don't immediately turn into superachievement days.

One more item to take into consideration here is the amount of income you earned in the same 30-day period. In other words, when you did this, you earned that. So, to earn more, you have to do more. The information from this will help you tremendously in your goal setting. If you desire a certain income level, you will get a good understanding of how productive you need to be to get there. Also, you'll begin to see how much of a time commitment is required to earn that level of achievement. If you are not willing to commit yourself, don't expect to earn the higher income. Also, as I mentioned before about families, you may need to help them understand that you can't make a million dollars in real estate and still be home for dinner every night. They, too, must be willing to make some adjustments in their lives if they want to benefit from the increased income you set your goals for.

Production graphs are one of the most valuable tools any business can have. And you, operating like a business, must learn to rely on them for tracking successes as well as failures. By utilizing the information on a simple graph, you can often recognize a slump before it has a drastic affect on your finances. You should also use production graphs to help you determine your future goals.

Take the daily total of points from the Daily Activity Chart and mark it on this chart. If you are going to do well in this business, it should reach a certain high level and stay there with some low points for days off. If your chart is very erratic, you're not putting enough into the business.

Please note that this graph can make you feel either fantastic or terrible depending on your activity. The important thing is that it's a reflection of your activity and not how you feel about it. Hopefully, you'll be elated with the activity, but if you're not, please realize that it's only pointing the way to what you need to be doing to make things better. Too many people have left real estate and still don't realize to this day why they didn't make it. They had no records to show them!

Now, you are fully armed to begin or improve your real estate career. You have been given the proper tools to conduct your business and keep the necessary files and records. What you do with it will determine the amount of success you achieve in your real estate career.

EXAMPLE

Please note that this graph can either make you feel fantastic or terrible depending on your activity. The important thing is that it is a reflection of your activity, and not how you feel about. We hope that you will be elated with the activity, but if you are not, we hope that it will show you that you need to do something about it, and then do it because in life everybody has problems. We are not judged by our problems, but by what we do about those problems, and doing something about a problem is a lot easier when you know what the problem is. The purpose of this graph is to let you know where the problem is. Too many people have left the selling profession and still don't realize why they didn't make it. A national survey taken recently pointed out that sales people spend an average of only 20 minutes a day talking to people who can buy. Can there be any doubt that you need to keep an eye on your activities.

AREA I:

Notice how this salesperson's production is up and down. This shows a lack of direction which can lead to frustration and irratic production. This person is trying, but is not motivated, and does not have a good work plan. Unless there is some change fast, he will soon be out of the business.

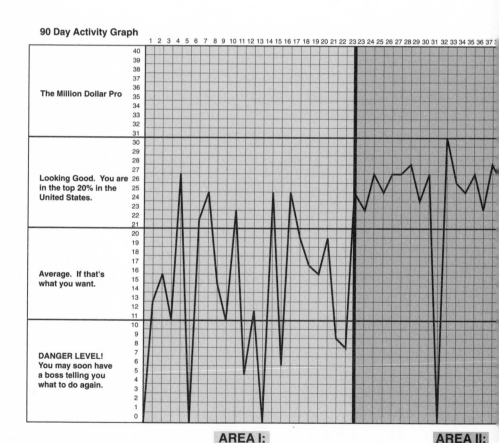

90 Day Activity Graph

AREA I: AREA II:

AREA II:

This person is a good steady worker, and is somewhat motivated, but is not doing the little extras that could make them the best. They're careful not to go over the 30 line. 20-30 is a good comfortable zone for them. There is no commitment to reach their full potential, although this person is a good strong money earner.

AREA III:

Strong highly motivated producer. Good goals - knows why they are working, and where they are going. They like to run their activity right off the chart. This type of day with that type of activity obviously gives them a great deal of satisfaction. Even on an off day they are in the above average area. You may also note that this person also needs less time off because selling is no longer work to them, it is a way of life, and a means to an end.

AREA IV:

This is where you will find thousands of salespeople. No goals and bad work habits, so they usually have but a "what's the use" attitude, as well as a self image that gets worse every day until they are out of sales. Remember, the average salesperson only spends 20 minutes a day in front of someone who can make a decision to buy... that's the average, so many salespeople are spending even less than that.

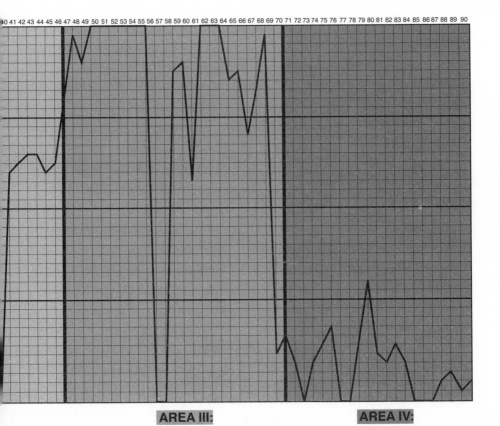

40 41 42 43 44 45 46 47 48 49 50 51 52 53 54 55 56 57 58 59 60 61 62 63 64 65 66 67 68 69 70 71 72 73 74 75 76 77 78 79 80 81 82 83 84 85 86 87 88 89 90

AREA III: AREA IV:

CHAPTER 29

How to Defeat Failure and Create a Winning Attitude

A champion, when asked what it's like to work in real estate, will enthusiastically say, "It's unbelievable!" That covers it either way, doesn't it?

Your goal in reading this book is to learn how to make more money. I hate to disappoint you, but you're not learning how, you're reading how. The only way to learn how to make more money from these pages is to master the material and then use it. This means that you practice the techniques, drill yourself on them, and rehearse every pause, gesture, and word. Then you go out, find people, and put your new knowledge to work.

How to Change Overnight

Some people are amazing. They spend between seventeen and seventy years cutting the grooves deeper on their personalities, and then they expect a seminar or a book to change them overnight. Let's talk for a moment about what's possible here.

First, I can't change you. Only one person can. Guess who? That's right—it's entirely up to you.

Second, you can decide at any time to master these techniques and use them to become more successful. In this sense you can change overnight—and you're really a different person the instant you commit yourself wholly to this goal.

However, your quick decision won't make any large and lasting impression on your life unless you follow your new ways of success—and avoid your old less-than-great habits—for twenty-one consecutive days. That isn't long to give your new money tree time enough to take root.

Now that you're seriously considering changing your life—and you are or you wouldn't have made it this far—please resolve to be happy. If you're ready to accept the challenge of change and start becoming the person you're dreaming of being, do it. If you're not ready, don't; stay the same as you are now. Either way, be happy. And, if you decide to change, give every new habit twenty-one days to take hold. Otherwise, reading this book is a waste of time.

Reject the Fear of Rejection

You won't put much effort into overcoming this challenge unless you admit to yourself that it's a big barrier to your future earnings. Sometimes the fear of rejection stops you from doing things, doesn't it? Or, if this fear doesn't actually stop you, it's always there, ready to help you find reasons for starting late, quitting early, and wasting time between calls.

How can you overcome this fear?

By selling yourself on the realities that'll make you a success, instead of on the realities that'll reinforce your fear. Let me explain.

There are many ways to look at how you're paid for taking a listing that sells. Let's talk about the two ways that relate to how you earned the fee.

We'll begin by assuming that you make $5,000 on the average listing after the split and after deducting the cost of any little fires you pay to put out instead of letting them burn the transaction down. Let's also say that you usually give your listing presentation in two hours.

One way to look at your listing activity is to say to yourself: "I make $2,500 an hour when I'm writing listings, but not one red cent the rest of the time."

Or you can say, "I've learned that meeting ten new people turns up one listing appointment, and from ten listing appointments I'm sure to get one listing that'll sell. This means that I meet one hundred people and hear ninety-nine nos to earn $5,000—so every no has to be worth $50 to me."

Which of those two ideas do you want to dwell on? Both propositions have an equal amount of truth in them. But the first drives out all feeling of accomplishment at taking the rejections and makes it much harder to continue taking them long enough to be successful.

The second idea lifts you up and makes it easy to keep on going. Jot down your daily progress:

DATE	NOS RECEIVED	EARNINGS
6/3	14	$700
6/4	15	$750

Talking to friends, relatives, and neighbors doesn't go on the tally—that's gravy. And only genuine home owners or those who could become home owners count. But if you'll use the techniques in this book with enthusiasm and confidence as you work with the husband or wife at one hundred homes, I guarantee you'll write one salable listing.

Actually, I believe you'll do better. In many parts of this continent, more than one listing opportunity will be found with every 10 people you meet. Also, when you've acquired professional skill with these techniques, you may regularly convert half of those opportunities into listings that'll sell. If your average fee is $5,000, this means that every no is worth $50, or more to you. And if your average take-home per listing sold is $7,000 (in many areas it's more) that increases the value each no has for you. At these prices, can you afford to let a single precious no get away from you?

The Cube of 20 Puts $10,000 a Month in Your Pocket

The sweetest part of my system for making rejection pay is that you decide how much you want to make—and then you go out and get the money. Put your own numbers into this speech, and then say it to yourself every morning as soon as you get up:

"Every no I get is worth $50 to me, and I make $10,000 a month meeting new people to get them. Since I also make lots of sales, I can only give parts of twenty days a month to meeting others. This means I've got to get twenty nos on each of those twenty days."

To make this work, use the figures that apply to you. Numbers you know aren't true won't push you. In the example, the agent may be working with an average earnings per listing sold of $3,000, but she knows from experience that she'll convert half her listing appointments into salable listings. Or she's getting one salable listing per ten appointments, and one appointment per ten new faces met, but her average take-home is $6,000 per listing sold.

The Creed of the Champion

The creed is all about believing in yourself. It's the central core of my philosophy. I hope you'll learn it word for word because if you'll live by this creed, it'll give a solid-fueled boost to your earnings and put the rest of your life on a higher plane.

> I am not judged by the number of times I fail but by the number of times I succeed, and the number of times I succeed is in direct proportion to the number of times I can fail and keep trying.

What counts isn't how many transactions fall out, how many doors slam, how many things don't work out, how many people go back on their word. What counts is how many times you pick yourself up, shrug, and keep on trying to make things go together.

Maybe you have financial challenges. I was flat broke when I started in real estate. If you've got one nice suit of clothes, you're that much ahead of me when I started. My first broker's training program went like this: "Hang in there." I know about the challenges, the obstacles, and the troubles of getting started in real estate because I did it the hard way.

But the problems are temporary if you take control of your thoughts and develop the right attitude. Do that and you'll soon see all your troubles fall off the scale. Only one thing counts after a few weeks of concentrated effort: your ability to brush the obstacles aside and keep on trying, learning, and perfecting your performance until you pile success on top of success and reach the highest levels you aspire to.

Recommendations for Continued Training

Understanding that no one can be an expert in everything, I recommend the following resources of excellent information that will continue to boost your career and your personal success.

PHYSICAL

Bailey, Covert. *Smart Exercise*. Boston: Houghton Mifflin, 1994.

Groeppel, Jack. *The Corporate Athlete*. New York: John Wiley & Sons, 1999.

EMOTIONAL

Canfield, Jack, Mark Victor Hansen, and Les Hewitt. *The Power of Focus*. Deerfield Beach, FL: Health Communications, Inc., 2000.

Carnegie, Dale. *How to Win Friends and Influence People*. New York: Simon & Schuster, 1936.

Hopkins, Tom. *The Official Guide to Success*. Scottsdale, AZ: Tom Hopkins International, 1982.

———. *Balance Your Life* (audio). Scottsdale, AZ: Tom Hopkins International, 1997.

Kennedy, Danielle. *WorkingMoms.Calm*. Mason, OH: South-Western Educational Publishing, 2002.

Mandino, Og. *The Greatest Salesman in the World*. Hollywood, FL: Frederick Fell Publishers, 1968.

Miller, John G. *QBQ! The Question Behind the Question*. Denver: Denver Press, 2001.

Rohn, Jim. *Seven Strategies for Wealth and Happiness*. Rocklin, CA: Prima Publishing & Communications, 1986.

Ruettiger, Rudy. *Rudy & Friends*. Henderson, NV: Legacy Communications, 1999.

———. *Dream Power*. Henderson, NV: Rudy International.

Salsbury, Glenna. *The Art of the Fresh Start*. Healthcom International, Inc., 1995.

Woititz, Janet. *Healthy Parenting*. New York: Fireside, 1992.

FINANCIAL

Clason, George S. *The Richest Man in Babylon*. New York: Penguin Books, 1926.

Ramsey, Dave. *Financial Peace*. Nashville: Lampo Press, 1995.

———. *The Total Money Makeover*. Nashville, TN: Thomas Nelson, 2003.

SPIRITUAL/RELATIONSHIPS

The Bible.

Bright, Bill. *Promises*. San Bernardino, CA: Here's Life Publishers, Inc., 1983.

———. *Transferable Concepts for Powerful Living*. San Bernardino, CA: Here's Life Publishers, Inc., 1985.

Dobson, James C. *Love for a Lifetime*. Portland, OR: Multnomah Press, 1987.

LaHaye, Tim and Jerry B. Jenkins. *Left Behind* series. Wheaton, IL: Tyndale House, 1996.

McDowell, Josh. *More Than a Carpenter*. Wheaton, IL: Tyndale House Publishers, 1982.

Sanborn, Mark and Terry Paulson. *Meditations for the Road Warrior*. Grand Rapids, MI: Baker Books, 1998.

SELLING CAREER, GENERAL

Duncan, Todd. *High Trust Selling*. Nashville: Thomas Nelson Publishers, 2002.

Mortell, Arthur. *World Class Selling*. Chicago: Dearborn Financial Publishing, Inc., 1991.

Tom Hopkins International. www.tomhopkins.com. Sales training tips, articles, books, tapes, free newsletter.

Ziglar, Zig. *Secrets of Closing the Sale*. Old Tappan, NJ: Fleming H. Revell Company, 1984.

———. *See You at the Top*. Dallas: We Believe, Inc., 1975.

SELLING CAREER, REAL ESTATE

Kennedy, Danielle. *Selling the Danielle Kennedy Way*. Danielle Kennedy International. (714) 498-8033.

———. *Seven Figure Selling*. Danielle Kennedy International. (714) 498-8033.

MANAGEMENT

Corpedia. www.corpedia.com. Online training courses with Peter Drucker, Tom Hopkins, and more.

Covey, Stephen. *First Things First*. New York: Simon & Schuster, 1994.

Drucker, Peter. *Management Challenges for the 21st Century*. New York: Harper Business, 1999.

Hopkins, Tom. *How to Gain, Train and Maintain a Dynamic Sales Force*. Scottsdale, AZ: Tom Hopkins International, 1987.

Index

Utility bills, 290, 299

VA (Veterans Administration), 111, 187–88, 316
Values, property, 7, 37, 45, 51–54. *See also*
    Market values
  based on CMA, 75, 78
  calculating, 179–83, 201–3
  ceiling/floor for, 171
  changes in, 164, 171
  FSBOs, 98
  mailings regarding, 119
  resale, 288
  research of, 45, 78, 101–3
Visual aid book, 215–21
Visual control board, 147–48
Vocabulary, slanting, 214

Wahlquist, Gary, 33
Walk-ins, 35

Warranties
  deeds, 112, 114
  home, 313
Water heater, 193–94, 212
Weather, 189, 278
Web sites, 15
  Brown and Bigelow, 159
  call to action and, 119
  Mapquest.com, 15, 147
  for maps/aerial photos, 147
  photos on, 58
Wolcotts forms, 111
Wolcotts forms, 111–12
Work, 154. *See also* Employment; Income
Wrap-up, as listing technique, 64

Yeses, minor, 62–65, 69–70

Zoning departments, 147